Mastering Foreign Exchange
& Currency Options

Mastering
Foreign Exchange
& Currency Options

A Practitioner's Guide to the
Mechanics of the Markets

FRANCESCA TAYLOR

FT
PITMAN
PUBLISHING

market editions

PITMAN PUBLISHING
128 Long Acre, London WC2E 9AN
Tel: +44 (0)171 447 2000
Fax: +44 (0)171 240 5771

A Division of Pearson Professional Limited

First published in Great Britain 1997

ISBN 0 273 62537 3

British Library Cataloguing in Publication Data
A CIP catalogue record for this book can be obtained from the British Library

10 9 8 7 6 5 4 3 2 1

Typeset by Pantek Arts, Maidstone, Kent.
Printed and bound in Great Britain by Bell and Bain Ltd, Glasgow.

The Publishers' policy is to use paper manufactured from sustainable forests.

The Author

Francesca Taylor is the Principal of Taylor Associates, a financial training company specializing in derivatives, capital markets, treasury training, accountancy and credit.

Francesca has worked in the City of London for 13 years and before that for four years with BICC plc, one of the UK's largest companies. It was while she was working at BICC that she learned her basic treasury skills. In a typical day she would need to liaise with banks, and transact money market and foreign exchange deals, as well as give advice on foreign currency rates for overseas tenders.

After four years at BICC she joined Midland Bank, and was working with them through "Big Bang" when Midland and Samuel Montagu joined forces to become Midland Montagu. Midland Montagu was in the forefront of the developing derivatives market, although the products were known then as "off-balance sheet" instruments, or risk management products rather than derivatives. She was one of the founders of the prestigious Financial Engineering Group, concentrating on marketing, selling, and troubleshooting the whole range of products to a client list which included central banks, major and minor commercial banks, corporations, and supranationals. It was in the mid to late 1980s that the derivatives and foreign exchange market really exploded, and it was Francesca's responsibility to make the Bank's customers aware of all the products and train them in the variety of ways in which they could be used.

After five years at Midland, Francesca became a Treasury Consultant, specializing in advising clients on all aspects of currency and interest rate risk management. She then spent some time as an interbank swap broker with Sterling Brokers in the City of London.

Over the course of her career Francesca has followed each of the four major careers within banking and finance. She has been a corporate, a banker, a broker, and a consultant. This leads her to be ideally placed to offer independent training and product education to clients, and to write books which are not bank marketing documents.

Her company Taylor Associates has been highly successful over the last four years and she has personally trained in major UK plcs, American and UK banks as well as "derivatives houses," both in the UK and Europe.

Francesca is also a designated speaker on the FOREX Association Diploma Course, and has spoken at major conferences both in the UK and in Hong Kong, Singapore, Malaysia, and Australia.

She is an associate member of the Association of Corporate Treasurers (ACT) and she has a B.Sc in Geology from Chelsea College, London University (now part of Royal Holloway), and a Masters Degree in Management Science from Imperial College, London.

CONTENTS

8 Spot Foreign Exchange – a Market Maker's Perspective

John Banerjee – Citibank N.A., London

9 Proprietary Trading

Tom Elliott – Nomura Bank International plc, London

10 The Role of the Forex Broker

Mike Plant – Harlow Butler Group

15 Practicalities of Trading Foreign Currency Options

David Ll. Jones – Royal Bank of Scotland

16 Hedging Foreign Exchange Risk

17 Technology and the Markets

David Joyce – Reuters plc

■ ■ ■

'Ultimately, everybody wishes to trade for profit, but is it a zero sum game?'

FOREWORD

"What are you?" "50–55, 10 by 20." "OK, mine, 20 at 55." What is all this? A secret code or some scientific formula? No, written above is a typical dealing conversation between a broker and a bank in the spot foreign exchange market – the details will become clear later.

For many years London has been at the center of the FX universe. Firstly, due to geography, where because of the global time zones we are roughly in the middle between the Far East and the US. Secondly, due to the high proportion of international banks and their proximity to the "euro-markets" (see Chapter 5 on *economics*). Thirdly, and most importantly, due to the high caliber of the staff with trading, dealing, and broking skills second to none. All in all, a very specialized and skilled marketplace.

> 'For many years London has been at the center of the FX universe.'

In the 1990s foreign exchange business continues to grow. The industry no longer remains the sole province of the market trader who buys or sells on instinct for profit, but also encompasses grammar school, university, and privately educated traders and arbitrageurs who may be looking for more subtle changes in the market.

Ultimately, everybody wishes to trade for profit, but is it a zero sum game? If one bank loses money, must another bank make money? There is a common understanding that a finite amount of foreign exchange circuits the globe terrifyingly fast, and traders deal with one another for gain. Foreign exchange brokers complement the market and position themselves to earn income from putting together willing buyers and willing sellers, providing anonymity, speedy transactions, and a thorough coverage of market participants.

Every three years in April, the Bank for International Settlements (BIS) in Basle, Switzerland, conducts a survey, the "Central Bank Survey of Foreign Exchange and Derivatives Market Activity." In 1996, for the first time, the survey also attempted to estimate the global activity in the derivatives markets. Twenty-six centers take part; these are noted in Appendix One. Any readers who would like a copy of the survey can contact the bank in their respective countries. Collectively, the banks show an increase in traditional FX turnover (spot, outright forward transactions and FX swaps) of some 45 percent, since the last survey in April 1992 (see Figure 1). This brings the estimated daily average figure

Fig 1

Reported foreign exchange market turnover in major centers in April 1989, April 1992 and April 1995*

(average daily turnover, in billions of US dollars)

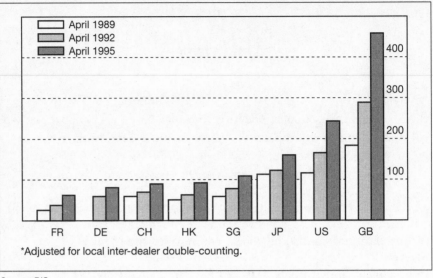

□ April 1989
◪ April 1992
▨ April 1995

FR   DE   CH   HK   SG   JP   US   GB

*Adjusted for local inter-dealer double-counting.

Source: BIS

to about USD1.2 trillion in April 1995, indicating a period of faster growth than was shown in the previous survey period.

The UK is the largest single center for foreign exchange trading and London tops the list with an average daily volume of USD464 billion, and accounts for almost one third of all foreign exchange turnover globally. In fact, daily FX turnover through London is greater than that of New York and Tokyo put together. Interestingly enough, more US dollars and Deutsche Marks are traded in London than in their own respective home countries. In the three-year survey period, London's turnover has increased by about 60 percent. But even this was overshadowed by the massive growth in France: up by 74 percent, but to a smallish figure of USD58 billion and Belgium: up by 79 percent to USD28 billion. Tokyo had been expected to show a decline due to the poor state of its economy, and competition from Singapore, but in fact saw continued solid expansion of 34 percent. Both the Singapore and Hong Kong markets showed strong performances. These particular survey figures exclude turnover in *over the counter* (OTC) foreign exchange options and futures, which is considerable.

'Daily FX turnover through London is greater than that of New York and Tokyo put together.'

The pattern of trading has changed slightly in the last three years and The Bank of England has highlighted the following trends:

- average daily turnover in London can be divided into USD186 billion in spot transactions and USD278 billion in forward transactions

- trading in USD/DEM continues to dominate the market with 22 percent of all transactions. Turnover in USD/JPY is now greater than in GBP/USD, and overall trades involving sterling fell 12 percent to 16 percent

- the proportion of business conducted through brokers remains constant at about 35 percent with 30 percent executed through traditional voice brokers and 5 percent through electronic brokers.

In the US the Federal Reserve Bank of New York reported its main trends:

- turnover volume in the three years 1992–5 has grown by 46 percent, an annualized rate of 13 percent

- the US dollar, the Deutsche Mark and the yen remain the most actively traded currencies

- the most traded currency pairs were USD/DEM with 30 percent of the volume, and USD/JPY with 20 percent.

Currencies in the emerging markets such as Hungary, South Africa, Thailand, and Russia are becoming increasingly attractive to trade as profit margins in the major currencies become squeezed. The pattern of trading also shows that the ten most active banks in London maintained their combined 44 percent share of the market, and that the top 20 banks accounted for 68 percent of the total, up from 63 percent three years ago.

The aim of the BIS derivatives market survey was to shed light on the size and structure of the global OTC derivatives market. Statistics were also collected from OTC market participants on their use of exchange-traded derivatives. The BIS estimates that about 90 percent of the intermediaries in the OTC market have contributed to the figures. The survey findings will understate the exchange-traded market figures, which are also available elsewhere from the exchanges direct. It has always been a problem to try to estimate the size of this OTC market as so many deals are proprietary, many are embedded in complex capital market structures, and many key players are loath to disclose their figures.

> 'Daily turnover in both OTC interest rate and FX derivatives is estimated to total USD880 billion.'

The survey shows that a good guide for OTC products is a total outstanding notional figure of about USD47 trillion (USD 40,637,000,000,000 plus a projected "gap" in reporting of USD6,893 billion) – this is more than twice the size of the figures previously estimated.

Derivatives business is global with more than half of all derivative transactions contracted with counterparties abroad. The OTC volumes are broken down into the four main underlying asset groups, notably, interest rates (USD28.9 trillion), FX (USD17.7 trillion), equity (USD0.6 trillion) and commodity (USD0.4 trillion), as shown in Figure 2.

Daily turnover in both OTC interest rate and FX derivatives is estimated to total USD880 billion per business day, and Figure 3 shows how this is split by country.

OTC currency options continue to be very successful as more and more banks, corporations, and institutions seek to hedge their currency exposures with derivative products as well as the more traditional spot and forward foreign exchange transactions. The disciplines of currency options and foreign exchange are very close and allow for considerable overlap, so this book will try to treat them with equal importance as each is complementary to the other.

> '[As a result of EMU] Paris and Madrid could risk losing 50 percent of their [FX] turnover.'

Fig 2

Estimated global amounts outstanding in OTC derivatives by market risk category at end-March 1995

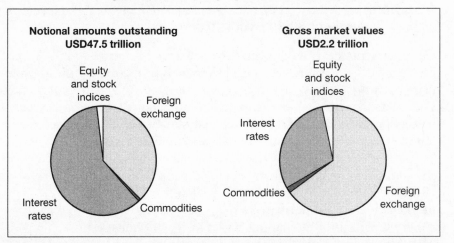

Notional amounts outstanding are useful for comparing OTC and exchange-traded business in relation to underlying markets. They are also relevant in assessing the risk to which firms might be exposed by price changes in the underlying markets. However, notional amounts outstanding do not reflect the payment obligations of the parties or the amounts at risk from counterparty default, which are better measured by gross market values. This indicator represents the cost which would have been incurred had contracts been replaced at prices prevailing on March 31, 1995. On that reporting date, the estimated global gross market value stood at USD2.2 trillion, compared with the preliminary total of USD1.7 trillion published in December 1995. Put in a broader perspective, this compares with a total stock of international securities outstanding (in OECD countries) of USD26.3 trillion, and of international banking assets (excluding securities holdings) reported to the BIS of USD8.3 trillion at end-March 1995. It is important to note, furthermore, that gross market values overstate the extent of the credit risk exposure in derivatives market given the existence of netting and collateral arrangements.

Source: BIS

Reported notional amounts outstanding at end-March 1995 and turnover in April 1995 of OTC foreign exchange and interest rate derivatives by country*

Fig 3

(in billions of US dollars)

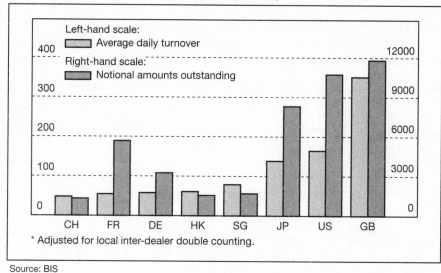

* Adjusted for local inter-dealer double counting.

Source: BIS

Future Developments

The real issues facing the foreign exchange and OTC currency options markets, are regarding how they will progress in the future, bearing in mind the increasing use of technology and the prospect of a single European currency. The final date for European economic and monetary union (EMU) has been set at January 1, 1999. Not all countries will meet the criteria; in fact, at the time of writing only a handful of countries will meet the stringent entry conditions. It will be difficult if not impossible to have a collective European currency with only a few members. The specter haunting the authorities is that some countries will be able to join on the due date, and others who wish to join will not yet be ready. This could lead to a two-tier EMU system, making things unworkable. The date itself may also drift – it already appears to be receding rapidly – or circumstances may change totally. Many politicians seem to be targeting EMU without a full knowledge or understanding of the implications, and some of these now have their reputations at stake. The "new" European currency even has a name. It appears that the name was chosen without reference or consultation with the inter-national banking and financial markets. The name of the currency will be the "Euro". This means that inevitably there will be trading in ". . . euro 'Euros,' " "euro" here signifying offshore trading of the new currency.

If EMU goes ahead the impact will be felt most strongly in the currency markets. The ACI (Association Cambiste Internationale) has released a paper warning of the following negative factors:

- EMU will result in lower aggregate profitability in the FX market, possibly with the elimination of niche currency markets together with a number of niche players

- the costs of transition are likely to be large and in the region of ECU 100 million to ECU 300 million per bank

- the loss of the intra-European FX volume will be about 25 percent, depending upon how many currencies are included

- the single currency will eliminate competitive advantage for many banks in their local markets and disturb many traditional banking relationships

- as EMU approaches so volatility will increase, with the likely possibility that currencies which join the EMU will depreciate while weaker currencies will appreciate.

Fig 4

Remember Paris?
Foreign exchange turnover, April 1995

(Daily average USDbn)

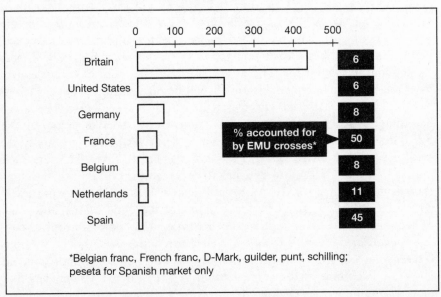

*Belgian franc, French franc, D-Mark, guilder, punt, schilling; peseta for Spanish market only

Source: Courtesy *The Economist*

Steven Bell, chief economist at Deutsche Morgan Grenfell, estimates that some financial centers will lose substantial foreign exchange business, especially Paris and Madrid where they could risk losing up to 50 percent of their turnover (see Figure 4). This is due to their high level of EMU "cross trading" – see Chapter 3 on *currency classifications*.

The increasing use of technology in the market for foreign exchange and currency options will bring its own risks and rewards. The human factor will remain an important decision-maker but increasingly dealers and traders will delegate the more mundane tasks to computer systems. For a more in-depth look at technology and the market, see Chapter 18.

One way and another a troubled time lies ahead for both traditional currency markets and the derivatives that require foreign exchange as part of their makeup.

ACKNOWLEDGEMENTS

Special thanks go to all of my contributors who are current market practitioners with "real" jobs, who have gone out of their way to find the time to sit down and write a chapter based on their experiences:

John Banerjee, Vice President, FX & Money Markets, *Citibank N.A.*
Jayne Dickinson, Far East and Exotic Markets, *Standard Chartered Bank, London.*
Tom Elliott, Deputy General Manager, *Nomura Bank International plc.*
David Jones, Senior Dealer, Currency Options, *Royal Bank of Scotland.*
David Joyce, Applications Marketing Manager, UK & Ireland, *Reuters plc.*
Mike Osborne, Director of Education, and Ann McGough, Business Development
   Manager, *The ACI Institute Ltd.*
Mike Plant, Managing Director, *Harlow Butler Group.*
David Simmonds, Senior Economist, *Ried, Thunberg & Co. Inc.,* London.
Ian K. Winter, Head of Technical Analysis, *ANZ, London.*

I would also like to offer my grateful thanks to everyone who has helped by providing market information and reading and advising upon the text, especially Derek Taylor of Harlow Butler and Adam Parkes of Chappel Ltd, and also to Lawrence Galitz who has let me reprint his derivation of the Black and Scholes option pricing formula.

I must also thank Andy Murfin, Senior Manager, Capital and Wholesale Markets Division; The Bank of England and, Georges Zuber, Chairman of the ACI Committee for Professionalism based in Geneva, for giving their approval for the inclusion of their respective codes of conduct.

I have tried to make this book as informative as possible by giving both sides of the story: the theory and the practice. This will I hope make the book easier to read and give the reader some "feel" for what it is like to work in a dealing room. The pre- and post-production staff at Pitman Publishing have all been exceptionally helpful, especially Richard Stagg and Linda Dhondy, and to them I am indebted.

Finally, I want to thank Derek, for his total support throughout this project, and Alex, my five-year-old son, for livening things up from time to time and by bringing me "creatures" from the garden. None of this could have been achieved without the help of my mother, Barbara, and Tina, both of whom ensured that things ran smoothly at home while I wrote this book.

■ ■ ■

'Foreign exchange has been with us for a long time . . . we must recognize that the markets today reflect the entire tapestry of preceding events.'

The Historical Perspective

Introduction

Foreign exchange has been with us for a long time; from your schooldays you may recall a mention in The Bible of moneychangers and moneylenders outside the temple in Jerusalem over 2,000 years ago. The two currencies were the Israeli shekel and the Roman dinari. The Romans were collecting taxes from the Jews in Bethlehem whose domestic currency was the shekel, yet payment was required in dinari. The Romans were setting the tax rates whilst others – the moneychangers – were setting the foreign exchange conversion rate.

Moving forward a little: in Italy in the Middle Ages, moneychanging and moneylending were carried out by prosperous families around the town square where the moneylenders would sit on benches. The Italian word for bench is "banco," which is how we derive the word for bank. In the twelfth century a group of wealthy Italian merchants came to London to set up a banking house. They came from Lombardy and left some years later – the result of a dubious credit decision. Although they are no longer in business they left behind their legacy – Lombard Street in the City of London.

More recently there have been a number of international agreements concerning foreign exchange, but before we look at them, we must recognize that the markets today reflect the entire tapestry preceding events. Some of the more notable foreign exchange milestones are described below.

1880–1914: The Two Gold Standards

This was a system of fixed exchange rates where currency parities were set in relation to gold. Under the *Gold Specie Standard*, gold was the internationally recognized sole medium of exchange and payment. Consequently, certain preconditions had to be met:

- the central bank must agree to sell and buy gold at a fixed price in unrestricted amounts
- anyone could melt down the gold to put it to different uses
- a holder of gold was entitled to have coins struck from bullion at the state mint, whatever the amount
- there had to be unrestricted import and export of gold.

It followed that under this standard the liquidity of a particular currency was linked to gold production, as the face value of the coin and the metallic value of the gold were the same.

Under the *Gold Bullion Standard*, money in circulation was either all paper or partly paper, with gold being used as the reserve asset. Paper money could be exchanged for gold, but not everyone wanted the gold equivalent. This meant that the issuing bank no longer needed to have full bullion coverage.

Accordingly, the volume of paper money in circulation was always greater than the holdings of the metal.

Between the War Years (1918–1939)

Wars are expensive. Finance in wartime economies could be met only by the creation of money. This in turn led to differential inflation in affected countries and created an obvious disparity in international price relationships. Corrective action required some countries to devalue and others to revalue. Inflation and devaluation were only two of the problems faced: the other main problem was the imposition of exchange controls in the first half of the 1930s. Governments were required to exercise control over currency flows in and out of the country, which in turn led to foreign exchange rationing. The outbreak of World War II forced all countries to introduce exchange controls, even those which had not imposed them earlier.

The Gold Exchange Standard (1944–1970)

To escape the danger of the devaluation/revaluation/inflation cycle experienced in the inter-war years, the US and the UK tried to create a "free, stable, and multilateral monetary system." The Bretton Woods agreement (signed in Bretton Woods, New Hampshire), proposed by the Americans and accepted in July 1944, effected this by using a method resembling the original Gold Standard concept. At the same time the International Monetary Fund (IMF) was founded to monitor the operation of this new system. The IMF's main objectives were:

• to establish stable exchange rates

- to eliminate existing exchange controls
- to bring about convertibility of all currencies.

Each member of the IMF set a parity for its currency relative to gold or the dollar, and guaranteed to maintain the rate within plus or minus 1 percent by central bank operations. Europe had been devastated by war and was slow to emerge from foreign exchange rationing, consequently liberalization took place very slowly. Currency convertibility eventually came into force on December 27, 1958.

The Bretton Woods agreement was effective for many years, although there was a wave of devaluations as early as 1949. The first real strains showed shortly after 1958 when convertibility had been achieved. The US's massive balance of payments deficit (USD11.2 billion) in the years 1958–60, caused a run on gold, pushing the price above USD35 per ounce for the first time since 1951, and central banks formed a gold "pool" to try and stabilize the market. Throughout this period economies were growing at divergent rates, leading to a series of revaluations. In 1961 both the Dutch guilder and the German mark were revalued due to large balance of payments surpluses, and in 1967 the British pound was devalued from a parity of £1 = USD2.80 to £1 = USD2.40. This caused another run on gold, ultimately forcing the central banks to abandon their "gold pool."

In the years that followed, social unrest in France in 1968 cost the Banque de France most of its currency reserves, and the franc was devalued by 11.1 percent, whilst in Germany massive inflows of capital caused a revaluation 9.3 percent.

The Collapse of Bretton Woods (1971–1973)

The collapse was swift, brought about mainly by a lack of confidence in the dollar. The American economy ran into trouble following President Johnson's attempt to finance the Vietnam War, increasing the US current account deficits, causing a dollar crisis in 1971, and on August 15, 1971 President Nixon finally abandoned dollar–gold convertibility. In mid-December 1971 the US declared its readiness to devalue the dollar, if the major Western European countries and Japan would revalue their own currencies. This cleared the way for a general return to fixed parities. On December 17 and 18, 1971, and within the framework of the **Smithsonian Agreement**, the US raised the gold price to USD38 per ounce, equivalent to a devaluation of 7.9 percent. Japan and Europe revalued their currencies by up to 7.66 percent. At the same time intervention points were widened to ±2.25 percent. Speculation soon started up again and in March 1973 Japan and the hard currency countries of Europe suspended their obligations to intervene in the market. Fixed exchange rates were effectively dead.

The Period Since 1973

As a result of the collapse of the fixed rate system many industrialized countries went over to exchange rates that "float." At the time this was considered to be a short-term measure but after a few years it became unthinkable to return to the old ways. Most countries have adopted a type of "managed" floating exchange rate with central bank intervention to try to control the currency if movements become too erratic.

In the years since the breakdown of Bretton Woods it has become increasingly difficult to manage currency risk as exchange rates have moved in a haphazard way, although in the eight years leading up to 1988 there had been two important trends for the dollar. First, way up and then way down, each lasting a number of years. It was hard to get it wrong as

Chart showing the depreciation of the Deutsche Mark against the US dollar 1979–1984

Fig 1.1

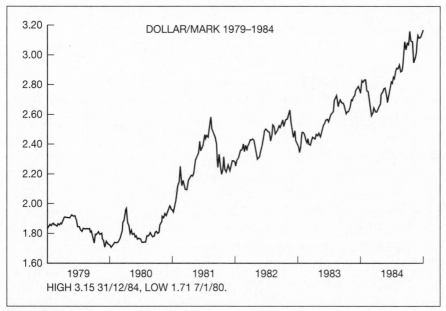

DOLLAR/MARK 1979–1984

HIGH 3.15 31/12/84, LOW 1.71 7/1/80.

Source: Datastream

the trends lasted a long time. Furthermore, until the Plaza Accord in September 1985, central bank intervention was largely regarded in the market as an opportunity to profit from the central bank's futile attempts to control market forces.

To appreciate more fully the dynamics of the market since 1985, let us examine an earlier period. Between 1979 and 1984 the Deutsche Mark depreciated almost in a straight line against the dollar from DEM1.73 to DEM3.15 or by about 82 percent (see Figure 1.1) there has probably not been a similar period where it was so easy to "get it right."

Towards the end of 1984 there was a general consensus that the dollar was seriously overvalued against most major currencies, and in September 1985 the finance ministers of the world's leading industrialized nations met to launch a coordinated effort to drive the dollar down. There was a deliberate correction (about 50 percent) to the dollar value but it was over by late 1987.

It has now been clearly established that forecasting exchange rates on the basis of a view about relative fundamentals such as inflation, external accounts, and interest rate differentials is of limited or no value to the hedger, trader, or arbitrageur, and is now reserved largely for end of year competitions.

■ ■ ■

'The recent survey conducted by the BIS shows a general increase in the volume of foreign exchange traded globally . . . and estimates that the daily average figure is in excess of . . . USD1,200,000,000,000.'

Background and Development of the Foreign Exchange Market

Introduction

What exactly is foreign exchange and what is being bought and sold? When people discuss foreign exchange they invariably refer to the value of one currency in terms of another. A typical comment might relate to the strengthening of the US dollar: this will have little impact on the Americans domestically, but it will allow them to buy foreign goods more cheaply. However, on the international market it will make their exports more expensive and possibly uncompetitive. In essence, our statement concerns the value of the dollar in the global marketplace, in terms of how much of other currencies can be bought with one single dollar, or how many dollars will need to be given up in return for a specific amount of a second currency.

Individuals and companies do not normally buy and sell currencies for their own sake; rather, they do so in order to pay for something else, such as goods and services. In that sense foreign exchange transactions are essentially a part of the payment mechanism, and it is to the commercial banks that individuals and companies have turned to convert foreign currency into domestic currency and vice versa. Incidentally, the market standard abbreviation for foreign exchange is FX or Forex.

The FX markets in a particular country tend to be located in the national financial centers, near their related financial markets. In the UK the market is in London, with very little activity taking place elsewhere in the country. A client in Birmingham may sell dollars to his local bank in return for sterling under a "retail" transaction, but ultimately the deal will be priced and processed through the treasury operation of the bank in London, which will have access to the "wholesale" or inter-bank markets.

In the US most of the activity centers around New York, although due to the immense size of the country there is a role to play for both Chicago and some of the West Coast banks in the late afternoon. Communication is effected by telephone, fax, and direct dealing electronic systems such as Reuters and Dow Jones Telerate.

There is no requirement for either of the parties to a foreign exchange transaction to be physically present in a specific location. This is because the foreign exchange markets are found in the dealing rooms of the commercial banks around the world. This is in contrast to some "exchange-traded" products where both parties have to be physically present in a building known as an exchange. FX is an Over the Counter (OTC) market, where the prices are negotiable, as are the amounts, the currencies, and the maturity dates. Each party must take on the other's credit risk, although with spot foreign exchange transactions this will ultimately become a risk on final settlement of the currencies.

Many dealing rooms in the major commerical banks employ over 150 *front office* traders, sales and marketing staff, and economists – some as many as 250. The front office is where the deals are struck and where the bank and the client enter into obligations to buy/sell their currencies. This is distinct from the *back offices* where the deals are processed. The *middle office* will include the information technology, legal, audit, financial control and compliance areas. Not all of these traders or support staff will be active in foreign exchange: some will be working within the money markets or deposit markets, or maybe bonds, derivatives or bullion. One thing is certain, to an outsider looking in, a dealing room is a chaotic place: traders may be speaking into more than one phone, and brokers' boxes, and shouting at one another, and anyone else who happens to be passing – all at the same time! Foreign exchange traders, especially in the spot market, are known to be noisy and this can sometimes offend the more gentle souls in a bank.

So just why is there so much going on? If we logically follow through the argument that foreign exchange is part of the payment mechanism, it would seem that the volumes of foreign trade must have increased beyond all recognition. Not so. Twenty–five years ago dealing rooms were more dignified and much less frantic. The real reason for change is not linked to the speed at which international capital flows are moving, or indeed the growth of international trade; rather, it is due to the decline of fixed exchange rates and the introduction of (managed) floating exchange rates.

The recent survey conducted by the Bank for International Settlements (BIS) shows a general increase in the volume of foreign exchange traded globally on a daily basis, and estimates that the daily average figure is in excess of USD1.2 trillion (USD1,200,000,000,000). Be careful – when we discuss trillions, the US trillion and the European trillion are not the same. In this context we use the US trillion with 12 zeros. Of this USD1.2 trillion only about 5–7 percent is "real," or non-speculative, although it could be argued that when banks operate in the interbank market they are mostly hedging existing positions, or those recently inherited from clients. The FX market exhibits continuous trading, conducted 24 hours a day around the world, and far outstrips the volume of actual trade flows.

Market Participants

The players within this market fall into a number of specific categories. The main group consists of domestic and international banks, which may be acting on their own behalf or for their customers. Central banks comprise the second group, and may be active in the market either intervening to support a currency or perhaps to suppress its value, or possibly for reserves management. Customers of banks who need physical foreign exchange to pay currency invoices, or sell forward the proceeds of a trade transaction, comprise the third group, they will generally have a real need for the currency. Unfortunately, they may suffer in the speculative flows when the FX traders start to operate. A fourth group of players exists: the high net worth (HNW) individuals, who may well be speculating with their own money for capital gain. Finally, there are the foreign exchange brokers acting as intermediaries between buyers and sellers. Generally the professional players can be subdivided into the following groups: the market makers, the central banks, the brokers, and then the clients – both commercial banks and corporate customers.

Market makers

These are the major banks, which will buy or sell a currency on a continuous basis 24 hours a day – not in the same center! They quote their own prices, ie to buy and to sell a specific currency, and they will quote a two-way price. The gap between their bid and offer prices should cover their costs and make them a profit. The recent BIS survey mentioned earlier showed a daily average turnover of USD464 billion in London. Business in the UK is quite widely spread but much of it is concentrated within a few major banks:

- the top 10 banks account for a combined 44 percent of the total figure – USD204 billion
- the top 20 banks account for a combined 68 percent of the total figure – USD315 billion.

When you bear in mind there are over 400 banks in the City of London this is a massive concentration of business with a few major banks. The big market players are:

- Citibank
- Chemical/Chase Manhattan
- UBS
- Bank of America
- HSBC Midland
- NatWest
- Fuji
- Bankers Trust
- Barclays.

Source: FX Week/Syntegra

Central banks

In the UK the central bank is The Bank of England. The Bank will not only supervise the market but will also intervene on the foreign exchanges to stabilize the exchange rate. In the US it is the Federal Reserve Bank of New York which fulfills this role and in Germany the Bundesbank. For a financial center to operate effectively the market must have confidence in the abilities of the central bank.

The brokers

These are institutions which act as intermediaries, as agents rather than principals, and which do not trade on their own account. There is evidence of a declining share of the market going through brokers all around the world and for London the figures in Table 2.1 provide an example.

Table 2.1

London brokers' market share of total FX turnover

1986	43%
1989	38%
1992	35%
1995	35%

Source: BIS

Brokers remain an important part of the market, and if an average 35 percent of all FX trades are dealt through a broker, that still accounts for more than USD350 billion per day. The new electronic broking services are estimated to have captured about 6 percent of the brokers' share of business, and are concentrated on a few currency pairs only. Like everything else over the last few years, there has been a degree of consolidation among the brokers as the smaller firms have been taken over and amalgamated with the bigger firms.

The big FX broking houses in London are:

- Harlow Butler Group
- Tullett and Tokyo
- Marshalls.

The clients – domestic, commercial, and foreign banks

Not all banks will wish to make markets in every single pair of currencies. Often one can find niche banks which may aggressively trade, say, Norwegian kroner and USD/DEM, but for everything else they rely on the market to provide them with prices, so in effect they are client banks most of the time. The distinction between foreign and domestic banks is subjective and is relative to where the client is based.

The clients – the customers

These may be financial institutions, hedge funds, multinational companies based in the UK or foreign subsidiaries based in Europe, or indeed anyone from anywhere, whether it be a major company or a private individual. The distinction between a customer and a market maker revolves solely around who is making the price and who is dealing on the price. Customers can buy or sell the foreign currency against their own domestic currency, or any other, with minimal regulation and with the certain understanding that the deal is being quoted and serviced in a highly professional manner.

Financial institutions

This group of companies can be regarded as institutions in the City of London or on Wall Street, or elsewhere in the world, whose major commodity is money and which buy and sell money or money equivalents, but which are generally not banks. Included in this group are the building societies, the insurance companies, the pension funds, and the unit trusts.

Hedge funds

This is an American term that crossed the Atlantic about five years ago. The name is a misnomer. A hedge fund does not hedge. It is a high-risk investment vehicle that speculates in the currency, equity, and commodity markets. The fund name that is familiar to most market practitioners is the Quantum Fund through which George Soros often operates in the markets, and through which he made good profits during the ERM crisis of September 1992 (Black Wednesday). There are many other hedge funds that speculate on the foreign exchanges. Hedge funds are now beginning to cause some concern among some of the regulators, as they are often based offshore and are consequently outside the jurisdiction of the central banks.

Multinational or domestic companies

There is a collective name given by banks to companies who are active – and sometimes not so active – in the financial markets: the "corporates." A corporate may range in size from BP Finance right down to a small engineering company based in Wigan, Lancashire. It is amazing but some large trading banks treat US investment houses as corporates rather than counterparty banks. Corporates usually have an underlying trade transaction for which they need to buy or sell currency. They will often be trying to "hedge" or risk manage their positions so as to minimize potential losses or to obviate them completely.

High net worth individuals (HNWs)

A whole industry has grown up with the sole purpose of managing the risks and assets of the private individual. To qualify as an HNW you need to have a fair amount of money that can be placed "under management": quite how much depends on the individual banks but it is usually assumed to be in the region of a minimum of USD250,000 to USD1,000,000. The banking service that these clients need will be vastly different from that required by, say, a major European corporate, and is known as private banking. A private bank may well concentrate on large mortgages, income enhancement, asset management, and investments, as well as offering speculative FX trading such as margin trading. This is where the client puts up collateral of, say, USD1 million, and the bank allows him to "gear up" and trade anything from five to 20 times his principal amount on the foreign exchanges.

Some Basic Definitions and Questions

What is a currency?   `Definition`

It is a medium of exchange, coins or notes, used to buy goods or services. Most countries have their own currency, issued by an official agency called a central bank or a monetary authority. In some countries, such as Hong Kong, private banks, such as the Hong Kong Shanghai Banking Corporation (HSBC) and Standard Chartered Bank, are authorized to issue currency.

What is a foreign exchange rate?   `Definition`

It is the ratio used to convert from one currency into another. A rate of 2.40 for GBP/DEM signifies that one pound is worth 2.40 Deutsche Marks, or that one pound will buy 2.40 Deutsche Marks.

What is a convertible currency?   `Definition`

A currency that can be freely bought or sold with no restrictions, or very few restrictions. Most currencies in the industrialized world are convertible or semi-convertible.

Definition

How are foreign exchange rates quoted?

Generally the SWIFT convention (see Appendix 2) is used: if a currency pair is written USD/JPY it signifies how many yen per dollar; if a currency pair is written GBP/FFR, it signifies how many French francs per pound sterling. In effect, it shows how many units of the second currency equal a specific amount, usually one unit of the first currency.

Definition

What is a foreign exchange transaction?

A deal where at a given moment two currencies are exchanged at an agreed rate. The exchange can be immediate or within a day or two: this is known as a **SPOT** *transaction.*

Alternatively, it may be for a future date – which is a **FORWARD** *transaction.*

Definition

What is the foreign exchange market?

It is a communication network linking all participants. This is now a global market but centers like London and New York tend to dominate.

Question: Why are banks involved with foreign exchange?

Answer: To make money! In theory any individual or corporation can run a foreign exchange operation, unless restricted by law. Banks, however, are well equipped to handle all aspects of foreign exchange activities.

Question: Is there a formal marketplace?

Answer: No. The market consists of the trading rooms of public and private institutions, their clients and the brokers. Participants in various institutions may see one another only occasionally.

Question: Is there a physical exchange of money?

Answer: Rarely. The vast majority of transactions involve electronic transfers where accounts are simultaneously credited and debited. The recent money-laundering regulations have also encouraged the banks to ask many more questions when they are asked to transact in "real" money or cash.

Question: How permanent is a given exchange rate?

Answer: The rate is valid until there is another rate. This can be a fraction of a second or it can be indefinitely if the exchange rate is controlled by the government. In the market, rates fluctuate constantly as they are affected by supply and demand

How Foreign Exchange Affects the Economy

Consumer prices
The prices of all imported products are directly affected by foreign exchange movements. In many countries a significant proportion of consumer goods are imports.

Wholesale prices
Staples and raw materials, from food to oil and metals, are major imports and therefore also subject to fluctuating prices due to foreign exchange developments.

Inflation
The pricing of imports will have a marked effect on inflation levels.

Export industries
The behaviour of the home currency in international markets is an important factor in determining the competitiveness of exports.

For instance, if a currency is overvalued, the price of that country's goods overseas will be relatively expensive, exports will suffer and jobs in export industries could be lost.

Domestic economy
All of the factors mentioned above can affect domestic developments.

Investor confidence
Patterns of savings and investments in the domestic economy can be greatly influenced by the degree of domestic and international confidence in the home currency.

Monetary policies
The pattern of international money flows (in or out), and to a lesser extent central bank interventions, may have a strong influence on the money supply, and therefore on monetary policies.

Interest rates

A change in monetary policies for the reasons shown above may result in changes in prevailing interest rates. For example, the desire to control inflation may lead to an increase in interest rates.

Leisure and tourism

Patterns of tourism are directly affected by currency fluctuations. When a country's home currency becomes strong, it becomes expensive for visitors.

The Role of the Central Banks

The Bank of England

The Bank of England, often called The Old Lady of Threadneedle Street, or simply The Bank, was founded in 1694 when the newly formed government under William of Orange raised a loan from a group of individuals who in return became the first Court of The Bank of England. It is reputed that this loan was needed to fund the war with France and was for £1.2 million with interest at 8 percent. Three years later, in 1697, the national debt had increased to £15 million. Two companies were soon contributing to the finances of the UK, making loans to the government in exchange for trading privileges these were, the East India Company and the South Sea Company. By the early eighteenth century these three groups practically controlled all of the nation's debt. The financial crisis of 1720 put an end to this arrangement and discredited the practice of financing the state with company funds. It also led to the increased importance of The Bank of England.

In 1844 The Bank was split into two separate departments: the Issue Department and the Banking Department. The Issue Department was given the authority to issue notes covered by government securities, and eventually became the sole bank with this privilege. The Banking Department is the banker for the government and the repository of the British monetary reserves (which may soon leave Britain's shores for Europe if/when the UK experiences EMU and joins the new European currency).

In 1946 The Bank of England was nationalized by the Labour government and placed under government ownership, the Treasury holding all the capital stock. In its banking role, The Bank will raise and lend funds like any other bank, and its main customers can be grouped into:

- private customers involved with commercial banking
- banking institutions such as discount houses and clearing banks
- overseas central banks and monetary authorities.

The US Federal Reserve System

The US Federal Reserve ("The Fed") was created by an Act of Congress in 1913. Until then there was only a decentralized system of banking providing the cash and credit requirements of the US economy. The Federal Reserve Act provided for 12 regional Federal Reserve banks to be located around the country. Each had its own Board of Directors which selected one person to be on the Federal Advisory Board which would meet in Washington four times a year. A Federal Open Market Committee (FOMC) was established later, controlled by the district banks.

The Federal Reserve has three components:

(1) *The Board of Governors* consists of seven members appointed by the US President, six of them for a term of 14 years; the seventh, the Chairman, serves a four-year term which can be renewed. No two Board members can come from the same Federal District. The Board is responsible for the supervision and regulatory compliance of all the regional banks, formulation of US monetary policy, and the supervision of US banks' activities outside the US.

(2) *The Federal Reserve Banks* – these are the 12 district banks, through which member banks can borrow funds. The districts are shown in Table 2.2.

Table 2.2

The Federal Reserve Districts

1st Reserve District: Boston	7th Reserve District: Chicago
2nd Reserve District: New York	8th Reserve District: St Louis
3rd Reserve District: Philadelphia	9th Reserve District: Minneapolis
4th Reserve District: Cleveland	10th Reserve District: Kansas City
5th Reserve District: Richmond	11th Reserve District: Dallas
6th Reserve District: Atlanta	12th Reserve District: San Francisco

The Federal Reserve Banks operate a clearing house arrangement. They also operate as fiscal agents for the US government, and hold deposits for member banks.

(3) *Member Banks* – of which there are about 5,750. Only half of the nation's banks are members and part of the Federal Reserve *system*. There used to be considerable advantages in being a member bank, but these have diminished as some of the privileges are now open to non-member banks. Privileges used to include access to the wire transfer facilities, receiving dividends on Fed Reserve Bank Stock, provision of aid and information and assistance.

The original 1913 Act paid scant attention to the institution of a national monetary policy to preserve economic stability, so the 1935 Banking Act transferred control of the FOMC to the Board from the district banks. The Committee comprises the seven governors of the Federal Reserve Board, and five of the 12 Chairmen of the Federal Reserve Banks, chosen by rotation. The FOMC operates through the New York Federal Reserve Bank, which carries out the day-to-day dealing operations.

The German Bundesbank

The Bundesbank was established just after World War II. A 1957 law ensured that it was independent and required to support general economic policy unless this conflicted with its own functions, which are to ensure:

• stable prices
• high employment
• balanced foreign trade
• constant and reasonable economic growth.

The Bundesbank is also particularly charged with protecting the value of the Deutsche Mark on the foreign exchanges. This formally defined role has its limitations or opportunities: the Bundesbank does not have to be consulted over fiscal policy. The unification of East and West Germany has led to an enlarged Bundesbank council, and the President of the Bundesbank can, should he wish, even attend cabinet meetings.

■ ■ ■

'The foreign
exchange market has
its own jargon . . .
"basket currencies,"
"exotics,"
"emerging markets"
. . . even "cross" or
proxy currencies.'

Currency Classifications

Introduction

The foreign exchange market has its own jargon as does the currency option market. It is quite likely that you will have heard references to the "five majors," "minor currencies," "basket currencies," "exotics," "emerging markets" or maybe even "cross" or "proxy currencies." In this section we will explain the various different classifications. One method of classifying currencies relates to the ease of conversion between them and what restrictions, if any, government or otherwise, might apply to their spot and forward markets. Generally there are three important subdivisions.

Key features

Broad classification of currencies

Major currencies
Freely available in the spot and forward markets.

Minor currencies
Freely available, although the spot market may from time to time lack liquidity. Restrictions can be imposed on the forward market in terms of maturity, ie not more than six months.

Exotic currencies
Spot rates are available, but may be restricted with regard to transaction amount or government intervention. The forward market could be lacking, intermittent, or very expensive.

Key features

Indications of currency classifications

Major currencies
US dollar, Deutsche Mark, Swiss franc, Japanese yen, Sterling, Dutch guilder, French franc, Belgian franc, ECU, Australian dollar, Italian lira, Spanish peseta, Canadian dollar.

Minor currencies
Irish punt, Finnish markka, Portuguese escudo, Austrian schilling, Singapore dollar, Greek drachma, Norwegian kroner, Swedish kroner, Danish kroner, Omani rial, Kuwaiti dinar, Luxembourg franc, Indian rupee.

Exotic currencies
Indonesian rupiah, Thai baht, Hong Kong dollar, Malaysian ringgit, Vietnam dong, Chinese renminbi, Philippines peso.

To get an idea of the total range of foreign currencies refer to Appendix Two where the full list of SWIFT codes/currencies is given.

Major Currencies

The top five major currencies in foreign exchange trading are the US dollar, Deutsche Mark, Japanese yen, Swiss franc, and British sterling. They should not be confused with similar abbreviations such as that for the G5 or G-7– the Group of 7 nations: US, France, Great Britain, Germany, Japan, Canada, and Italy. Each of the top five major currencies exhibits complete currency convertibility in large amounts, with an active long dated forward market sometimes up to five years forward.

Minor Currencies

These are the currencies where there is complete convertibility but where there may be difficulties executing the full amount in a large transaction, for example in excess of USD50 million equivalent. Alternatively, the forward market may only go out for say 12 months or a year, or it may be relatively expensive.

It is quite hard to distinguish whether some currencies belong in the major or the minor section – and a lot of politics is involved.

Exotic Currencies

The exotics, or "erotics" as they are sometimes known, were originally from the Far East, but now can be taken to include African currencies as well. Exotics include the currencies of Taiwan, Korea, and Vietnam, as well as the more familiar currencies of Singapore, Malaysia, and Hong Kong. Trade in exotic currencies flourishes and one of the foremost banks making markets in this area is Standard Chartered Bank. See the next chapter: "Far East and Exotic Markets."

Emerging Market Currencies

The term "emerging market currency" can cover a multitude of sins. Generally these are the currencies of the newly "Westernized" old Eastern Bloc countries, such as Poland, the Czech Republic, Slovakia and Hungary (as well as Russia), together with some of the South American currencies, notably the Venezuelan bolivar, the Chilean peso, and the Argentine peso, and the South African Rand.

Cross Currencies

The definition of a cross currency is where a foreign exchange market price is made in two currencies, not involving the US dollar. Historically, the US dollar has been used as the medium of exchange, between currencies, but about ten years ago the FX market started to expand the use of direct "cross" dealing.

Consider a company based in the UK and selling goods to Germany and receiving payment in Deutsche Marks. Before "crosses" evolved to their current level, it would have been necessary for the company to sell the Deutsche Marks for dollars and then sell the dollars for sterling. This would have involved not only paying away the "bid-offer spread" but also the possibility of running a potential dollar exposure if the two deals were not transacted simultaneously, not to mention further complications with forwards and options, etc. The major traded crosses are:

- DEM/JPY
- GBP/DEM
- DEM/CHF
- DEM/FFR
- DEM/ITL
- DEM/ESP

Notice that the DEM is an integral part of cross-trading.

As the growth of cross markets continued, more and more banks were faced with customers requiring both cross currency rates and cross derivatives. By 1990 the market had grown enormously, leading to a common trading practice where some cross rates are used to quote other less well traded crosses. For example, the best way to get a close rate in GBP/JPY is to carry out the following two transactions.

Spot:
DEM/JPY   72.17–19

Spot:
GBP/DEM   2.2685–90

(72.17 x 2.2685 = 163.72)
(72.19 x 2.2690 = 163.80)

Spot:
GBP/JPY   163.72–163.80

This method of quoting currencies is used where some crosses, for example GBP/JPY, never really developed into a major traded market. For further details on how to calculate cross currency rates see the section in Chapter 6 on the *Mechanics of spot foreign exchange*.

Cross currency arbitrage

This is one of the advantages of cross currency trading. It applies mainly to banks and brokers which are set up for the purpose. In simple terms, if the currency that is being dealt is DEM/JPY, and a counterparty sells the bank Deutsche Marks against yen, the bank has the option of either:

(1) selling the Deutsche Marks on to another counterparty;
(2) trading out through the dollar, by selling Deutsche Marks, buying dollars, then, selling dollars and buying yen.

If you can transact at a better rate through using the direct market (through the US dollar), then cross currency arbitrage is possible, sometimes known as triangular arbitrage.

Currency Baskets

Composite or basket currencies were developed to assist companies and financial institutions in their foreign exchange hedging. The two main basket currencies are the SDR and the ECU, although it can be argued that the Scandinavian currencies also effectively move as one basket.

The ECU

The European Monetary System (EMS) started operating on March 13, 1979 as a successor to The Snake. At the time of its birth all nine members of the European Community (EC) were signatories to the EMS although the UK did not initially join the Exchange Rate Mechanism

(ERM). Austria, Finland, and Sweden all joined the EMS on January 1, 1995 but, as yet, of the newcomers only Austria has joined the ERM.

The ECU (European Currency Unit) was originally developed from a need of the original member countries of the EC for a common measure of value which, clearly, for political reasons could not be one of the national currencies. The ECU is made up of specified amounts of each Community currency, frozen when the Maastricht Treaty came into force in November 1993. These amounts did not change when the Austrian schilling entered the the ERM.

The prime objective of the EMS is is to help member countries reduce exchange rate volatility, control inflation, and coordinate exchange rate policies. The ERM is the mechanism devised to limit the fluctuation of participating currencies to agreed bands around central rates. It ensures that if a currency pair weakens/strengthens outside its agreed bands the two central banks concerned will attempt to bring it back into line. Consider DEM/ITL, if the Italian lire weakens too far, the central banks in Italy and Germany must intervene to protect it. In some cases all of the central banks in the EMS act in concert to achieve this aim, through intervention in the foreign exchange markets.

The **official** ECU is a unit of account within the EMS recording amounts of foreign exchange intervention, very short-term borrowing, and as a means of settlement between central banks. It is also used as a reference point to measure the divergence of one currency from the others within the ERM. It is calculated using officially set exchange rates to the ECU. The relative amount of each currency depends upon the individual country's share of EC trade, its percentage share of GNP, and the importance of its foreign exchange reserves.

The **private** ECU is used for market transactions and can vary by up to 1.5 percent from its theoretical value depending upon market conditions.

Composition of the ECU

The ECU is composed of fixed amounts of the member currencies. The amount of each currency within the ECU remains fixed, but the actual weight can change due to currency fluctuations against the US dollar. For example, if the Dutch guilder appreciates against the US dollar it also appreciates against other ERM currencies, thus increasing its weighting within the ECU. To calculate the weights of each currency within the ECU at any point in time, the procedure shown in Figure 3.1 can be used.

Although the UK was part of the ECU from the early days it did not become a member of the ERM until October 8, 1990, when it was given agreed bands of movement ± 6 percent around the central rates. This allowed for a possible total movement of 12 percent from the top of the band to the bottom of the band before intervention was required. Against the Deutsche Mark the middle rate for GBP/DEM was 2.95, giving a top side of 3.1270 and a bottom side of 2.7730.

How to calculate the weights of each currency within the ECU at any point in time

Fig 3.1

	Fixed Amount (1)	USD Spot Rate (2)	USD Equivalent (3)	% in ECU (4)
DEM	0.6242	1.45	0.43	2.37
FRF	1.332	5.00	0.27	20.5
GBP	0.08784	1.54	0.14	10.6
ITL	151.8	1597	0.095	7.2
NLG	0.2198	1.62	0.14	10.6
BEF/LRF	3.431	29.81	0.12	9.1
ESP	6.885	123.12	0.056	4.3
DKK	0.1976	5.62	0.035	2.7
IEP	0.008552	1.58	0.0135	1.0
PTE	1.0393	152	0.009	0.7
GRD	1.44	240	0.006	0.5
Total			1.3145	100*

Calculation: (1)/(2)=(3) (or (1) x (2) in the case of GBP & IEP)
Sum (3) = 1.3145
(4) = (3) / sum (3)
* does not sum to 100 due to rounding errors
Calculated as at December 15, 1995

Source: "Guide to International Economic Policy" – Citibank

On September 15, 1992 sterling left the ERM. This date has gone down in economic history as Black Wednesday – or White, depending on your viewpoint. Under the ERM arrangement a country must protect its currency and maintain it within the respective bands. If currency intervention is unsuccessful, the next step is for the authorities to increase domestic interest rates up to a point where the currency stabilizes as other foreign exchange market players begin to purchase the (now) high yielding currency for the income. This helps the central bank, as it is not then alone in purchasing the currency as the speculators will pile in. If the UK had not been extracted from the ERM by the then Chancellor of the Exchequer, Norman Lamont, domestic UK interest rates would have increased from 10 percent to 15 percent overnight – an increase of 50 percent.

The Italian lira was also forced out of the ERM in September 1992; the Irish punt, the Spanish peseta, and the Portuguese escudo were all devalued within the mechanism (the escudo twice), and increasingly during 1993 there were speculative assaults on the French franc. On August 1, 1993 the ERM was effectively downgraded when the permitted fluctuation bands were widened to ±15 percent, except for the guilder and the

Deutsche Mark, whose bands remained at ±2.25 percent. In my opinion, the ERM is now in a state of limbo as the bands have been made so wide as to be effectively meaningless.

The SDR – special drawing right

The SDR is the unit of account of the International Monetary Fund (IMF). It can be thought of as an international reserve asset. It was created in 1969 and first allocated in 1970 to the IMF's members to supplement existing reserve assets. A total of SDR 21.4 billion has been allocated in six tranches. The value of the SDR is based on a basket of major currencies. The weights last changed on January 1, 1996, and as at that date the value of the SDR will be the sum of the values of the amounts of each currency shown in Table 3.1.

Table 3.1

The SDR Basket

Currency	Amounts	Weight from 1.1.96 (%)	Previous Weight 1991–5 (%)
USD	0.582	39	40
DEM	0.446	21	21
JPY	27.2	18	17
FRF	0.813	11	11
GBP	0.105	11	11

The SDR interest rate is calculated weekly and is a weighted average of the yields on specified short-term domestic money market instruments.

Uses of SDRs

Members with balance of payments problems may use SDRs to acquire foreign exchange. They can also be used for transfers between members and may be used under special arrangements determined by the IMF.

Proxy Currencies

Many exotic and some minor currencies have a proxy or similar currency that trades in a similar way. It is often necessary to revisit the trade flows of a country to establish which is the current closest currency proxy. This proxy currency can be used to facilitate hedging. For example, if a company wished to hedge an exposure in UAE dirhams against sterling, the bank may take a little time finding the rate as it is not that well traded a currency. In this case the real exposure is GBP/USD, and this is the exposure that should be hedged. The connection between the US dollar and the UAE dirham is very close, as it is linked. A graph of USD/AED is almost a straight line, as shown in Figure 3.2a, yet the graph of GBP/USD is one of almost continual movement, shown in Figure 3.2b. If you combine the two graphs together you can see that GBP/AED is almost as volatile as GBP/USD but with a different scale (see Figure 3.2c). Here the proxy currency is the US dollar.

There are a number of satellite currencies that are linked officially or unofficially with the US dollar, likewise with the Deutsche Mark. It is the underlying main currency that is seen as the major trading currency which can provide "proxy" hedging if required, ie will cover the real exposure, not the perceived exposure. For example, the satellite currencies to the US dollar include not only the OPEC currencies (oil based) but also those nations trading heavily with the US either for commercial or historical reasons, as well as the major recipients of aid funds denominated in US dollars (see Figure 3.3).

It could now be argued that post-Black Wednesday the European Community currencies are no longer quite so closely linked with the Deutsche Mark, but how long that will be the case remains to be seen. With EMU on the horizon, this may all be swept away with the

US dollar/UAE dirham

Fig 3.2a

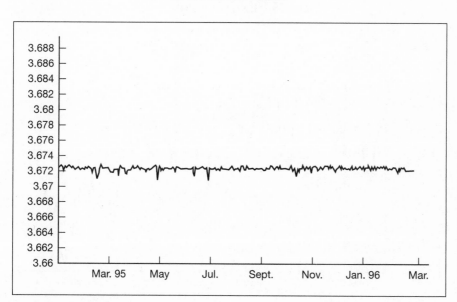

Source: Reuters Technical Analysis

Fig 3.2b

Sterling/US dollar

Source: Reuters Technical Analysis

Fig 3.2c

Sterling/UAE dirham

Source: Reuters Technical Analysis

Major currency relationships

Fig 3.3

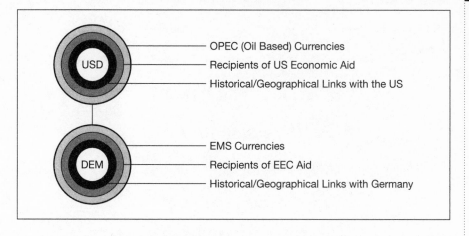

introduction of the new "Euro" currency, but before that, under the terms of the Maastricht Treaty, the UK is required to rejoin the European Monetary System for a period of two years. There is a certain amount of hostility to this at the time of writing.

■ ■ ■

'As the Asian and
African economies
continue to develop,
financial and
corporate investors
are increasingly
attracted to the
financial markets of
these regions.'

Far East and Exotic Markets

JAYNE E DICKINSON

Far East & Exotic Markets
Standard Chartered Bank, London

Introduction

Non-Deliverable Foreign Exchange Forwards

North East Asia

South East Asia

South Asia

Africa

Introduction

Several terms are now used to refer to those currencies previously referred to as "exotic." With the dramatic developments of the foreign exchange markets of Asia and Africa over the last few years, the term "exotic" has become just one of a collection of phrases used to describe these dynamic markets.

Other terms currently used include: emerging, regional, and where the term "emerging" has become inappropriate the markets are now being described by their geographic location.

As the Asian and African economies continue to develop, financial and corporate investors are increasingly attracted to the financial markets of these regions. In Asia particularly, economic dynamism and potential high returns from such fast-growing economies have proved a significant incentive for international investment funds looking to increase their exposure in the region.

As familiarity with these regions increases investors are now looking beyond the more established markets such as Singapore, Malaysia, Hong Kong, Thailand, and Indonesia towards the less developed markets such as the Philippines, Taiwan, Korea, and Vietnam.

With a wide range of developments currently in progress in Asia and Africa's foreign exchange markets, the risk of distorted flows having a negative impact on their economies is growing and finance ministries and central banks are keeping a close eye on such developments. An understanding of the complexities of these markets and regulatory environments is essential for any investor seeking to do business in these regions.

An increasing number of more complex products are now available to help investors looking to limit their investment risk. Asia is beginning to experience the widespread introduction of derivative products and as currency deregulation accompanies financial market developments, currency options and interest rate derivatives will play an increasing role in risk management.

A summary of some of the key exchange control issues and availability of prices for overseas investors follows. The currencies covered have been segregated by region. The tables summarize current exchange control restrictions and refer to the availability of prices from the offshore customer's perspective. For example, "purchase only" indicates that offshore customers are only permitted to buy the currency from banks.

It must be remembered that due to the dynamic and sometimes volatile nature of the markets covered, conditions can change and it is always worth checking with an expert in these currencies for current exchange control details.

Non-Deliverable Foreign Exchange Forwards

As Asia's high growth economies continue to attract offshore investment, demand for facilities to hedge several currencies previously considered "unhedgeable" is growing. Limited foreign access to certain local currency markets has fueled demand for an offshore alternative and we are now seeing the development of a market in "non-deliverable" forwards.

The non-deliverable forward provides a hedge for profit and loss exposure to a change in a "local" currency's exchange rate against US dollars or another major currency, without the requirement for any physical transfer of the local currency.

The product is conceptually similar to an outright forward transaction. The difference is that the deal is agreed on the basis that net settlement will be made in US dollars or another fully convertible currency.

Non-deliverable forward markets have already developed for several Asian currencies, whilst non-deliverable hedging may be negotiated for many African currencies.

North East Asia

The sustained high economic growth of this region has resulted in significant developments in the foreign exchange regimes of the countries involved, although they each have retained quite unique characteristics. Table 4.1 summarizes the position.

Whilst the **Hong Kong dollar** has been linked to the US dollar at a rate of HK$7.80 per USD1 since October 1983, under normal market conditions the exchange rate is generally freely determined by the market. The forward and derivative markets are also extremely liquid and under normal conditions deals of substantial size can usually be easily absorbed by the market.

In contrast the foreign exchange markets of South Korea, China, and Taiwan remain restricted, with foreign access extremely limited.

The exchange rate of the **Korean won** is determined under a "managed floating" system under which the Bank of Korea uses market intervention to influence the exchange rate whenever it deems it necessary. Exchange controls do not permit non-residents to trade the won unless they are investors in the equity market. Even foreign investors are subject to restrictions and are permitted to trade the won only up to the limit of their outstanding equities.

Similarly, the **New Taiwan dollar** remains a restricted currency and overseas financial institutions are not permitted to trade in it. Foreign parties may purchase New Taiwan dollars for inward investment but exchange controls dictate that transactions must be covered through a local bank. In the domestic market the Taiwan dollar is permitted to float although the central bank uses market intervention whenever necessary to influence the currency's movements. The central bank of China appears committed to liberalizing the foreign exchange controls and significant developments are expected. Customers are able to hedge positions through the non-deliverable forward market.

Access to *China*'s foreign exchange market and the opening of foreign exchange accounts are subject to the approval of the State Administration of Exchange Control (SAEC). Although the extent of such controls has been relaxed gradually over recent years, numerous controls remain and offshore access to the market remains extremely limited. The People's Bank of China does, however, appear committed to liberalization and has announced that the yuan/renminbi should be fully convertible on the current account by the end of 1996. Full convertibility on the capital account will take considerably longer.

On March 1, 1996 the central bank introduced an experimental scheme permitting foreign funded enterprises (FFEs) to trade foreign exchange at designated banks without prior approval in four zones within China and, as a further step towards convertibility on the current account, the privilege was extended to further regions from July 1, 1996.

Table 4.1

Country	Currency	Availability of spot cover	Availability of forward cover (deliverable)	Currency options
Hong Kong	Dollar(HKD)	Two-way market	Liquid market out to 6 months. Prices available out to 5 years	Yes–limited market beyond 1 year
South Korea	Won (KRW)	Purchase won only-must be equity related	Not available	No
Taiwan	Dollar (TWD)	Purchase TWD only-must be investment related	Not available	No
China	Renminbi (CNY)	Purchase renminbi only	Not available	No

Non-deliverable forward prices may be available where access to the local physical market is restricted.

South East Asia

The South East Asian economies and foreign exchange markets remain very diverse. Singapore, Malaysia, and Thailand have already experienced significant deregulation and liberalization of their economies, whilst the Philippines and Vietnam are still relatively undeveloped markets. However, both the Philippines and Vietnam attract substantial investor interest with further liberalization of the markets expected. Table 4.2 summarizes the position.

The **Indonesian rupiah** exchange rate has been determined on a "managed floating" basis since September 1986 using a basket of the currencies of Indonesia's major trading partners. Bank Indonesia fixes a daily intervention band indicating the rates at which it will buy and sell US dollars against the rupiah. The band is currently fixed 192 rupiah wide. However, Bank Indonesia reserves the right to intervene in the market at any time even when USD/IDR is trading within the intervention band.

The **Malaysian ringgit** is also pegged to a basket of the currencies of Malaysia's major trading partners. Although the exact composition is unknown the Japanese yen, Singapore dollar, and the US dollar are known to carry heavy weightings. However, in practice the ringgit tends to track its basket only loosely and moves in reaction to the substantial commercial and speculative flows evident both on and offshore.

The Monetary Authority of Singapore (MAS) manages the **Singapore dollar** exchange rate in line with its target of non-inflationary growth, using a weighted basket of the currencies of Singapore's trading partners (particularly those of the US, Japan, and Malaysia.) The MAS views destabilizing swings of the exchange rate negatively and strongly discourages speculative trading and the internationalization of the Singapore dollar. Trading in the Singapore dollar is extremely competitive both on and offshore.

The level of the **Philippine peso** is also usually determined by market conditions although the central bank, Bangko Sentral, keeps a close eye on the market and uses intervention on a selective basis when considered necessary to maintain orderly conditions. However, under normal market conditions the volatility of the peso against the US dollar is low. Although locally there is an active market in the peso, liquidity outside local trading hours remains thin; overseas banks may buy pesos freely but may be requested to provide commercial details when selling pesos.

Since the last devaluation of the **Thai baht** in 1984, the currency has floated against a basket of currencies, with the estimated composition: roughly 85 percent on the US dollar, 10 percent on the Japanese yen and 5 percent on the Deutsche Mark.

Table 4.2

South East Asian currencies

Country	Currency	Availability of spot cover	Availability of forward cover (deliverable)	Currency options
Indonesia	Rupiah (IDR)	Two-way market	Liquid market out to 1 year. Prices available out to 5 years	Yes
Malaysia	Ringgit (MYR)	Two-way market	Liquid market out to 1 year. Prices available out to 5 years	Yes-limited by central bank restrictions
Singapore	Dollar (SGD)	Two-way market	Liquid market out to 1 year offshore. Prices available out to 5 years	Limited to onshore trades
Philippines	Peso (PHP)	Purchase of pesos unrestricted. Sales may require commercial details	Restricted to commercially backed deals. Need central bank approval to sell and buy peso in the swap or sell pesos outright	No
Thailand	Baht (THB)	Two-way market	Liquid market out to 1 year. Prices available out to 5 years	Yes
Vietnam	Dong (VND)	Purchase of dong only	Development of forward market currently being analyzed	No

Non-deliverable forward prices may be available where access to the local physical market is restricted.

During local time, the Bank of Thailand controls the exchange rate, through a separate legal entity, the Exchange Equalization Fund (EEF). The EEF acts as last resort for local commercial banks between 8.30 am and 12.00 noon Bangkok time, setting a daily exchange rate against the

US dollar and guaranteeing local commercial banks a price 2 satang either side within this time. The daily fixing rate is generally used to realign the Thai baht against its basket when required in line with the Bank of Thailand's policy of exchange rate stability. Sporadic speculation of changes to the basket system have resulted in temporarily increased Thai baht volatility. However, consistent with the Bank of Thailand's policy of exchange rate stability any changes are expected to be gradual.

Although the **Vietnamese dong** remains subject to exchange controls and is not currently convertible outside Vietnam, the potential of this currency market attracts substantial international interest. Locally any currency speculation is discouraged by the tight central bank control over the exchange rate and strict exchange control regulations, consequently volatility remains low. The State Bank of Vietnam fixes the exchange value of the dong against the US dollar on a daily basis and permits transactions up to 0.5 percent either side of the official rate.

South Asia

Despite the spectacular development of several Asian economies, Southern Asia remains one of the poorest areas of the East and is dependent on economic and infrastructure development if the region is to progress significantly. Despite examples of commitment to reform, continuing political uncertainty continues to hamper the region's advance. With the stability of the currencies of this region a cause for concern, progress towards the liberalization of these markets is likely to remain limited. Table 4.3 summarizes the position.

The **Bangladesh taka** is fully convertible on the current account. However, offshore participation in the taka market remains limited. Overseas counterparties are able to buy unlimited taka but they are permitted to sell only taka received as capital gains from investments in local stocks. The only exception is for foreign air and shipping lines, which can also sell taka against remittances of their surplus earnings.

Significant offshore demand for the **Indian rupee** has resulted in the development of a limited offshore market due to continuing restricted access to the local market. Indian-based banks can sell rupees to offshore parties but are not permitted to buy rupees from them.

The **Pakistan rupee** market also remains heavily restricted, with non-residents permitted to buy rupees only for commercial transactions. Locally the rupee is managed under a floating exchange rate system, whereby the State Bank of Pakistan sets rates at which it will buy and sell US dollars against rupees with authorized dealers. The rate is changed on an irregular basis only and may remain unchanged for several weeks or months.

Table 4.3   **South Asian currencies**

Country	Currency	Availability of spot cover	Availability of forward cover (deliverable)	Currency options
Bangladesh	Taka (BDT)	Purchase of taka unrestricted. Sales restricted to taka received as capital gains from investments in local stocks.	No	No
India	Rupee (INR)	Two-way market – limited liquidity	Limited deliverable market	No
Pakistan	Rupee (PKR)	Purchase of rupees unrestricted. Sales must be equity related and require details	No	No
Sri Lanka	Rupee (LKR)	Purchase of rupees unrestricted. Sales must be equity related	Two-way prices available for equity-related transactions. Details must be provided.	No

Non-deliverable forward prices may be available where access to the local physical market is restricted.

Exchange controls also limit foreign access to the **Sri Lankan rupee** market. Although no exchange controls exist on the current account, regulations restrict transactions on the capital account to trade and equity-related based deals. Each morning the Central Bank of Sri Lanka announces daily buying and selling rates for transactions with local commercial banks. Local commercial banks provide a limited foreign exchange market using the central bank's rates as a guideline for setting spot rates.

Africa

Although much of the focus of the "emerging/developing" markets remains on Asian currencies, the rate of development and continuing deregulation of several of Africa's foreign exchange markets suggest that they cannot be ignored by investors seeking new opportunities.

Economic reforms and currency and financial market deregulation continue to open Africa up to the global investor community with investors encouraged (or cautioned) by the development of the South African rand market.

Africa still faces the challenge of establishing the long-term credibility of international investors to facilitate its development. However, opportunities are already emerging and looking at a sample of Africa's markets can give an idea of their potential (see Table 4.4).

Table 4.4

A selection of African currencies

Country	Currency	Availability of spot cover	Availability of forward cover (deliverable)	Currency options
Kenya	Shilling (KES)	Two-way market – liquidity limited. Sales of shillings must be commercially backed	Limited two-way market for commercially backed transactions	No
Malawi	Kwacha (MWK)	Purchase of kwacha only	No	No
Seychelles	Rupee (SCR)	Purchase of rupees only	No	No
Tanzania	Shilling (TZS)	Purchase of shillings only	No	No
Uganda	Shilling (UGS)	Two-way market – limited liquidity	No	No
Ghana	Cedi (GHC)	Two-way market permitted but sales of cedis limited by local shortage of foreign exchange	Bank of Ghana looking at feasibility of establishing a forward market	No
Botswana	Pula (BWP)	Two-way market – liquidity limited	Foreign parties only permitted to lend pula into the center – consequently can only access one side of swap via arbitrage	No
South Africa	Rand (ZAR)	Two-way market	Liquid market out to 1 year. Prices available out to 5 years	Yes – limited
Zambia	Kwacha (ZMK)	Two-way market in theory – sales of kwacha limited due to lack of liquidity	No	No
Zimbabwe	Dollar (ZWD)	Two-way market. Sales of ZWD subject to investment details	Limited outrights available subject to investment details and liquidity	No

Non-deliverable forward prices may be available where access to the local physical market is restricted.

■ ■ ■

'An exchange rate is determined by the interplay of supply and demand.'

The Economics of Foreign Exchange

DAVID SIMMONDS

Senior Economist,
Ried, Thunberg & Co Inc, London

Introduction

A foreign exchange rate is the price of one currency in terms of another. A rate will thus tell us, for example, how many Deutsche Marks are needed to purchase one US dollar. It is always important to remember that an exchange rate involves two currencies and can therefore be influenced by economic, financial, or political developments in either of the two countries in the relationship. As with any price, an exchange rate is determined by the interplay of supply and demand. This takes place in the global foreign exchange market, which in economic terms can be described as a "perfect" market.

There are four criteria that have to be fulfilled for a market to be "perfect":

(1) There must be freedom of entry and exit from the market.
(2) The product must be homogeneous.
(3) Each participant must be seeking to maximize profit.
(4) There must be freedom of information within the industry.

Let us look at each of these in turn.

Entry into the foreign exchange market is generally relatively easy, especially following the abolition of exchange controls in the major economies. Both companies and individuals can trade foreign exchange with very few restrictions, although in their dealings with banks they will be subject to credit considerations, with banks themselves being supervised by central banks or other agencies.

The products being traded are undoubtedly homogenous or identical in that a purchaser of Deutsche Marks for dollars from one bank would be able to purchase them from any other bank.

There are problems with the third requirement in that the various participants in the market are not necessarily seeking profits in the same way and, in the case of governments, may not be seeking a profit at all. The attitude to profit differs because of the different time horizons of participants. A spot interbank dealer has a profit horizon of only a few minutes, an institutional investor will be judged by performance over months, while a corporate treasurer may simply have a mandate from the company to cover its currency requirements as and when they arise. In this case the corporate treasurer's activities may not even be regarded as being those of a profit center. Over recent years a new development in the market has been the growth of so-called "hedge funds." Such funds use computer-generated technical models to seek profits in any financial market and as such have become important "movers and shakers" in the foreign exchange market. Unlike banks they are not market makers and are not committed to being active in any one market at any time. Finally, when central banks/governments (collectively called the authorities) intervene in the FX market they are not usually seeking to make a profit but, rather, to influence the value of their currency for the "benefit" of the economy and society as a whole.

The fourth issue–that of the freedom of information flows–brings in the concept of the "efficient market" hypothesis. A market is said to be "fully efficient" if the current price results from a consideration of all available news about the past and influences on the future. There is little doubt that spot rates are based on all the available information and therefore are traded in a "fully efficient" market but this is not the case for forward exchange rates. These are not based on all available information, but instead are calculated from interest rate differentials plus a risk premium. This will be discussed in more detail later.

Why Buy and Sell Currencies?

There are a number of reasons why governments, industrial and commercial companies, financial institutions, and individuals should want to supply and demand non-domestic currencies. The main reasons are:

- trade in goods and services
- flows of short-term deposits
- investment in financial assets (bonds and equities)
- investment in physical assets (e.g. factories)
- the use by central banks of reserves.

The relative importance of these has altered over the years and even now varies from time to time and from currency to currency. In the 1950s the bulk of activity on the foreign exchange market was the result of trade in goods and services. With the development of Eurocurrency deposit markets from the mid-1960s onwards, flows of short-term money became an important influence. More recently, the abolition of capital controls, improved communications and technology, together with an increase in the volume of investable funds, such as those of pension funds, has meant that flows of long-term capital into bonds and equities have become increasingly important. Various theories have been developed to try to explain what determines the levels of exchange rates.

In the Beginning was Purchasing Power Parity

The oldest attempt to explain exchange rates is the purchasing power parity (PPP) theory. The pen that was used to produce the first draft of this text would be just as useful in New York City or Frankfurt as it is in London. However, the currency used to pay for it would be different – dollars in New York, Deutsche Marks in Frankfurt, and pounds sterling in London. Suppose that the price of the pen was £1.25 in the UK and $1.88 in the US. This would indicate an equilibrium exchange rate of $1.50 per £1. By comparing this with the actual market price of the currency, it is possible to say if the currency is over or undervalued. In this example just one product was used but, if a basket of many goods is taken, an indication of an equilibrium exchange rate can be obtained. This type of calculation is carried out from time to time by international organizations such as the OECD. The result is, of course, only as representative as the basket of goods that has been used.

Purchasing power parity also gives an indication of the effect that inflation has upon exchange rates. Going back to the earlier example, if over the subsequent year the price of the pen increased by 15 percent in the UK to £1.44, but rose by just 5 percent in the US to $1.97, this would give a new equilibrium exchange rate of $1.37 per £1. The value of the high inflation currency, sterling, would have fallen in terms of the low inflation dollars. This illustrates the importance of looking at economic developments in both countries.

Note that the example of the pen was chosen deliberately as it is the type of product that is universal. One of the drawbacks of PPP is that many goods cannot be transferred from one country to another in order to take advantage of exchange rate differentials. It thus applies only to tradeable and not nontradeable goods. A car, for example, although cheaper, after allowing for the exchange rate in another country, may have the steering wheel on the wrong side, while differences in television transmission systems mean that a US television will not work in Europe. In addition, there are problems in deciding which is the correct measure of inflation to use when assessing relative exchange rate movements, given that there is a choice of consumer prices, wholesale prices, producer prices, traded goods prices and unit labour costs. Even if a particular index is chosen there may be problems as a result of differing tastes, and therefore index weightings, when comparing one country to another. A further difficulty is that when applying relative price changes in different countries to the exchange rate, it is necessary to start from a year in which the exchange rate is in "equilibrium." It is, however, extremely difficult to judge when this occurs at the time, and can only really be confirmed retrospectively. Finally, and most importantly, PPP tells us nothing about the determination of the flows of capital that dominate today's foreign exchange rate market. Many believe, however, that although PPP is of little use in forecasting short-term exchange rates, it is very important over the long term of five, ten, or more years.

Fig 5.1

Exchange rate and purchasing power parity

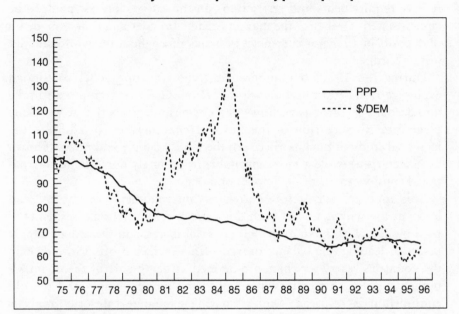

Source: DATASTREAM

Figure 5.1 shows the actual dollar/Deutsche Mark exchange rate since 1975 together with the ratio of US consumer prices to those in Germany. It can be seen that over the period as a whole the exchange rate is now close to where PPP would have predicted, but that there have been times, e.g. 1985, when the dollar was substantially overvalued.

An extension of PPP is the use of "real" exchange rates which show inflation differentials between countries. There is not, however, agreement as to which measure of inflation should be used, but there is a strong argument that relative wage costs give a good indication of a country's competitiveness. For this reason real exchange rates are taken as a measure of competitiveness.

And Then There Were Deposits

A Eurocurrency deposit is a currency held at a bank outside its country of issue. It is, for example, a sterling deposit at a bank in Paris. This market started in the late 1950s as a result of the unwillingness of state banks in the Soviet Union to hold dollar deposits in the US for fear that they would be "blocked" for political reasons. Instead the funds were placed with banks in Europe, which then lent them to their customers. The market quickly developed with dollars accumulating as a result of US trade deficits. The attraction of holding the deposits in banks outside the US was that this enabled US monetary controls, in particular bank reserve requirements and restrictions on the rate of interest paid, to be circumvented. Over time the market became broader and is now made up of deposits in all major currencies in banks throughout the world and not just in Europe.

During the 1970s a number of alternative approaches to foreign exchange rate determination were developed. These attempted to take into account the increasing flows of short-term deposits that were taking place after the creation of the Eurocurrency market. In addition the increased study of the links between the money supply and prices (known as monetarism) made a move inevitable from purely domestic to international considerations of the impact of money.

This approach is therefore known as "international monetarism" and looks at the willingness of both domestic and international residents to hold money. With fixed exchange rates, an increase in the money supply is seen as leading to a balance of trade deficit, which is offset by a drop in the country's reserves, which are defined as being part of the country's money supply. This results in a fall in the money supply and the old equilibrium is restored. Under floating exchange rates the analysis is somewhat different. An increase in the money supply is seen as being followed by a rise in domestic prices. With PPP assumed to hold continuously, this leads to an equivalent drop in the floating exchange rate. Observation of real world exchange rates, however, shows that rates frequently diverge from what were assumed to be their PPP levels.

An important development of the monetary model by Professor Rudiger Dornbusch of the Massachusetts Institute of Technology (MIT) attempted to resolve this dilemma. Dornbusch made a distinction between asset markets, where prices can react instantaneously to events, and goods markets, where prices are "sticky." In these goods markets prices are slow to react in the short term, although eventually the prices and the exchange rate will move in proportion to the change in the money supply as happened above. There are several possible reasons for prices being "sticky." Wages, for example, are often subject to review only on an annual basis, while supplies of raw materials may be bought on long- term fixed price contracts that cannot be readily altered. The analysis is based on the assumption that over the "long term" PPP will apply, but not continuously as with fixed rates. In these circumstances, in the short term, a rise in the money supply will result in a fall in domestic interest rates (an increase in the supply of any product will generally result in a fall in prices). This fall will make the domestic currency less attractive. It will therefore depreciate, but those holding it will require to be compensated for the lower domestic rates by a future appreciation. The currency will therefore have "overshot" its long-term equilibrium level, but will over time move to this level.

Although this "sticky price" model is more sophisticated and provides an insight into why exchange rates may over or undershoot, it has a number of drawbacks. First, it had problems associated with the definition of the money supply and the erratic velocity of circulation as a result of the instability in the demand for holding money. Secondly, the assumption in many models that PPP held continuously was clearly unjustified. Thirdly, and most importantly, it assumed that wealth was held just in the form of domestic or foreign money. Holdings of bonds and equities were ignored.

FX Rates With a Full Range of Assets

The international monetary approach has thus given way to the wider approach of portfolio balance. This has the advantage that it can be adapted to embrace a greater range of assets and it thus includes money, bonds, and equities. Under portfolio balance, it is assumed that investors have a desired mix of money, domestic bonds, foreign bonds, domestic equities, and foreign equities. Furthermore, it is assumed that, although the foreign assets (by definition) are denominated in a foreign currency, the investor is interested only in their value in the domestic currency. Thus a depreciation of the currency raises the domestic value of the foreign bonds.

Let us work through an example of how the portfolio model operates. Suppose that the monetary authority increases the supply of domestic money. This will lead to domestic interest rates falling, which will make domestic bonds more attractive with their price tending to rise. At the same time, however, the lower interest rate will make the domestic bonds less attractive to foreign investors, and this will lead to an outflow of funds and a depreciation of the exchange rate. This in turn will boost the value of domestic holdings of foreign assets. The balance of the portfolio will be restored. A similar simulation can be carried out in the case of changes in fiscal policy. The impact on the exchange rate, however, will be less clear cut. Changes in the issuance of either public sector debt, as a result of budget deficits, or private sector debt, as a result of balance of payments deficits, can also be considered. As with other models, the portfolio approach is best at suggesting how a currency will react to a change of policy or behavior, rather than predicting exactly where a spot rate will be in the future.

Are Forward Rates Forecasts?

Another approach is to look at forward exchange rates. By definition, a forward exchange rate gives the price of a currency at a future date. If markets were completely efficient, forward exchange rates would be forecasts based on information such as statistics and political developments that are expected to affect the currency over the period. Studies, however, show that economic forecasters can, on average, beat the forward rate. Why should this be? The answer is that forward rates are not forecasts but are based on an arithmetic calculation using the spot rate when the transaction is arranged and a forward margin based on the interest rate differential between the two currencies over the period until the contract matures, together with a risk premium. Forward rates at any other price would allow the counterparty to make an automatic profit. (This is discussed in detail in Chapter 7.) The relationship between spot and forward rates can be seen in Figure 5.2. The interest rates used to calculate forward rates are not allowed to find their own level but are set to a greater or lesser extent by the domestic monetary authorities, either the government or the central bank, using domestic considerations. They are not therefore set purely by market forces particularly at the very short end of the maturity curve. This is because the monetary authorities have a monopoly on the creation of money and can use this power to determine the level of interest rates in their economy.

On the face of it, then, there is little reason to suppose that forward rates are a forecast, but this raises the question of why interest rates differ from one country to another. As noted above, this is partly the result of differing official policies, and also as a result of differing inflation rates and the credibility of official policy. In brief, and very simply, interest rates can be characterized as being made up of two components: a real return and compensation for inflation. Thus a country with high inflation will tend to have high interest rates, when compared with a low inflation economy. This in turn will result in the high inflation economy having a relatively high forward discount on its currency which will make it worth less in the future. This, of course, is the same prediction as would have been made under PPP.

Spot and forward rates

Fig 5.2

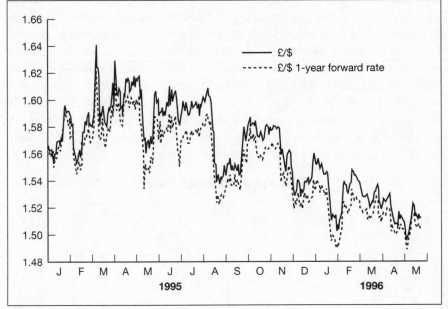

Source: DATASTREAM

Relative Interest Rates

There are some cases in which an exchange rate is dominated by flows of short-term deposits. One example of this is the Deutsche Mark/Swiss franc relationship. In this case, changes in interest rate differentials may give a good indication of how the exchange rate will move. This, of course, assumes that the direction of causation is from interest rates to exchange rates, but there may well also be a feedback in the other direction. A more sophisticated way of looking at this is to take inflation into account and adjust the interest rates accordingly. However, although domestic residents will be concerned by the inflation rate in their own country, they will not be bothered by the inflation rate in the other country except to the extent that it influences the exchange rate either through PPP or because the authorities try to counter the high inflation through high interest rates. Looking at relative real interest rates can be useful, but this approach can be overwhelmed by other flows. For example, during late 1995 the Swiss franc was boosted against the Deutsche Mark by inflows that resulted from concerns that the Deutsche Mark was going to be subsumed into a European single currency that would be subject to greater inflation than the Deutsche Mark has been under the Bundesbank. Lower Swiss interest rates had no impact on reducing these flows.

While considering interest rates, it is important never to forget that exchange rate changes are calculated in simple percentages but interest rates are quoted as a percentage per annum. Thus the return from an exchange rate movement of 1 percent during a day is considerably greater than that from a three-month Eurodeposit with a rate of say 10 percent per annum. This explains why the raising of short-term interest rates to extremely high levels does not necessarily protect a currency from expectations that it will be devalued. As can be seen from Figure 5.3 Irish Call money rose to a relatively high level in late 1992 as a result of speculation that the punt was to be devalued. In some cases overnight rates of as high as 1,000 percent have been seen in money markets.

Fig 5.3

Irish overnight deposit rate

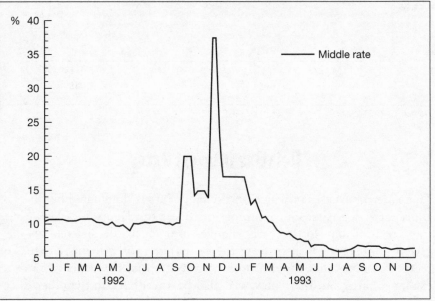

Source: DATASTREAM

As already noted, high inflation countries tend to have high interest rates and depreciating currencies. There are periods, however, when their currency is, for one reason or another, expected to remain relatively stable. This combination of high interest rates and a stable currency encourages inflows of short-term capital. On occasions investors borrow a low interest currency and then convert it into the high yielding currency in order to take advantage of the high interest rates. (Note that because forward rates are based on the interest rate differentials, the protection of a position through a forward contract would mean giving up the interest rate advantage.) By contrast, in volatile market conditions, historically stable "hard" currencies, such as the yen or Swiss franc, will appear more attractive despite their relatively low interest rates.

A Few Words on Technical Analysis

Another approach to exchange rates is the use of technical analysis, which is discussed in detail in Chapter 11. In the very short term, technical analysis methods, such as moving averages, give a good indication of supply and demand pressures in a market. Charts and associated techniques can thus provide useful information. To some extent charts can become self-fulfilling prophecies. If market participants are using similar techniques they will react in the same way at the same time and this will produce the expected movement. The use of chart patterns to make predictions into the future is perhaps more problematic. Essentially chartists are saying that history repeats itself. A similar belief underlies econometric models. Those who look at currencies from a fundamental perspective would argue that, while charts are useful in the short term, they cannot deal with longer-term developments such as changes in fiscal policy. The counter-argument is that time is made up of a succession of discrete short terms and that it is therefore fruitless to make forecasts based on the long term.

What Moves Exchange Rates – Economic News and Statistics?

Whichever model of exchange rate determination is thought to be most relevant, it is clear that economic developments are important. Economic news gives an indication of what is happening in an economy and how the economy might develop in the future. Economies are rather like supertankers at sea. They both have considerable forward momentum and are slow to respond to commands, which in the case of the economy include fiscal changes and interest rate adjustments. Because of this forward momentum, markets have a good idea of where an economy is going, but will nonetheless react, possibly dramatically, to shocks from statistics which lead to changes in those expectations.

Economic news

There are various types of economic news.

The **stance of a government's economic policy** has an important influence on exchange rates. Declarations by governments and central banks give an indication of official policy and may include remarks on the exchange rate. These are studied closely to see if the policies put forward are consistent and credible. Markets are not gullible and are not taken in by promises to carry out policies that are impractical or will be impossible to carry out because they lack public support.

Other **business news** may also be important. For example, a cross-border takeover may involve a large currency transaction that will not only have a one-off impact on the market, but may also be a precursor of similar deals, especially if a particular country is seen as offering good investment opportunities. Note that investment in physical assets, such as factories and machinery, once made is difficult to withdraw when compared with investment in financial assets.

Statistics

Statistics give an indication of what has happened in the past, and this forms the basis for forecasting what might happen in the future. Statistical releases can be broken down into several different groups.

First come those that deal with the **size and growth of the overall economy**. Gross domestic product (GDP) measures this, but because it is generally calculated only quarterly needs to be supplemented by other, monthly figures, such as industrial production and retail sales. Growth is an important influence on unemployment.

Secondly, there are several **measures of inflation** or changes in prices. Overall inflation is measured by the GDP deflator, while other measures such as the consumer (or retail) price index, producer prices, and import prices give information about what is happening in key parts of the economy. Wage and earning statistics give an indication of the effect of labor costs, with unit labor costs also taking account of productivity changes.

Thirdly, **balance of payments** statistics give an indication of international flows to and from a country. The current account is made up of trade in goods and services, and also includes payments of interest and dividends. Flows of capital are included in the capital account. Note that not all the transactions included in the balance of payments involve an FX transaction. Exports, for example, may be paid for in the currency of the exporting country or that of a third country, with oil, for example, being paid for in US dollars.

Fourthly, **financial statistics** show financial developments. These statistics include a country's budget deficit/surplus or the public sector borrowing requirement (PSBR) and money supply statistics. It is believed by monetarists that there is a link between money supply and future price inflation. The strength of this link varies from country to country and is thought by the German Bundesbank to be particularly close in Germany, where it forms a very important influence on interest rate policy.

Foreign exchange statistics

Information and statistics are available about exchange rates themselves. FX prices are readily available from screens and newspapers, but note that these prices are indicative and do not necessarily represent actual deals. In addition, because the FX market does not have fixed hours of activity there cannot be definitive opening and closing prices as in a stockmarket or futures exchange. Some central banks hold daily fixings for their currencies against other units, and publish the price at which market supply and demand balances.

Effective exchange rates attempt to show the overall impact of changes in spot rates, by linking exchange rate movements to trade flows. An effective exchange rate index for a country weights the importance of other currencies in terms of volumes of trade. Thus a change in sterling against, say, the US dollar will have a greater impact than a movement of sterling against the Australian dollar. Such indexes are compiled by several organizations and as a result of different weightings produce slightly different results. The overall picture, however, should be broadly similar. In the UK, for example, the sterling index is published at hourly intervals during the working day by The Bank of England, with those for other currencies published on a daily basis.

Surveys of overall activity in the global FX market are carried out at three-yearly intervals by central banks under the auspices of the Bank for International Settlements (BIS). The 1995 survey is discussed in the Foreword.

FX market reaction to data releases

In many countries, notably the US and the UK, a calendar of future releases is published, sometimes covering several months ahead. In others, however, particularly Germany, the day and time of the release are not known. Thus only around ten minutes' notice is given of the release of German M3 figures. Whereas positions can be taken before US and UK figures in the knowledge that they can be closed ahead of a release, this cannot be done with German statistics. Markets normally have a forecast of each release and will react only if the actual figure is significantly different from this forecast.

With many statistical releases, the reaction of the foreign exchange market will take place in two stages. The first reaction will be based on economic theory, while the second will depend on how the authorities are expected to react. Thus higher than anticipated inflation could be expected to lead to a currency depreciating as higher prices will make a country's exports less competitive, but the realization that rising inflation should lead to the government raising interest rates will encourage inflows of short-term deposits. Note, however, that higher interest rates will tend to slow the economy and could thus have an adverse impact on equities. Short-term bonds will react unfavorably to higher interest rates, but long-dated stocks are likely to be helped by the government's move to dampen inflationary forces. As the range of transactions in the FX market has broadened, it has become more difficult to judge the reaction to news and statistics. This has made the use of economists and analysis services more important.

Observation of statistics shows that economies move in cycles of boom and bust or peaks and troughs. Various theories have been put forward for these patterns, ranging from the influence of sunspots to the effect of investment. Market reaction to statistics will depend partly on where an economy is within the business cycle. Thus a sharp increase in industrial output may be welcomed when an economy is in recession, as it suggests that a recovery is taking place that will boost company profits, but a similar rise when the economy is booming may lead to concerns over shortages of capacity within the economy and thereby give rise to fears of higher inflation.

What Moves Exchange Rates – Politics?

Politics is another factor that has an important influence on foreign exchange rates. While the business cycle is unpredictable in timing and amplitude, it is played out against the background of the political cycle. In some countries, e.g. the US, this cycle is very rigid, with set dates for elections, but in others, such as the UK, it is more flexible with the government having discretion on the timing of the election, subject to a latest date by which voting must take place. Economic factors are a major consideration for voters and governments therefore tend to try to maximize the "feel-good" factor of rising incomes and falling unemployment as elections approach.

It would be naive to pretend that markets do not prefer center-right governments, because these tend to allow the corporate sector more freedom. Generally the market is looking for consistency and continuity of policies. Changes of government or leaders call this continuity into question and this can cause exchange rate volatility. A good knowledge of a country's political system is needed to be able to assess the importance of opinion polls and elections. Thus, in many European countries, voting in the elections for the European Parliament is seen as being an opportunity to register a protest vote, rather than as an opportunity to change the government of the country. A poor result for the ruling party may, therefore, have a minimal influence on domestic politics and policies, unless the poll is very close to the general election.

What Moves Exchange Rates – Intervention?

Given the importance of foreign exchange rates to an economy, a government has to have a policy on its currency. This will vary from country to country ranging from allowing the unit to float freely, on the grounds that the market knows best, to having a currency that is fixed against another unit. Few currencies are truly floating or completely fixed and most countries undertake "dirty floating" with reserves of gold and foreign currency used from time to time to influence the value of the currency.

The Exchange Rate Mechanism (ERM) forms part of the European Monetary System (EMS). In its current form each of the participating currencies has a central rate against the European Currency Unit (ECU), which is made up of a basket of the currencies of the members of the European Union in 1989. These ECU rates are used to calculate central rates, and bands of ±15 percent, against each of the other currencies. A combination of intervention, interest rate adjustments and general economic policy is used to keep a currency within its band. Should these fail, then devaluations/revaluations can take place. (Note that strictly a devaluation refers to an administered change in a fixed central rate, whereas a downward movement of a floating rate is a depreciation.) The ERM is thus a hybrid system that contains elements of both fixed and floating exchange rate systems.

Intervention can be both verbal and actual. Verbal intervention takes place when the authorities make statements intended to influence the value of a currency. Actual, physical, intervention takes place when reserves of gold and other currencies are used to purchase the domestic currency and, by increasing the demand for it, boost its value. However, reserves are finite and unlimited intervention to support a currency cannot therefore be carried out, because eventually the reserves will run out and all borrowing facilities will be exhausted.

Intervention can also be carried out to reduce the value of a currency. The domestic authority can literally produce extra money and, by increasing the supply of the currency, reduce its value. Note, however, that this printing of money has implications for the country's money supply and, if the country is following a money supply target, the extent of this intervention will have to be limited. This is, for example, the case in Germany where the Bundesbank sets annual targets for the growth of the money supply aggregate, M3. Thus in July 1993 the Bundesbank made it clear that it was not prepared to use a "blank cheque" to support the French franc.

Given the size of the global foreign exchange market, the influence of central bank intervention will always be limited. Central banks know that their finite reserves will have only a modest impact and that they will rarely be able to turn around a currency. They can, however, seek to influence their currency and encourage markets to assess whether a movement is justified or not. Coordinated intervention, carried out by two or more central banks acting together, tends to be more effective than when a single bank is acting alone to support its currency. This is because it shows that there is international agreement on the need for the value of a currency or currencies to be altered. Often such action is carried out by the Group of Seven (G-7) industrialized countries acting together. Intervention, backed up by appropriate changes in national economic policy, may be effective, but intervention by itself rarely has more than a relatively short-term impact.

Figure 5.4 shows movements in GBP/DEM and the UK's reserves over the period 1987 to 1993. During 1987 the government followed a policy of shadowing the DEM with sterling being sold in an attempt to prevent it from appreciating over DEM3.00. As a result the UK's reserves rose substantially. There then followed a period of more modest intervention, apart from in 1989 while the currency was weakening. During the period of the UK's membership of the ERM intervention was again relatively modest, but there were very large falls in late 1992 as a result of the government's ultimately unsuccessful attempt to keep sterling within its bands.

A country will try to hold its reserves in the currencies that will prove most effective when it is intervening. Historically the foreign exchange market has been dominated by dollar trading and the US unit has therefore formed the bulk of reserves. Over recent years, however, this has been changing as a result of the growing importance of the Deutsche Mark and the yen. Within the ERM, most intervention is done through the Deutsche Mark. European countries have therefore been tending to change the mix of their reserves, with the proportion of dollars falling and that of Deutsche Marks rising. Similarly in Asia, countries have replaced dollars with yen as trade with Japan has become more important.

Central banks are likely to continue to intervene almost entirely through the traditional spot and forward markets. This is because they are unwilling to take the unlimited losses that could come from the use of options. However, central banks will increasingly look to the options market for information on market expectations.

What Moves Exchange Rates – Sentiment and Rumors?

Sentiment is a word that is frequently used in the FX market, but is almost impossible to define. To some extent it is based on a long-term view of a country and represents confidence that it will maintain policies

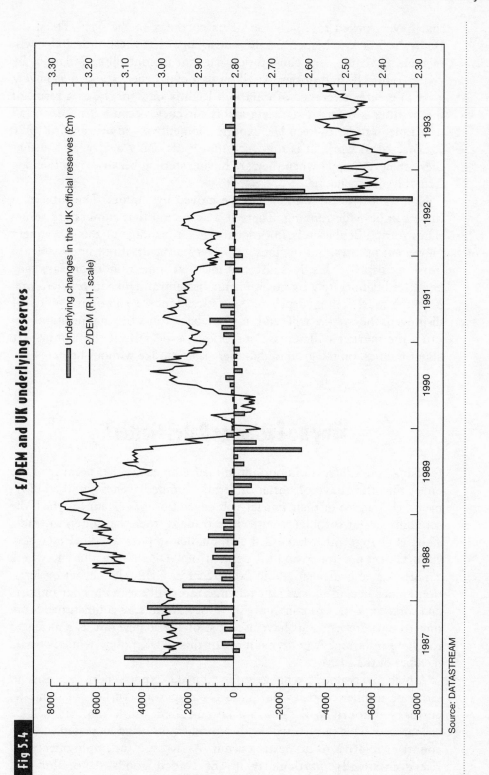

Fig 5.4

£/DEM and UK underlying reserves

Legend:
- Underlying changes in the UK official reserves (£m)
- £/DEM (R.H. scale)

Source: DATASTREAM

that have worked for the good of its currency in the past. Thus, the Deutsche Mark is helped by the knowledge that the Bundesbank will remain, by virtue of its constitution, vigilant in controlling inflation. By contrast, the UK authorities, based on past experience, are seen as having a much greater tolerance of inflation. Rightly or wrongly, as a result of this sterling is regarded as being a soft currency, because it needs to fall over time in order to keep UK exports competitive – in other words, PPP is expected to work. It is this view that leads many dealers to say that they are never happy when they are buying sterling because over the long term it is always falling.

In the short term, markets can be moved by rumors. The subject of these can be wide-ranging. There is a suspicion that rumors are sometimes started deliberately in order to take advantage of the subsequent movement in rates, but obviously it is very difficult, if not impossible, to prove or disprove this. It is also possible that some rumors or leaks may be started deliberately by governments or central banks in order to prepare the market for surprising statistics. Once a rumor is denied or disproved, the market will tend to move back to its original position, but often the market will remain suspicious, especially if the rumors are about politics, on the ground that there is no smoke without fire.

Why Do Exchange Rates Matter?

Exchange rates have an important influence on economies because of the effect that they have on inflation, trade competitiveness, and employment. The degree of their impact will depend on the extent to which the economy is self-sufficient, with little trade, rather than open to trade. Thus exchange rates have a much smaller impact on the US, where exports account for around 8 percent of GDP than in the UK where exports are equivalent to about 20 percent of GDP. The impact on inflation comes because a strong exchange rate will mean cheaper imports and force exporters to contain costs if they are to stay competitive. From time to time governments have used a strong exchange rate as a means of reducing inflation. A good example of this is UK policy while it was a member of the ERM.

A high, overvalued exchange rate will make exports more expensive in terms of another currency but imports cheaper in terms of the domestic currency. Exports will therefore be curtailed, while imports will be encouraged. This in turn will lead to production being increased in other countries relative to domestic output. As a result, unemployment will rise domestically, particularly in the traded goods sector, but fall internationally. A weak exchange rate will have an analogous effect, but in reverse. Note that the exchange rate does not affect just trade in goods, but has an impact on services such as tourism. The fall of sterling relative to the French franc over the period since sterling's withdrawal from the ERM in September 1992 has led to French holidays becoming more expensive relative to those in the UK and this, together with good weather in the UK, has encouraged a change in holiday patterns, with UK resorts benefiting. Workers have votes, and politicians know that employment is a key issue in general elections. Thus over time there will be a tendency for politicians to try to keep the currency close to, or even perhaps a little weaker than, its equilibrium level in terms of employment in goods and services. This process, however, will be slow and erratic.

Another reason exchange rates matter is that it is thought by many business leaders and politicians that exchange rate volatility reduces international trade. It is argued that the uncertainty created by this volatility discourages businesses from selling to other countries. This is, of course, despite the existence of a wide range of hedging products. To encourage trade within the European Union, politicians set up the ERM in 1979, which seeks to limit exchange rate movements. This is one of the motivations for the move towards the "Euro" single currency. In addition, within an area such as the European Union, politicians want to control rates in order to prevent countries from using devaluations/depreciations to increase their employment at the expense of other members.

The economics of foreign exchange will remain at the center of debate within Europe over the coming years. A reduction in the number of European currencies as a result of the creation of the Euro will boost the attention given to hitherto "exotic" currencies such as those of the rapidly expanding South East Asian economies. Looking into the future, there could be a polarization of the world into three economic blocs centered around the Euro, US dollar and Japanese yen. Whether or not this results in more or less currency volatility will depend on the degree of cooperation and coordination between the blocs.

'The spot foreign
exchange markets
are driven purely by
supply and demand.'

The Mechanics of Spot Foreign Exchange

Introduction

The spot foreign exchange markets are driven purely by supply and demand. Nevertheless, it is important to remember that demand can be artificially stimulated by such things as rumor, expectation, intervention, and even charts (technical analysis). It is also quite possible that a number of influences will operate simultaneously, thus masking any individual effect. Market confidence is also a key factor, as without it the traders in the banks may start to have second thoughts about the ability of the market or a particular bank to fill their respective orders. It is a zero sum game – almost! The overhead that used to be paid by the central banks is now being funded by the corporation and the private individual.

Throughout this book I shall use the SWIFT (Society for Worldwide Interbank Financial Telecommunication) codes for the currencies. A full list of the SWIFT codes can be found in Appendix Two. When discussing exchange rates I shall also adopt the market convention – where references are made in relation to how many units of the second currency are equivalent to one (or a specified) unit of the first. For example, USD/NLG will be quoted as the number of guilders per dollar, and DEM/JPY the number of yen per Deutsche Mark.

Timing

Spot FX is generally dealt or transacted today (the dealing date), for *value* two business days later (the value date); that day must be a business day in each of the two countries to apply. The term value date is used to denote the day on which funds must be received or paid with "good value" into a nominated bank account. Over the Christmas and New Year periods, where some countries often have different scheduled bank holidays, it is quite possible for the value date on a spot deal to be four or five actual days away to cover the two business days in each territory, and longer if a weekend intervenes. Two business days are required to transfer the currencies – this allows for the different time zones and for the completion of all necessary paperwork and settlement procedures. We could now argue that with the increasing use of technology two days is overly long for the settlement of a spot transaction, but it is has become tradition.

There are some notable exceptions. A trader dealing USD/CAD without qualification would expect delivery on the next working day. This is known as "Funds." A spot price can, however, be requested as an alternative. In order to keep the value dates the same, some FX transactions involving the Australian market, if dealt early enough in their morning, are for one working day ahead only. This provides continuity with the US market, where the actual day of the week has not yet changed. After midnight *London* time, all Australian market prices will have the usual spot value.

Other complications arise when dealing in some of the Middle East currencies; this is where the banks are closed on the Friday but open on the Saturday, by when the rest of the market is closed. Consider a USD/SAR spot transaction dealt on Wednesday for value Friday, but the local Saudi market is closed. This deal could have a split settlement date, with the dollars settled on the Friday and the Saudi riyal settled on the Saturday; alternatively, it may be dealt Wednesday for value Monday, and have the same value date as a spot deal that was dealt on the Thursday for value Monday.

Cross currencies, which are currencies that are not traded through the dollar, for example Deutsche Marks against yen, also require two business days for the settlement. So in the case of Deutsche Marks and yen, we would need two clear business days in Japan, and Germany. There is, however, a strong argument that we will also require two business days in the US, as many cross currency traders may trade out of or into their positions through the dollar, and if the US markets were closed, there would be a mismatch on settlement.

Quotations

Direct vs indirect

Foreign exchange has very specific ways of quotation and it is necessary to become familiar with these. Domestically, most countries use a method known as *direct* quotation: this is when the foreign currency is quoted in Deutsche Mark terms in Germany but in French franc terms in France, etc. There are exceptions to the rule: in the UK everything is quoted against sterling, with sterling as the base currency. This is because for many years the UK did not have the decimal system and it was easier to quote this way round. Eventually, in 1971, the UK adopted decimalization , but this method of quotation is still used.

In the US all domestic prices are quoted on a *direct* basis in their equivalent dollar terms, so, for example, a Deutsche Mark may be worth USD0.6667, but on the international foreign exchange markets the same rate would be quoted the other way around as USD/DEM at 1.5000.

Internationally, it is convention in the global FX market to quote most currencies against the dollar, with the dollar being the base currency; this is in practice an *indirect* method of quotation for the Americans, sometimes known as the European method.

Generally, most currencies are quoted against a US dollar base, except currencies like sterling, the Australian dollar, and the ECU, where they themselves are the base against the various "foreign" or "quoted" currencies. Using the dollar base simplifies currency trading a great deal: it will allow a trader to compare rates more easily. He could ask a German bank in Madrid their rates for Deutsche Marks, and he could also inquire the same of a French bank. Both rates will be quoted back to him as indications against a dollar base currency, rather than, firstly, a quote against Spanish pesetas and, secondly, a quote against French francs.

Should anyone need to, the way to convert an indirect quotation into a direct quotation is to calculate the reciprocal: this is rarely required for major currencies but is occasionally used for minors. An example is shown below.

Example

Consider a USD/DEM quotation of 1.4856–61

This can be converted to DEM/USD by taking 1 and dividing by 1.4861 equalling 0.6729, and by taking 1 and dividing by 1.4856 to make 0.6731. These rates will still be quoted in line with market practice, with the smaller number on the left, see section below on *procedures and practices – banks*.

In the above case of DEM/USD the two sides of the quotation need to be reversed, resulting in 0.6729–0.6731. The important factor here is that as the quotation is reversed the bank also operates in the reverse. So, instead of buying the dollars and selling the Deutsche Marks on the left-hand side of the quotation, as is normal, with the direct quotation the bank buys the Deutsche Marks against the dollar on the left, and sells the Deutsche Marks against the dollar on the right.

Changing the price

When a market maker quotes a client, whether it is another bank or a corporate client, his price will only be good until he changes it. It is not uncommon for a trader to want to change his price before he has managed to voice his/her rate. Among market makers and major clients it is market practice when quoting two-way rates to quote only the last two figures. For example, if the USD/DEM rate is 1.5330–35, the trader will quote 30–35. In a fast-moving market the trader may get as far as saying thirty–thirty ... *change* – he does not complete the quotation as he wishes to change his price. His next price may be, say, 33–38.

There are some markets and some times where the foreign exchange rates are fairly stable and where the trader may be happy with his price for hours, but as soon as you hear the all important "*change*" or "*off* " you know the price is changing.

> *When dealing on the telephone with banks, it is vital that the client does not put the bank's dealer on "hold." If the bank is placed on hold while a second call is made or received (usually because the client is seeking a competitive quote), and the dealer shouts "change", no one will hear the new rate. This can lead to confusion.* **Tip**

Significant figures

Another area where mistakes can be made concerns how many significant figures should be quoted after the decimal point. Generally most currencies run to four figures after the point, but as usual there are exceptions, notably:

- USD/JPY: 100.50–60
- USD/LIT: 1600.00–70
- USD/BEF: 30.535–545

> *If you are ever unsure how many figures are required after the decimal point check how many appear in the standard spot quotation.* **Tip**

Foreign Exchange Market Information

Because foreign exchange prices move very quickly it is important for all market participants to have access to up–to–date prices, preferably "real-time" prices and feeds. These can be provided by the various commercial operators, such as Reuters, Dow-Jones Telerate, and Knight Ridder. Publications such as the *Financial Times* also carry a very good market page within the Companies and Markets section, covering FX and money rates. But, remember, this information is historical as it is a day old before it appears in print. A selection of various data forms is shown in Figures 6.1 and 6.2.

Fig 6.1   **Extract from the _Financial Times_ – January 30, 1996**

POUNDSPOT FORWARD AGAINST THE POUND

Jan 29		Closing mid-point	Change on day	Bid/offer spread	Day's Mid high	low	One month Rate	%PA	Three months Rate	%PA	One year Rate	%PA	Bank of Eng. Index
Europe													
Austria	(Sch)	15.7551	−0.0045	478 – 623	15.7822	15.7285	15.7116	3.3	15.6676	2.2	–	–	106.3
Belgium	(BFr)	46.0513	−0.0209	315 – 710	46.1740	46.0050	45.9463	2.7	45.7413	2.7	44.9013	2.5	108.5
Denmark	(DKr)	8.6735	+0.0089	689 – 780	8.6816	8.6583	8.6602	1.8	8.6361	1.7	8.5383	1.6	109.4
Finland	(FM)	6.8663	+0.0181	588 – 738	6.9010	6.8440	6.8619	0.8	6.8538	0.7	–	–	85.7
France	(FFr)	7.7001	+0.0044	965 – 036	7.7265	7.6803	7.6895	1.6	7.6716	1.5	7.5977	1.3	109.6
Germany	(DM)	2.2405	−0.0007	395 – 415	2.2453	2.2354	2.2357	2.5	2.2255	2.7	2.1828	2.6	110.7
Greece	(Dr)	371.426	+0.55	011 – 841	371.961	368.949	–	–	–	–	–	–	65.8
Ireland	(I£)	0.9648	+0.0005	639 – 656	0.9662	0.9633	0.9639	1.1	0.9626	0.9	0.9588	0.6	97.9
Italy	(L)	2413.17	+3.81	200 – 434	2421.32	2403.62	2420.32	−3.6	2435.07	−3.6	2494.22	−3.4	72.8
Luxembourg	(LFr)	46.0513	−0.0209	315 – 710	48.1740	46.0050	45.9463	2.7	45.7413	2.7	44.9013	2.5	108.5
Netherlands	(Fi)	2.5102	−0.0001	088 – 116	2.5151	2.5055	2.504	3.0	2.4913	3.0	2.4405	2.8	108.6
Norway	(NKr)	9.8181	+0.0038	098 – 263	9.8455	9.7808	9.808	1.2	9.7865	1.3	9.7053	1.1	98.8
Portugal	(Es)	233.129	−0.129	984 – 274	233.809	232.718	233.554	−2.2	234.459	−2.3	–	–	95.4
Spain	(Pta)	189.935	−0.151	840 – 031	190.346	189.686	190.345	−2.6	191.21	−2.7	194.665	−2.5	81.7
Sweden	(SKr)	10.5371	+0.0814	273 – 469	10.5761	10.4508	10.5391	−0.2	10.5425	−0.2	10.5556	−0.2	85.1
Switzerland	(SFr)	1.8238	+0.0112	226 – 250	1.8274	1.8183	1.8175	4.1	1.8045	4.2	1.7515	4.0	114.1
UK	(£)	–	–	–	–	–	–	–	–	–	–	–	83.2
Ecu	–	1.2262	+0.0016	255 – 269	1.2288	1.2243	1.2248	1.4	1.222	1.4	1.2104	1.3	–
SDR†	–	1.036870		–	–	–	–	–	–	–	–	–	–
Americas													
Argentina	(Peso)	1.5077	+0.0054	072 – 081	1.5083	1.5015	–	–	–	–	–	–	–
Brazil	(R$)	1.4754	+0.0053	748 – 760	1.4765	1.4686	–	–	–	–	–	–	–
Canada	(C$)	2.0103	+0.0042	793 – 812	2.0815	2.0720	2.079	0.7	2.0766	0.7	2.0687	0.6	83.4
Mexico	(New Peso)	11.1419	−0.0175	314 – 524	11.1632	11.1091	–	–	–	–	–	–	–
USA	($)	1.5079	+0.0049	075 – 083	1.5085	1.5015	1.5069	0.8	1.505	0.8	1.4952	0.8	96.6
Pacific/Middle East/Africa													
Australia	(A$)	2.0379	+0.0043	366 – 391	2.0440	2.0270	2.0397	−1.1	2.0436	−1.1	2.0643	−1.3	87.1
Hong Kong	(HK$)	11.6614	+0.041	575 – 652	11.6655	11.6111	11.6555	0.6	11.6462	0.5	11.6117	0.4	–
India	(Rs)	54.2015	+0.1403	193 – 837	54.2840	53.9880	–	–	–	–	–	–	–
Israel	(Shk)	4.7367	+0.0028	319 – 415	4.7415	4.7210	–	–	–	–	–	–	–
Japan	(Y)	160.742	+0.415	624 – 860	160.910	160.090	159.997	5.6	158.487	5.6	152.442	5.2	137.1
Malaysia	(M$)	3.8580	+0.0187	562 – 597	3.8600	3.8353	–	–	–	–	–	–	–
New Zealand	(NZ$)	2.2572	+0.0006	554 – 589	2.2602	2.2511	2.2606	−1.8	2.2691	−2.1	2.3016	−2.0	105.8
Philippines	(Peso)	39.4655	+0.1258	362 – 948	39.4950	39.4360	–	–	–	–	–	–	–
Saudi Arabia	(SR)	5.6554	+0.0186	536 – 572	5.6575	5.6317	–	–	–	–	–	–	–
Singapore	(S$)	2.1390	+0.0093	376 – 403	2.1405	2.1296	–	–	–	–	–	–	–
South Africa	(R)	5.5103	+0.0155	077 – 128	5.5135	5.4925	–	–	–	–	–	–	–
South Korea	(Won)	1181.06	+0.42	067 – 145	1181.86	1176.67	–	–	–	–	–	–	–
Taiwan	(T$)	41.4462	+0.1842	291 – 632	41.4640	41.2357	–	–	–	–	–	–	–
Thailand	(Bt)	38.2102	+0.1254	850 – 354	38.2360	38.0600	–	–	–	–	–	–	–

† Rates for Jan 26 Bid/offer spreads in the Pound Spot table show only the last three decimal places. Forward rates are not directly quoted to the market but are implied by current interest rates. Sterling;ing Index calculated by the Bank of England. Base average 1990 = 100. Index rebased 1/2/95. Bid, Offer and Mid–rates in both this and the Dollar Spot tables denved from THE WM/REUTERS CLOSING SPOT RATES. Some values are rounded by the F.T.

Source: Reuters

Extract from the *Financial Times* – January 30, 1996

Fig 6.2

DOLLAR SPOT FORWARD AGAINST THE DOLLAR

Jan 29		Closing mid-point	Change on day	Bid/offer spread	Day's mid high	Day's mid low	One month Rate	%PA	Three months Rate	%PA	One year Rate	%PA	J.P Morgan index
Europe													
Austria	(Sch)	10.4484	−0.0374	463 – 504	10.4975	10.4460	10.4329	1.8	10.4009	1.8	10.2784	1.6	106.1
Belgium	(BFr)	30.5400	−0.1145	350 – 450	30.6820	30.5300	30.488	2.0	30.3875	2.0	30.025	1.7	108.0
Denmark	(DKr)	5.7520	−0.013	505 – 535	5.7745	5.7500	5.747	1.0	5.7375	1.0	5.7595	−0.1	108.5
Finland	(FM)	4.5536	−0.0029	498 – 573	4.5862	4.5490	4.5486	1.3	4.5399	1.2	4.5111	0.9	85.0
France	(FFr)	5.1065	−0.0139	055 – 075	5.1355	5.1035	5.1024	1.0	5.0968	0.8	5.078	0.6	108.9
Germany	(DM)	1.4859	−0.0053	856 – 861	1.4930	1.4855	1.4837	1.8	1.4788	1.9	1.4599	1.7	109.8
Greece	(Dr)	246.320	−0.445	110 – 530	247.210	245.410	247.995	−8.2	251.245	−8.0	266.07	−8.0	65.3
Ireland	(I£)	1.5630	+0.0044	620 – 640	1.5645	1.5570	1.5635	−0.3	1.5639	−0.2	1.56	0.2	–
Italy	(L)	1600.35	−2.74	000 – 070	1608.00	1597.90	1607.2	−5.1	1619.25	−4.7	1677.35	−4.8	72.4
Luxembourg	(LFr)	30.5400	−0.1145	350 – 450	30.6820	30.5300	30.488	2.0	30.4	1.8	30.095	1.5	108.0
Netherlands	(Fl)	1.6547	−0.0055	642 – 652	1.6713	1.6639	1.6617	2.2	1.6552	2.3	1.6321	2.0	107.8
Norway	(NKr)	6.5111	−0.0189	073 –148	6.5445	6.5010	6.5088	0.4	6.5006	0.6	6.4836	0.4	97.7
Portugal	(Es)	154.605	−0.595	550 – 660	155.310	154.550	154.98	−2.9	155.75	−3.0	159.355	−3.1	95.2
Spain	(Pta)	125.960	−0.515	930 – 990	126.650	125.930	126.355	−3.8	127.09	−3.6	130.58	−3.7	81.1
Sweden	(SKr)	6.9880	+0.0312	833 – 926	7.0412	6.9500	7.0051	−2.9	7.0345	−2.7	7.172	−2.6	84.9
Switzerland	(SFr)	1.2095.	+0.0035	090 – 100	1.2157	1.2076	1.2061	3.4	1.1989	3.5	1.1714	3.2	113.9
UK	(£)	1.5079	+0.0049	075 – 083	1.5085	1.5015	1.5069	0.8	1.505	0.8	1.4952	0.8	82.6
Ecu	–	1.2298	+0.0024	294 – 301	1.2302	1.2244	1.2301	−0.3	1.2305	−0.2	1.2311	−0.1	–
SDR†	–	0.68767	–	–	–	–	–	–	–	–	–	–	–
Americas													
Argentina	(Peso)	0.9999	+0.0003	998 – 999	0.9999	0.9998	–	–	–	–	–	–	–
Brazil	(R$)	0.9785	+0.0003	783 – 786	0.9787	0.9783	–	–	–	–	–	–	–
Canada	(C$)	1.3796	−0.0018	793 – 798	1.3825	1.3785	1.3798	−0.1	1.3799	−0.1	1.3849	−0.4	82.6
Mexico (New Peso)		7.3890	−0.036	840 – 940	7.3940	7.3840	7.3913	−0.4	7.3944	−0.3	7.3993	−0.1	–
USA	($)	–	–	–	–	–	–	–	–	–	–	–	97.7
Pacific/Middle East/Africa													
Australia	(A$)	1.3514	−0.0016	510 – 519	1.3555	1.3500	1.3534	−1.8	1.3569	−1.6	1.3756	−1.8	88.1
Hong Kong	(HK$)	7.7335	+0.0018	330 – 340	7.7345	7.7325	7.7342	−0.1	7.736	−0.1	7.763	−0.4	–
India	(Rs)	35.9450	−0.025	000 – 900	35.9950	35.9000	36.095	−5.0	36.4	−5.1	37.87	−5.4	–
Israel	(Shk)	3.1413	−0.0084	389 – 436	3.1530	3.1369	–	–	–	–	–	–	–
Japan	(Y)	106.600	−0.075	550 – 650	107.050	106.450	106.115	5.5	105.28	5.0	101.945	4.4	137.9
Malaysia	(MS)	2.5585	+0.004	580 – 590	2.5595	2.5535	2.5594	−0.4	2.5655	−1.1	2.589	−1.2	–
New Zealand	(NZ$)	1.4968	−0.0045	961 - 977	1.4992	1.4955	1.4999	−2.5	1.5057	−2.4	1.5303	−2.2	–
Philippines	(Peso)	26.1725	−0.0025	600 – 850	26.1850	26.1600	–	–	–	–	–	–	–
Saudi Arabia	(SR)	3.7505	–	503 –507	3.7508	3.7503	3.751	−0.1	3.7517	−0.1	3.755	−0.1	–
Singapore	(S$)	1.4185	+0.0015	180 –190	1.4205	1.4170	1.415	3.0	1.409	2.7	1.3835	2.5	–
South Africa	(R)	3.6543	−0.0017	535– 550	3.6565	3.6535	3.6831	−9.4	3.7346	−8.8	3.9578	−8.3	–
South Korea	(Won)	783.250	−2.3	200 – 300	785.000	782.800	786.25	−4.6	789.75	−3.3	808.25	−32	–
Taiwan	(T$)	27.4860	+0.032	820 – 900	27.4900	27.4700	27.506	−0.9	27.546	−0.9	–	–	–
Thailand	(Bt)	25.3400	–	300 – 500	25.3550	25.3240	25.4387	−4.7	25.6425	−4.8	26.525	−4.7	–

†SDR rate per $ for Jan 26 Bid/offer spreads in the Dollar Spot table show only the last three decimal places. Forward rates are not directly quoted to the market but are implied by current interest rates. UK, Ireland & ECU are quoted in US Currency. J.P. Morgan nominal indices Jan 25: Base average 1990 =100

Source: Reuters

The reason information is so very important relates back to one of the favorite sayings in the market: "every single piece of known information is already discounted in the price."

So why do markets and prices move?

It all comes down to what we don't know. So the bank with access to faster market information will have the opportunity to change its prices ahead of other market players, assimilating the new information, and will have a competitive advantage, assuming of course that it has moved its price the right way!

Procedures and Practices-Banks

As already mentioned it is market practice to quote only the last two figures of a price. If the exchange rate at a particular point in time is GBP/USD: 1.5050–55, we can expand out the price to form GBP/USD: 1.5050–1.5055. A spot trader is likely to quote only 50–55, the client is expected to know the rest. This represents the bid–offer spread on the two currencies in question: basically, how the bank buys and sells pounds against dollars (the base currency against the "foreign" currency). In a perfect world, the bank trader would deal simultaneously with two different parties on his or her prices, and would see the 5-pip differential as his profit. Each 0.0001 is known as a "pip." Interbank rates can be quoted with a 2- to 5-pip spread, corporate transactions will have a wider spread, sometimes as much as 10 pips, to reflect the different credit risks of the two parties. See Figure 6.3 which illustrates a Reuters page used by many corporate clients.

Let us examine the following rate for "cable." This refers to the original way in which banks dealt with one another 30 or so years ago. Then, the only way to ask for and receive prices in GBP/USD was to send messages down the transatlantic submarine cable, and the term "cable" has stuck.

True story *I found out recently that the use of the cable did not come free. One of the UK merchant banks remarked to me that they had the use of the cable for, I think, 30 or so minutes each afternoon, at a yearly cost of £30,000! That was a lot of money in those days.*

Reuters page showing major currencies quoted against the dollar

Fig 6.3

1605 BARCLAYS BANK PLC LONDON TEL 283 – 0909 TX 887841 BAXX					
	Spot	**1 MTH**	**2 MTHS**	**3 MTHS**	**6 MTHS**	**12 MTHS**
STG	1.5312/22	12.5/10.5	23/20	31/28	61/56	130/120
DEM	1.4684/94	25/23	49/47	72/69	143/138	267/257
CHF	1.1970/80	39/36	78/74	111/106	214/206	400/385
NLG	1.6446/56	31/28	63/58	90/85	178/170	325/310
FRF	5.0350/00	50/44	95/85	127/117	225/210	110/360
JPY	105.03/13	42.4/41.4	87.5/85.5	125/122	238/234	442/436
XEU	1.2592/99	6/7	12.5/14.5	18.5/20.5	36/41	66/73
ESB	123.63/73	40/44	69/75	98/106	187/197	360/380
ITL	1554.5/6.0	58/65	115/125	170/182	325/350	600/640
BEF	30.18/22	5.7/4.7	11/9.5	16/14	31/26	56/50

Source: Reuters (courtesy Barclays Bank plc)

Spot Rate: GBP/USD: 1.5355-65
Alternatively this can be written: £/$: 1.5355-65

The bank will always quote their price, bid first and offer second. The bid being "55" for the base currency, which is sterling, and the offer being "65." This can be termed as how the bank buys sterling and sells dollars @ 1.5355; or how the bank sells sterling and buys dollars @ 1.5365.

It is obviously important to establish which is the base currency, in the case above it is sterling. The other currency is referred to as the "quoted" or the "foreign" currency. Back to our example: as this is a *direct* quotation, the bank will sell the foreign currency (the dollar) on the left and buy it on the right. It is worth noting that many users of foreign exchange (clients) ask for their prices in "foreign currency" terms rather than base currency terms. A UK corporate who wishes to sell his dollars receivables against sterling will almost certainly ask for a price to sell the dollars, rather than a price where he can buy sterling (see Figure 6.4).

The same "rules" apply when dealing with currencies quoted on an *indirect* basis, for example USD/DEM at a spot rate of 1.4860–65 (see Figure 6.5).

By following these simple rules, dealing on the wrong side of the price should be avoided. Another way to reinforce this technical point is to remember that a dealer wants to make money out of his trading, in that, he will wish to buy the base currency as cheaply as possible, for as few dollars as possible, and when selling his pounds on to the next player he wants to sell them as expensively as possible. The difference will be his profit. A bank will always deal at the most advantageous rate to itself.

Traders, when dealing interbank, may transact a deal with simply one word, "Mine" or "Yours:" this is in relation to the base currency. So if the spot rate was DEM/JPY: 71.15–20, and a trader shouted "Mine, 10," he would have bought 10 million Deutsche Marks against yen at 71.20 (dealing on the counterparties' "offer" rate). The problems arise when inexperienced dealers shout "Mine," with no amount given. Each currency pair has a market accepted amount for a *regular* trade. These are shown in Table 6.1. Our inexperienced dealer may shout "Mine" and be told, "OK you got 20" "But I only wanted 5!!"

Fig 6.4

Spot quotations GBP/USD

Spot rate: GBP/USD: 1.5355–65

Base currency is sterling
Foreign/quoted currency is US dollar

1.5355	1.5365
(bid)	(offer)

Bank bids for £ against $ Bank offers £ against $
Client buys $ and sells £   Client sells $ and buys £

Fig 6.5

Spot quotations USD/DEM

Spot rate: USD/DEM: 1.4860–65

Base currency is US dollar
Foreign/quoted currency is Deutsche Marks

1.4860	1.4865
(bid)	(offer)

Bank bids for $ against DEM   Bank offers $ against DEM
Client buys DEM and sells $ Client sells DEM and buys $

Tip

It is vital to establish what your dealing amount is. This will vary from bank to bank, and from trader to trader. If you agree to make prices in 10 million, and someone tries to deal with you in 20 million, you are only committed to deal in 10, but you may want to do the full amount. Quotations are assumed to be for "regular" amounts, unless otherwise specified.

Regular dealing amounts in major currencies

Table 6.1

GBP/USD	£5 million
USD/JPY, USD/CHF, USD/DEM, etc	US$10 million
DEM/JPY	DEM20 million

Now we know which side of the price we are on we must consider another market convention where banks, for simplicity, run their trading room positions in US dollars. And although they may be trading USD/CHF, they will generally say they are long of US dollars rather than short of Swiss francs. This allows positions across many currencies to be traded, with the US dollar as the common denominator for running the positions. This is still the case even if the foreign exchange bank itself is not dollar based. A bank's position across many different currencies can then be valued in dollars and may look something like Table 6.2.

Potential dealing room position

Table 6.2

Currency	Long	Short	Rate
GBP/USD	**$4,546,500**	3,000,000	1.5155
USD/DEM	**$5,000,000**	7,450,000	1.4900
USD/CHF	3,000,000	**$2,480,363**	1.2095
USD/ITL	**$2,500,000**	4,000,000,000	1600.00
USD/JPY	1,060,000,000	**$10,000,000**	106.00
Overall US dollar position	**=**	**short US$433,863**	

This can help the banks to monitor their exposure, by seeing at a glance whether they are long or short in dollar terms.

Procedures and Practices–Clients

The bank's clients will always be trying to get the best deal for themselves and, naturally enough, their aims are totally opposite to those of the banks. Few corporate customers can deal on the finest terms. A client may want to deal for an uneven amount, possibly below the minimum amount for which competitive rates are available. This may leave the bank with an amount to cover on less favorable terms unless it has other customer business to go against it.

The bank may also have to add together a series of smaller deals and cover the aggregate amount, leaving itself exposed to changes in the exchange rate. In addition, the bank must also take into account the credit risk: that the client will fail to fulfill its side of the bargain. This may leave the bank with an unbalanced position and exposed to market movements. It also begs the question, is there a credit risk or a settlement risk? Banks seem to be equally divided on this point.

Let us go back to the cable rate – spot rate: GBP/USD: 1.5355–65. A client who needs to purchase dollars will be trying to buy as many dollars as he can with his pounds, and will be trying to get as numerically high a rate as possible. The client will be buying the dollars where the bank is selling the dollars, yet the bank will be trying to quote as numerically low as possible.

Larger amounts can generate more attractive rates, but not always. Obviously the rate quoted to a client will reflect the transaction amount, in that a rate to sell USD75,700 may not be too competitive – it is too small for a pure interbank quotation. On the other hand, a rate to sell USD5,000,000 will get a very good rate. But what if the sale amount was USD1,000,000,000? It could then be argued that this is too large for a one-off deal, and for safety the bank may quote a worse rate, to give it time to cover the entire transaction in the market.

Tip

On some occasions when clients need to convert a smaller amount, say USD20,000 to sterling they may find that they will achieve a more favorable rate by using the bank's "sheet rates." These are the rates set by the foreign exchange dealers at the start of the day, sent to the various London and regional branches, and they generally remain good for the whole day, unless "referred" if the market becomes very active. The advantage of using sheet rates is that the rate will not be adjusted unfavorably by the traders for the small size of the transaction, so the original sheet rate may turn out to offer a better exchange rate. All clearing banks offer a similar service for smaller amounts.

True story

A young trainee had joined the treasury of a large Middle Eastern multinational company. He had joined as the "tea boy" and was working his way up. He hadn't been with the company that long when they gave him the opportunity to place his first deal. He had watched how the dealers worked, and his job was to place a deposit in Deutsche Marks over the weekend. It was late in the afternoon on

True story

*Friday, he carefully checked the screen rates, and chose the bank with the best price. He called them up and asked if the price on the screen was still good, it was – so he took a deep breath and said "Yours, 800 million Marks." He was rather hurt to get the reply, "Thanks, now **** *** !" I thought they'd be pleased he said rather naively.*

NB: Normal dealing amount is DEM10 million.

Look at the data from Figure 6.2 (from the *Financial Times*) showing the value of different currencies quoted against the dollar. From the data the rates in Table 6.3 have been extracted.

Example

Major currency spot rates against the US dollar

Table 6.3

Currency	Bid	Offer
GBP/USD	1.5075	1.5083
USD/JPY	106.55	106.65
USD/CHF	1.2090	1.2100
USD/DEM	1.4856	1.4861
USD/FRF	5.1055	5.1075
USD/NLG	1.6642	1.6652

1. A German manufacturer of heavy equipment sells his goods into the US and invoices in USD; he needs to convert the dollars to his own domestic currency.

   Client sells dollars, bank buys dollars, quotation is 1.4856.

2. A French importer of American "off-road" vehicles pays for the goods in US dollars, as part of his contract.

   Client buys dollars, bank sells dollars, quotation is 5.1075.

3. UK client sells USD2,500,000, for pounds. How much do we get?

   Rate quoted 1.5083, making a total of £1,657,495.

4. A Dutch exporter sells goods to America, and invoices in guilders.

   Client sells dollars, bank buys dollars, quotation 1.6642.

5. Client purchases FRF10,000,000, How many dollars are required for payment?

   Rate quoted 5.1055, making a total of USD1,958,672.

Quick fix exercise (1)

1. A client is trying to buy dollars and sell Deutsche Marks, and has contacted three different banks for prices. He has been quoted:

Bank A USD/DEM 1.4830–40
Bank B USD/DEM 1.4832–42
Bank C USD/DEM 1.4825–35

At what rate should he deal?

Using Table 6.3:

2. Where does the bank sell Swiss francs to a client against US dollars?

3. You buy 1,000,000,000 yen, from a client against dollars, at which rate and how many dollars will you pay out?

4. A client wishes to buy USD5 million with pounds, what rate will he be quoted and   how much sterling will he need?

For answers, refer to the end of the chapter.

Calculating Cross Currency Rates

As mentioned earlier, it is market practice for most currencies to be quoted against the dollar in terms of the number of units of the currency for each single US dollar. This is the **indirect** method of quotation. Rates quoted the other way round, such as GBP/USD, are **direct** quotations. A "cross rate" is a rate of exchange between two currencies where neither is the dollar. There are three different ways of calculating cross rates, dependent upon whether you have two **indirect** quotations, two **direct** quotations, or one of each.

Two indirect quotations

The two exchange rates must be cross divided.

Spot: USD/DEM: 1.5337–1.5342

Spot: USD/ITL: 1535–1536

Example

$1536 \div 1.5337 = 1001.50$: how the client can sell ITL, and buy DEM.
$1535 \div 1.5342 = 1000.52$: how the client can buy ITL, and sell DEM.

The bank of course will be on the other side of the price:

Spot: DEM/ITL 1000.52–1001.50

Two direct quotations

The two exchange rates must be cross divided.

Spot: GBP/USD: 1.5400–1.5405

Spot: AUD/USD: 0.7914–0.7919

1.5400 ÷ 0.7919 = 1.9447: how the client can buy AUD and sell GBP.
1.5405 ÷ 0.7914 = 1.9465: how the client can sell AUD and buy GBP.

The bank of course will be on the other side of the price:

Spot: GBP/AUD: 1.9447–1.9465

An indirect quotation and a direct quotation

The same side of each exchange rate must be multiplied.

Spot: GBP/USD: 1.5400–1.5405

Spot: USD/CHF: 1.2650–1.2660

1.5400 × 1.2650 = 1.9481: how the client can buy CHF and sell GBP.
1.5405 × 1.2660 = 1.9503: how the client can sell CHF and buy GBP.

The bank will, as in the previous examples, be on the other side of the price:

Spot: GBP/CHF: 1.9481 – 1.9503

Quick fix exercise (2)

1. Given the following rates calculate where a UK exporter would sell Deutsche Mark receivables for sterling.

Spot: GBP/USD: 1.5400–05
Spot: USD/DEM: 1.5337–42

2. A bank has quoted the following spot rate:
DEM/JPY: 71.13–15
Where will the client buy yen?

3. Calculate the Deutsche Mark/peseta cross from the following rates:

Spot: USD/DEM: 1.5337–1.5342
Spot: USD/ESP: 128.95–128.98

For answers, refer to the end of the chapter.

Conclusion

To recap, spot foreign exchange is driven totally by supply and demand; this can be influenced by any number of factors acting individually, on either one or both of the currencies, or multiple factors acting in concert upon one or both currencies. Some factors will be more or less important depending upon the time of year, a political agenda, or other third party influences. Major currencies can become minor currencies, weak currencies can become strong and vice versa. In times of crisis there may often be a "flight to quality" into currencies such as the US dollar, the Deutsche Mark, and the yen. The currency markets are ever changing and participants with access to *state of the art* information systems are arguably better placed to profit from market movements than those with the less up-to-date inputs. See Chapter 18 on *technology and the markets*.

Answers to quick fix exercises

(1)

1. From Bank C at 1.4835.

2. 1.2090.

3. 106.55, USD9,385,265.

4. 1.5075, £3,316,749.

(2)

1. 1.5405 × 1.5342 = 2.3634: how the client can sell DEM and buy GBP.

2. 71.13.

3. 128.98 ÷ 1.5337 = 84.10: how the client can sell ESP, and buy DEM.
   128.95 ÷ 1.5342 = 84.05: how the client can buy ESP, and sell DEM.

Spot: DEM/ESP: 84.05–84.10

■ ■ ■

*'Forward foreign
exchange is naturally
more complex than
spot FX, as the extra
dimension of relative
interest rates comes
into play in the
pricing.'*

The Mechanics of Forward Foreign Exchange

Introduction

Foreign exchange can be bought or sold by many different market participants using many different currencies in most countries around the world. It can be bought or sold value *spot*, which, as we saw in the previous chapter, generally means a two-business-day value period, or it can be transacted for delivery on a future date, in which case it is a *forward* transaction.

Forward foreign exchange has been available at commercial banks for many years, but the explosive growth occurred in the late 1970s and early 1980s. Before World War II it was possible to get forward prices, but the market was quite small and volumes did not increase until some years later. It could also be argued that the development of the pocket calculator in the mid-1970s made forward pricing that much easier and that in turn helped the interbank market to progress rapidly.

Background

There are two distinct types of forward transaction: the *forward outright* (or outright forward) transaction and the *FX swap* – not to be confused with currency swaps which are one of the range of derivative currency products. Outright forward deals are used mostly by corporate customers to hedge their currency risk, whereas the professional interbank market will trade "swap points" or "differentials" among themselves.

Theoretically, the spot price and the forward price of a currency could be the same, but it is highly unlikely. Ordinarily, the forward rate is either higher or lower than the spot rate, indicating that something has been added or subtracted from the underlying spot exchange rate – these are known as the differentials or the "points." Quoting forward differentials, called premiums and discounts, rather than quoting an all-in forward price has advantages. Firstly, forward differentials can remain unchanged for longish periods, even though the spot rate may be very volatile. Secondly, the outright forward rate is not of much interest to the interbank dealer who is quoting only the points.

Question:
Just what are these differentials and why are they so important ?

Answer:
Let us consider a trade where a bank has agreed to sell sterling to a customer in 12 months' time, and buy Deutsche Marks in return.

The bank could fix the rate now based on the current spot rate, but that may well move in the next 12 months. The bank, however, is committed to hand over the sterling in 12 months' time, but may end up receiving less Deutsche Marks than it needs to buy the sterling at the then prevailing rates. This could lead to a foreign exchange loss on the Deutsche Marks.

Question:
How does the bank protect itself against this loss?

Answer:
The FX risk on the forward sale of sterling can be offset by a spot purchase of sterling now. This ensures that the bank has the sterling available and has fixed the exchange rate with which to buy them. But what should they do with this sterling as it is not required for 12 months?

Firstly, the resulting sterling must be put on deposit in the money markets for 12 months, yielding an interest income. Secondly, with what do we fund the purchase of the sterling? The bank must borrow Deutsche Marks from the money markets for 12 months, to buy the sterling spot. The Deutsche Marks will be repaid by the customer's funds in 12 months' time. There will be a funding cost for this position.

Figure 7.1 shows the bank's transactions.

Fig 7.1

Group of transactions that make up the bank's forward hedge

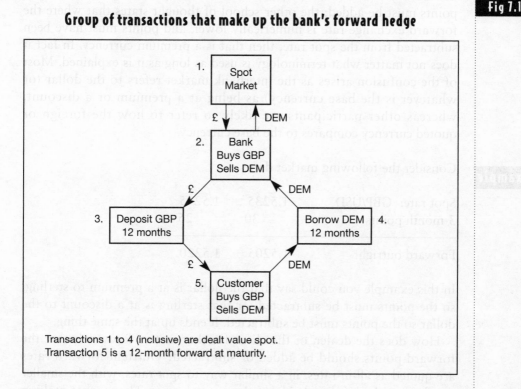

Transactions 1 to 4 (inclusive) are dealt value spot.
Transaction 5 is a 12-month forward at maturity.

If we group the transactions in Figure 7.1 together: the forward rate consists of a combination of the current spot rate plus or minus the appropriate differential for the maturity (see Figure 7.2). This will be examined in more detail later in the chapter.

Fig 7.2

Components of a foreign exchange forward transaction

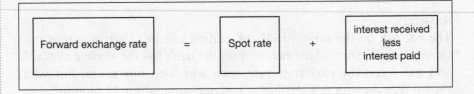

Premiums and Discounts

These refer to the forward points, which need to be added or subtracted from the spot rate. There can be an element of confusion when using these terms. One school of thought is that if the forward exchange rate is numerically higher than the spot rate the currency is at a premium, so the points must be added; the other school of thought states that where the forward exchange rate is numerically lower, and points must have been subtracted from the spot rate, then that is a premium currency. In fact it does not matter what terminology is used as long as it is explained. Most of the confusion arises as the interbank market refers to the dollar (or whatever is the base currency) as being at a premium or a discount, whereas other participants are likely to refer to how the foreign or quoted currency compares to the base currency.

Example

Consider the following market data:

Spot rate: GBP/USD	1.5235	1.5245
3-month points	30	25
Forward outright	1.5205	1.5220

In this example you could say that the dollar is at a premium to sterling, so the points must be subtracted, or that sterling is at a discount to the dollar so the points must be subtracted. It ends up at the same thing.

How does the dealer, or the client for that matter, know whether the forward points should be added or subtracted? Outright forward rates are quoted as all-in rates, in a similar way to spot rates, with the smaller number on the left-hand side of the quoted price. The market making bank will always buy the base currency as cheaply as possible, and sell the foreign or "quoted" currency as expensively as possible to achieve the best deal for itself (in this example the base currency is sterling and the quoted currency is the US dollar).

This is achieved by having the larger points figure on the left in the case of premium "quoted" currencies, and the larger figure on the right in the case of discount "quoted" currencies. Using our example to re-state the position, the dollar is at a premium to sterling so the points must therefore be subtracted; this gives the forward outright rate as GBP/USD 1.5205–20.

Forward prices will always exhibit a larger bid–offer spread than spot prices. The example above illustrates a bid–offer spread on the spot rate of 10 pips, but a 15–pip spread on the forward. The same is true even if we use a currency pair where the dollar or another currency is the base, as shown below.

Consider the following market data:

Example

Spot rate: USD/ITL	1535	1536
3-month points	20	23
Forward outright	1555	1559

In this example the base currency is the US dollar and the quoted currency is the Italian lira. The larger figure is on the right, as is the case of discount "quoted" currencies. The lira is at a discount to the dollar so the points must be added, giving a forward outright rate of USD/ITL 1555–1559. Alternatively, we could have said that the US dollar is at a premium to the lira. On both occasions the points are added. This shows a bid–offer spread on the spot rate of 1 lira, with a 4-lire spread on the forward.

A *"quick and dirty" way of remembering whether to add or subtract the points relates to the sequence of the numbers when you look at the bid–offer spread on the differentials:* **Tip**

- *If the points sequence is high/low (145–135) subtract the points.*
- *If the points sequence is low/high (20–23) add the points.*

Calculating Differentials

The outright forward rate is not a dealer's assessment or forecast of what the spot rate will be on a predetermined future date. It is a simple calculation involving the current spot rate plus or minus the current interest rate differentials at that same moment in time. The forward rate is not a predictor of what the spot rate will be in the future.

As mentioned in the previous chapter: the market has a saying: *"that every single piece of known information is in the price."* If there were no changes in the data available, and every item of data had been assimilated in the price, and all we experienced was the passage of time, and nothing whatsoever changed, then the current spot rate may well turn out to be the actual spot rate on a specific date in the future. But, as we know, life is not like that; every change, however minute, is reflected in the price, making exchange rates very volatile.

It must also be borne in mind that when pricing any financial instrument the market will always consider the cost of the hedge as the minimum price for the deal.

As stated previously, the interbank market will quote exchange rate forwards not in terms of an outright rate but, rather, in terms of spot rates and differentials (or swap points). The differential or forward swap is an exchange of one currency for another currency on one date to be reversed on a given future date. This can also be achieved by borrowing one currency for a given period while lending the other currency for the same period.

The swap rate will reflect the interest rate differential between the two currencies, converted into foreign exchange terms, using a calculation based on Eurocurrency interest rates (unless otherwise stated).

The logical extension of this is that it is the perceived change in a country's inflation rate that will increase or decrease the number of forward points. The argument is that, when a country experiences inflation, there is a natural tendency by the authorities to increase domestic interest rates to try to combat it, so rates overall increase.

Let us consider the facts. Do we agree that a parallel transaction to calculate the forward differential of a currency pair could also be achieved by borrowing one currency for a given period while lending the other currency for the same period? The rationale for this close association is that a trader should not be able to make a profit by "round-tripping," i.e. by borrowing and lending currencies for the appropriate period, then reconverting through the exchange rate the principal plus interest and ending up with more money than he started with.

Consider the following simultaneous transactions:

(a) borrow NLG for three months from spot value date;
(b) sell NLG and buy USD value spot;
(c) invest the dollars just purchased for three months from spot value date;
(d) sell forward now the USD principal and interest maturing in three months' time, into NLG.

Basically, the market will adjust for the price of (d) so that there will be no profits or losses. It can be argued that interest differentials, or forward points or swap points, whatever you wish to call them, are merely a "balancing item" to ensure that arbitrage does not take place. If the four rates are not in line, then *round-tripping* or *arbitrage* will occur, when for a short period of time the four transactions above may generate a profit, until such time as market forces bring the rates back into line.

The four transactions (a) to (d) above are more meaningful if we convert them to a formula:

(a) Borrow NLG100 at a rate of A% per annum. The total amount of principal and interest, (repayable in three months) will be:

$$100 \times \left(1 + \frac{A}{100} \times \frac{Days}{360} \right)$$

(b) Sell NLG100 for USD at the spot rate to give USD (100/spot).

(c) Invest USD (100/spot) at B%. The principal and interest returned (in three months' time) will be:

$$(100/spot) \times \left(1 + \frac{B}{100} \times \frac{Days}{360} \right)$$

(d) Sell forward this last amount at the forward rate to give:

$$(100/spot) \times \left(1 \times \frac{B}{100} \times \frac{Days}{360} \right) \times \textbf{Forward outright}$$

Equating the principal and interest in (a) and (d) we get:

$$100 \times \left(1 + \frac{A}{100} \times \frac{Days}{360} \right) =$$

$$(100/\text{spot}) \times \left(1 + \frac{B}{100} \times \frac{Days}{360} \right) \times \text{Forward outright}$$

making:

$$\text{Forward outright} = (\text{Spot}) \times \frac{1 + \dfrac{A}{100} \times \dfrac{Days}{360}}{1 + \dfrac{B}{100} \times \dfrac{Days}{360}}$$

also:

$$\text{Forward differential} = (\text{Forward outright} - \text{Spot})$$
$$(\text{Forward swap})$$

$$= \frac{(\text{Spot}) \times \left\{ \dfrac{A - B}{100} \right\} \times \left\{ \dfrac{Days}{360} \right\}}{\left\{ 1 + \dfrac{B}{100} \times \dfrac{Days}{360} \right\}} \qquad \textbf{Equation 7.1}$$

NB: If the interest rate at B% and the number of days are sufficiently small, the following approximation can be made, which I shall call Equation 7.2.

$$\textbf{Forward swap} \approx (\text{Spot}) \times \frac{(\textbf{Interest rate differential})}{(\qquad 100 \qquad)} \times \frac{(\textbf{Days})}{(360)}$$

$$\textbf{Equation 7.2}$$

This formula can be reversed as follows:

$$\textbf{Interest rate differential} \approx \frac{(\textbf{Forward swap} \times 100 \times 360)}{\text{Spot} \times \text{Days}}$$

Worked example (1)

Consider the following market data:

30-day NLG interest rate: 3.5%
30-day USD interest rate: 5.5%
Spot USD/NLG: 1.49

Example

Using Equation 7.1:

$$\text{Forward swap} = \frac{1.49 \times \frac{-2}{100} \times \frac{30}{360}}{1 + \frac{5.5}{100} \times \frac{30}{360}} = 0.00247 \text{ or } 25 \text{ points}$$

Using Equation 7.2:

$$(\text{Approximate swap}) \approx 1.49 \times \frac{-2}{100} \times \frac{30}{360} = 0.00248 \text{ or } 25 \text{ points}$$

But if we extend the maturity of the forward transaction the relationship breaks down as shown below.

Example

Worked example (2)

Consider the following market data:

1-year NLG interest rate: 3.625%
1-year USD interest rate: 5.25%
Spot USD/NLG: 1.49

Using Equation 7.1:

$$\text{Forward swap} = \frac{1.49 \times \frac{-2}{100} \times \frac{365}{360}}{1 + \frac{5.25}{100} \times \frac{365}{360}} = 0.02869 \text{ or } 287 \text{ points}$$

Using Equation 7.2:

$$(\text{Approximate swap}) = 1.49 \times \frac{-2}{100} \times \frac{365}{360}$$

$$= 0.03021 \text{ or } 302 \text{ points}$$

NB: The day count convention is 360 days as this is market practice for both Euroguilders and Eurodollars, so we are using the Actual/360 calculation. It should also be borne in mind that the interest differentials must be calculated using gross (not net) interest rates, for otherwise the costs/receipts are exaggerated.

Procedures and Practices

FX swaps or differential prices are quoted as two-way prices in the same way as other rates, but technically we should use the correct side of the underlying foreign exchange rate and relevant money market prices for the calculations. It is, however, far easier to use mid-prices throughout to calculate the mid-price of the swap and then to spread the two-way price around this middle rate. When a deal is done, only one price is dealt, (the swap price); the actual transaction will be written out as two deals because there will be two separate settlements:

- a settlement on the spot value date
- a settlement on the forward value date.

Consider the following three-month forward swap quote:

USD/CHF: 110–100

110	100
Client buys CHF spot	Client sells CHF spot
Client sells CHF forward	Client buys CHF forward

A specific spot rate will be needed to complete the calculation to arrive at the settlement rates. The exact spot rate that is used is not that important as long as the near and far sides of the swap preserve the differential.

When you consider where the forward foreign exchange rates are derived from, it is easy to see how close the relationship is between money market interest rates and foreign exchange rates.

Calculating Outright Forwards

The technology that the banks use for quoting forward and spot rates is becoming increasingly sophisticated, and will vary from bank to bank. As with all fast moving markets it is vital for the traders to have access to completely up-to-date current market information, in order for them to maintain their competitiveness. The Reuters and Dow-Jones Telerate networks offer both information services and dealing technology. It is also market practice for the market making banks to exhibit their current rates on screens for distribution around the market. A sample of the information is shown in Figure 7.3.

Reuters page showing major currencies quoted against sterling

Fig 7.3

1715 BARCLAYS BANK PLC LONDON			283 0909 TX 887841 BAST		
	SPOT	1 MTH	2 MTHS	3 MTHS	6 MTHS	12 MTHS
STG	1.5392/02	13/11	24/21	34/31	68/63	153/143
DEM	2.2321/52	55/48	108/99	157/147	304/289	588/558
CHF	1.8168/96	72/66	143/136	209/200	394/378	753/722
NLG	2.4996/29	65/59	128/119	189/179	364/347	691/661
FRF	7.6590/718	131/113	252/227	339/308	622/566	1219/1124
JPY	160. 50/77	77/72	152/145	224/217	428/417	808/790
ITL	2375. 4/9.4	67/82	147/168	223/248	416/463	754/832
BEF	45.88/98	13/9	24/19	34/29	65/55	127/108
ESP	187.96/25	37/47	79/93	118/135	220/243	399/444
XEU	1.2099/15	16/13	31/26	44/39	87/77	170/155

Source: Reuters (courtesy Barclays Bank plc)

Figure 7.3 is a "monitor" page published by Barclays Bank plc through the Reuters network and available to most market participants. Some screens however, will be available only on a *selective access* basis. This gives contributors the chance to ensure that their information does not go directly to their competitors.

The page quotes major currencies spot and forward against sterling and uses the SWIFT codes to identify them. The first currency on the left-hand side is shown as STG: how can you quote STG against sterling? In fact, this actually means GBP/USD. The first column shows the spot rates with the bid-offer spread, and the rest of the page displays the forward differentials out to 12 months. Using Figure 7.3 above we can calculate outright forward rates:

(1) Calculate the two-month forward for cable:

Spot: GBP/USD	1.5392–1.5402
2-month points	24–21
Outright	1.5368–1.5381

NB: The points sequence goes high/low, so the points are subtracted.

(2) Calculate the two-month forward for GBP/DEM:

Spot: GBP/DEM	2.2321–2.2352
2-month points	108–99
Outright	2.2213–2.2253

NB: The points sequence goes high/low, so the points are subtracted.

| Tip | *Remember to incorporate the correct amount of zeros into the differential before adding or subtracting the points from the spot rate. Market information screens are notorious for leaving off the zeros. If the sequence is 145/135 for GBP/USD, check the number of significant figures after the decimal point when the spot rate is quoted – it is four. So the forward points are actually 0.0145/0.0135.* |

(3) Calculate the two-month forward for GBP/FRF:

Spot: GBP/FRF	7.6590–7.6718
2-month points	252–227
Outright	7.6338–7.6491

NB: The points sequence goes high/low, so the points are subtracted.

Figure 7.3 gives the forward differentials for specific monthly periods. These are known as "straight" dates or "calendar" dates. Sometimes it may be necessary to transact a deal for a date that is in between these dates; these are known as "broken" dates. A forward foreign exchange transaction can be arranged for any day in the future as long as it is a business day in both currencies. The forward swap points or differentials are then calculated by interpolating between the given dates on either side, as shown later in the section.

Calculating "Straight Date" Forwards (Against Sterling)

A client wishes to buy CHF3 million forward for six months against sterling.
Consider the following market information:

Spot GBP/CHF	1.8168–96
Transaction date	Thursday February 29, 1996
Spot value date	Monday March 4, 1996
Forward value date	Wednesday September 4, 1996
6-month points	394–378

The Swiss franc is at a *premium* to sterling so the points will need to be subtracted, this can be seen as the number sequence is high/low. When calculating rates for outright forward transactions, if you use the right-hand side of the spot rate you also use the right-hand side of the forward differential, and vice versa.

First, we must decide on the correct side of the spot rate. As our client is buying the Swiss francs he is on the left-hand side of the rate at GBP/CHF at 1.8168.

Second, we need to use the left-hand side of the forward differential, which is 394 points or 0.0394.

Third, we need to put all the components together:

Spot GBP/CHF:	1.8168
6-month points:	.0394
Outright	1.7774

The Swiss francs will cost £1,687,858.67 (3,000,000 divided by 1.7774)

Quick fix exercise (1)
Using the data in Figure 7.3:
1. Calculate the one-month outright forward rate for a client who wishes to sell US dollars and buy sterling.

2. A client wishes to buy forward 10 million French francs with sterling for a period of six months. How much will he be charged?

3. A client wants to sell forward DEM2 million against sterling for three months. How much will she receive?

For answers, refer to the end of the chapter.

Calculating "Broken" Date Forwards (Against Sterling)

A customer of the bank needs to sell forward USD5 million for value May 29, 1996.

Consider the following market information:

Spot GBP/USD	1.5392–02
Transaction date	Thursday February 29, 1996
Spot value date	Monday March 4, 1996
Forward value date	Wednesday May 29, 1996
2-month points	24–21
3-month points	34–31
Day count – 2 months forward	64 days (May 7, 1996)
Day count – 3 months forward	92 days (June 4, 1996)
Day count – May 29, 1996	86 days

NB: May 4 is a Saturday; the following Monday is May 6 which is a bank holiday in the UK so the next business day is May 7, 1996.

It is possible to work out the straight date forwards for either two or three whole months, but our date falls between them both. It is necessary to *interpolate* between month 2 and month 3 and calculate the number of points per day and add or subtract as required. The dollar is at a *premium* to sterling so the points will need to be subtracted – this can be seen as the number sequence is high/low. When calculating rates for outright forward transactions, if you use the right-hand side of the spot rate remember to use the right-hand side of the forward differential.

First, we must decide on the correct side of the spot rate. As our client is selling dollars he is on the right-hand side of the rate at GBP/USD 1.5402.

Second, we need to calculate the number of points between month 2 and month 3, and then calculate the number of points per day, using the formula: 3-month points less 2-month points, divided by the number of days (May 7–June 4). This gives:

$$\frac{(0.0031 - 0.0021)}{(92 \text{ days} - 64 \text{ days})} = \frac{0.0010}{28} = 0.000036 \text{ points per day}$$

Third, we need these extra points for an additional 22 days between the two-month forward value date and May 29, 1996:

$$(0.000036 \times 22 \text{ days} = 0.000786)$$

Fourth, we need to put all the components together:

Spot GBP/USD:	1.5402
2-month points:	.0021
Extra 22 days' points:	.0008
Outright	1.5373

The USD5 million will generate £3,252,455.60 (5,000,000 divided by 1.5373).

> When calculating the number of points per day, do not round the significant figures to the final number of decimal places required until the last calculation has been concluded. Do not round after each stage.   **Tip**

Quick fix exercise (2)

Using the data in Figure 7.3: a UK company director needs to pay a bill of USD2.2 million, due on December 10. He wishes to lock in the rate now as he is concerned about the weakness of the pound. The transaction date is March 18, 1996. How much sterling will the dollars cost?

For answer refer to the end of the chapter.

Calculating "Straight Date" Forwards (Against the US Dollar)

For those readers who feel uncomfortable with using sterling as a base currency, this and the next section provide similar examples using the US dollar as the base – as is more normal in the international markets.

A client wishes to buy DEM3 million forward for six months against US dollars.

Consider the following market information:

Spot USD/DEM	1.4684–94
Transaction date	Thursday February 29, 1996
Spot value date	Monday March 4, 1996
Forward value date	Wednesday September 4, 1996
6-month points	143–138

The Deutsche Mark is at a *premium* to the dollar so the points will need to be subtracted. This can be seen as the number sequence on the forward differential is high/low.

First, we must decide on the correct side of the spot rate. As our client is buying the Deutsche Marks he is on the left-hand side of the rate at USD/DEM 1.4684.

Second, we need to use the left-hand side of the forward differential, which is 143 points or 0.0143

Third, we need to put all the components together:

Spot USD/DEM:	1.4684
6-month points:	.0143
Outright	1.4541

The Deutsche Marks will cost USD2,063,131 (3,000,000 divided by 1.4541).

Quick Fix Exercise (3)
Using the data in Figure 6.3 on page 75:

1. What rate will the bank quote to a client who wishes to sell forward for one month NLG5 million against dollars and how many dollars will the company receive?

2. A client needs to buy £875,000 two months forward. How many dollars will he need, and when will he pay for the sterling?

3. A UK corporate wishes to sell forward for nine months CHF2,250,000 against US dollars. How many dollars will it receive?

For answers refer to the end of the chapter.

Calculating "Broken" Date Forwards (Against the US Dollar)

A customer of the bank needs to sell forward NLG10 million for value July 15, 1996.

Consider the following market information:

Spot USD/NLG	1.6446–56
Transaction date	Thursday February 29, 1996
Spot value date	Monday March 4, 1996
Forward value date	Monday July 15, 1996
3-month points	90–85
6-month points	178–170
Day count – 3 months forward	92 days (June 4, 1996)
Day count – 6 months forward	184 days (September 4, 1996)
Day count – July 15, 1996	133 days

Our date falls between the three- and six-month rates. It is therefore necessary to *interpolate* between month 3 and month 6 and then to calculate the number of points per day, multiplied by the number of days, and then to add or subtract as required. The guilder is at a *premium* to the US dollar so the points will need to be subtracted – this is evidenced by the high/low number sequence. When calculating rates for outright forward transactions, if you use the right-hand side of the spot rate you also need to use the right-hand side of the forward differential.

First, we must decide on the correct side of the spot rate. As our client is selling guilders he is on the right-hand side of the rate at USD/NLG 1.6456.

Second, we need to calculate the number of points between month 3 and month 6, and then calculate the number of points per day, using the formula: 6-month points less 3-month points, divided by the number of days (June 4 – September 4). This gives:

$$\frac{(\,0.0170 - 0.0085)}{(\,184\ \text{days} - 92\ \text{days})} \quad = \quad \frac{0.0085}{92} \quad = \quad 0.000092\ \text{points per day}$$

Third, we need these extra points for an additional 41 days between the three-month forward value date and July 15, 1996:

$$0.000092 \times 41\ \text{days} = 0.003772\ (\text{or } 0.0038)$$

Fourth, we need to put all the components together:

Spot USD/NLG: 1.6456
3-month points: .0085
Extra 41 days' points: .0038
Outright   .6333

The NLG10 million will generate USD6,122,573.93 (10,000,000 divided by 1.6333).

Problems With Interpolation

The examples above work well because the forward value date is some way away from both the two- and three-month value dates. If the broken date had been two months and, say, three days forward, then when we calculate the average number of points per day it may give a misleading answer. Had the average number of points per day calculation been made over a longer period – say 30 to 60 days – it could well give a different answer.

This method of interpolation also assumes that the relationship is linear between the two end dates, when it may not be, but in the absence of further information this is the obvious assumption.

> **Tip** *When interpolating I have always found it easier to start with the full number of figures after the decimal point. In the example above the two-month forward differential was quoted as 24–21. If you do the calculation first and then add the zeros afterwards you can sometimes trip yourself up. I would always add the zeros first to make the points 0.0024–0.0021, and then commence the calculation.*

Short Date Forwards

The spot exchange rate for the particular pair of currencies is used as the base from which to calculate the forward rates. Forward foreign exchange is anything more than two days forward, although value dates up to one month in the future are known as "short-dates." An illustration of some short dated transactions is shown in Figure 7.4 courtesy of Swiss Bank Corporation.

The terminology used in the short date foreign exchange forward market is based on the deposit market, as forward swaps are quoted on the basis of the relevant deposit/loan rates. In the deposit market the following abbreviations are used:

Terminology

Overnight	A loan or deposit from today until "tomorrow"
Tom-next	A loan or deposit from tomorrow to the "next" day (spot)
Spot-next	A loan or deposit from spot until the "next" day
Spot-a-week	A loan or deposit from spot until a week later

In the deposit market "tomorrow" means the "next working day after today," and "next" means the "next working day following."

In the foreign exchange market the swaps are calculated:

Terminology

Overnight	A swap today against "tomorrow"
Tom-next	A swap "tomorrow" against the "next" day
Spot-next	A swap spot against the "next" day
Spot-a-week	A swap spot against a week later

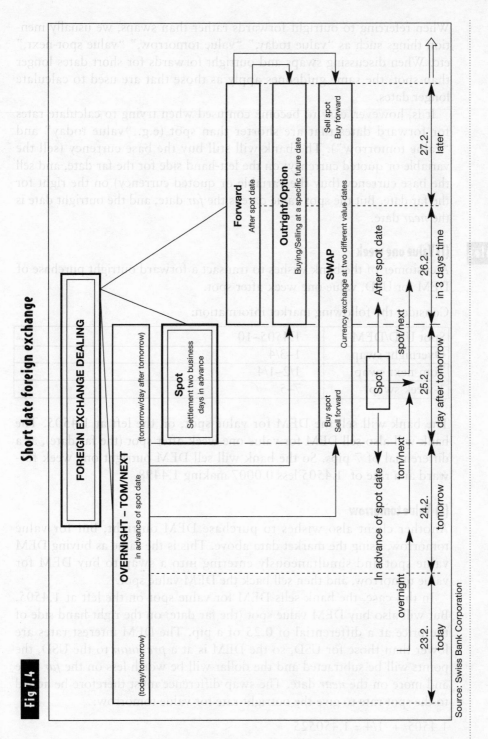

Fig 7.4

Short date foreign exchange

FOREIGN EXCHANGE DEALING

OVERNIGHT – TOM/NEXT
in advance of spot date
(today/tomorrow)
(tomorrow/day after tomorrow)

Spot
Settlement two business
days in advance

Forward
After spot date

Outright/Option
Buying/Selling at a specific future date

SWAP
Currency exchange at two different value dates

Buy spot
Sell forward

Spot

Sell spot
Buy forward

today   tomorrow   day after tomorrow   After spot date   in 3 days' time   later
23.2.   24.2.   25.2.   26.2.   27.2.

overnight   tom/next   spot/next

In advance of spot date

Source: Swiss Bank Corporation

When referring to outright forwards rather than swaps, we usually mention things such as "value today," "value tomorrow," "value spot-next," etc. When discussing swaps and outright forwards for short dates longer than spot, the same guidelines apply as those that are used to calculate longer dates.

It is, however, easy to become confused when trying to calculate rates for forward dates that are shorter than spot (e.g. "value today" and "value tomorrow"). The bank will still buy the base currency (sell the variable or quoted currency) on the left-hand side for the far date, and sell the base currency (buy the variable or quoted currency) on the right for the far date. But the spot value date is the *far* date, and the outright date is the *near* date.

Examples

(1) Value one week

A customer of the bank wishes to transact a forward outright purchase of DEM for USD, value one week after spot.

Consider the following market information:

Spot USD/DEM	1.4505–10
Overnight swap	1–3/4
Tom-next swap	1/2–1/4
1-week swap	7–5

The bank will sell the DEM for value spot, on the left at 1.4505. The bank will also sell DEM for value one week after spot (the far date), at a differential of 7 pips. So the bank will sell DEM outright one week forward at a rate of 1.4505 less 0.0007 making 1.4498.

(2) Value tomorrow

Another client also wishes to purchase DEM outright, but for value tomorrow, using the market data above. This is the same as buying DEM value spot and simultaneously entering into a swap to buy DEM for value tomorrow, and then sell back the DEM value spot.

In this case, the bank sells DEM for value spot on the left at 1.4505. But will also buy DEM value spot (the far date) on the right-hand side of the price at a differential of 0.25 of a pip. The DEM interest rates are lower than those for USD, so the DEM is at a *premium* to the USD, the points will be subtracted and the dollar will be worth less on the *far* date and more on the *near* date. The swap difference must therefore be added to the spot rate to give the outright rate for value tomorrow:

1.4505 + 1/4 = 1.450525

The other side of the calculation is 1.4510 + 1/2 = 1.45105.

(3) Value today

The customer wishes to buy DEM value today, using the same market data shown above. This will involve three separate transactions:

- buying DEM for value spot, entering into a swap to buy DEM value tomorrow
- sell DEM back for value spot (tom-next), and entering into a swap to buy DEM value today
- sell DEM back for value tomorrow (overnight).

The price is therefore calculated at: 1.4505 + 1/4 + 3/4 = 1.4506

> **Tip**
>
> When calculating forward dates with value shorter than spot, remember to reverse the swap points and procede exactly as for a longer dated transaction. In example (2) above, this would mean points of 1/4 – 1/2; the outright rate is then 1.4505 + 1/4 on the left, and on the right it is 1.4510 + 1/2, giving a bid–offer price of 1.450525 – 1.45105.

Cross Rate Forward Outrights

Just as in spot foreign exchange some currencies are quoted on a *direct* basis and others on an *indirect* basis, so the same applies to forward rates. When calculating cross rate outright forwards, the method used will depend upon whether the two particular rates are both direct, both indirect, or one of each.

Two indirect quotations

The two exchange rates must be cross divided.

Example

Spot:	USD/DEM	1.3539–1.3545
6-month swap		155–150
6-month outright		1.3384–1.3395

Spot:	USD/DKK	5.3535–5.3550
6-month swap		100–150
6-month outright		5.3635–5.3700

5.3635 ÷ 1.3395 = 4.0041: how the client can sell DKK, and buy DEM.
5.3700 ÷ 1.3384 = 4.0123: how the client can buy DKK, and sell DEM.
The bank of course will be on the other side of the price:
Forward cross rate DEM/DKK: 4.0041–4.0123

Two direct quotations

The two exchange rates must be cross divided.

Example

Spot:	GBP/USD	1.5075–1.5083
1-month swap		12–10
1-month outright		1.5063–1.5073

Spot:	AUD/USD	0.7397–0.7402
1-month swap		20–15
1-month outright		0.7377–0.7387

1.5063 ÷ 0.7387 = 2.0391: how the client can buy GBP, and sell AUD.
1.5073 ÷ 0.7377 = 2.0432: how the client can sell GBP, and buy AUD.
The bank of course will be on the other side of the price:
Forward cross rate GBP/AUD: 2.0391–2.0432

An indirect quotation and a direct quotation

The same side of each exchange rate must be multiplied.

Example

Spot:	GBP/USD	1.5075–1.5083
3-month swap		33–31
3-month outright		1.5042–1.5052

Spot:	USD/CHF	1.2090–1.2100
3-month swap		111–106
3-month outright		1.1979–1.1994

1.5042 × 1.1979 = 1.8019: how the client can sell GBP, and buy CHF.
1.5052 × 1.1994 = 1.8053: how the client can buy GBP, and sell CHF.

The bank of course will be on the other side of the price:
Forward cross rate GBP/CHF: 1.8019–1.8053

Quick fix exercise (4)

1. Calculate the cross rate forward outright given the following information:

Spot:	**GBP/USD**	**1.5075–1.5083**
3-month swap		33–31
Spot:	**USD/NZD**	**1.4968–1.4983**
3-month swap		90–100

2. Calculate the cross rate forward outright given the following information:

Spot:	**USD/CHF**	**1.2090–1.2100**
3-month swap		111–106
Spot	**USD/NZD**	**1.4968–.4983**
3-month swap		90–00

For answers refer to the end of the chapter.

Cross Rate Forward Swaps

This becomes a little more complicated. When calculating cross rate forward swaps or differentials, the method used will also depend upon whether the two particular rates are both direct, both indirect, or one of each, and now we need to use a mid-rate spot.

Two indirect quotations

To calculate the forward differentials between two indirect rates, it is necessary to cross divide the mid-spot rate, and also cross divide the forward rates (based on the mid-spot rate), and then subtract one from the other.

Example

Spot: USD/DEM		1.4865–1.4875
1-month swap		55–50
Spot: USD/NKR		6.3230–6.3240
1-month swap		40–30

USD/DEM		USD/NKR
1.4870	[Mid-spot]	6.3235
55–50	[Swap]	40–30
1.4815–1.4820	[Outright]	6.3195–6.3205

Cross spot rate: $\dfrac{6.3235}{1.4870} = 4.2525$

Cross forward outright: $\dfrac{6.3195}{1.4820} = 4.2642$

$\dfrac{6.3205}{1.4815} = 4.2663$

Subtract one from the other: 4.2642 – 4.2525 = 0.0117

4.2663 – 4.2525 = 0.0138

1-month DEM/NKR swap: 117–138

Two direct quotations

To calculate the forward differentials between two direct rates, it is necessary to cross divide the mid-spot rate, and also cross divide the forward rates (based on the mid-spot rate), and then subtract one from the other.

Spot:	AUD/USD	**0.7386–0.7391**
1-month swap		60–50
Spot:	GBP/USD	**1.5108–1.5118**
1-month swap		40–35

AUD/USD		**GBP/USD**
0.7388	[Mid-spot]	1.5113
60–50	[Swap]	40–35
0.7328–0.7338	[Outright]	1.5073–1.5078

Cross spot rate: $\dfrac{1.5113}{0.7388} = 2.0456$

Cross forward outright: $\dfrac{1.5073}{0.7338} = 2.0541$

$\dfrac{1.5078}{0.7328} = 2.0576$

Subtract one from the other: 2.0541–2.0456 = 0.0085

2.0576–2.0456 = 0.0120

1-month GBP/AUD swap: 85–120

An indirect and a direct quotation

To calculate the forward differentials between a direct and an indirect rate, it is necessary to multiply the mid-spot rate, and also multiply the same side of the forward rates (based on the mid-spot rate), and then subtract one from the other.

Spot:	USD/DEM	**1.4865–1.4875**
1-month swap		55–50
Spot:	GBP/USD	**1.5108–1.5118**
1-month swap		40–35

USD/DEM		**GBP/USD**
1.4870	[Mid-spot]	1.5113
55–50	[Swap]	40–35
1.4815–1.4820	[Outright]	1.5073–1.5078

Cross spot rate: $1.4870 \times 1.5113 = 2.2473$

Cross forward outright: 1.4815 × 1.5073 = 2.2331
1.4820 × 1.5078 = 2.2346

Subtract one from the other: 2.2331 – 2.2473 = 0.0142
2.2346 – 2.2473 = 0.0127

1-month GBP/DEM swap: 142–127

Option Dated Forwards

So far we have examined foreign exchange forward transactions with a single maturity date. These comprise by far the majority. Occasionally, however, a client may be unsure of the exact timing of a currency receipt, although he is sure it will arrive by the end date. In this case he will request from his bank an "option dated forward," not to be confused with a currency option. A currency option allows the client to walk away from the deal, an option dated forward must be fulfilled by the end date.

Option dated forward

November 10
A client knows he must sell sterling and buy US dollars some time between December 12 and February 12, and asks for a quote on an option dated forward contract.

Example

Current market data   GBP/USD

Spot	1.5310–1.5320	value November 12
1-month	1.5272–1.5284	value December 12
3-month	1.5200–1.5215	value February 12

In this example it is the three-month bid rate which exchanges the smallest number of US dollars for sterling.

Simultaneously, the bank dealer will enter into an offsetting contract to match their position and lock in a spread. In this case the one-month bid rate gives the maximum amount of US dollars and locks in a spread of 72 points (1.5272–1.5200).

Advantages and disadvantages

The client in our example has locked in an exchange rate, good for the period, and is now no longer concerned about the timing of the delivery, as he has no exchange rate or interest rate risk. Unfortunately, the size of the spread on the deal is massive.

The bank has taken on the client's risk and has charged a wide spread to do it. The bank's total income may be eroded if the company delivers the sterling after December 12, as the bank will have to cover the shortfall in sterling by a series of *overnight swap* transactions. The bank is also exposed to adverse interest rate movements and will have additional transaction costs.

Conclusion

Forward foreign exchange is naturally more complex than spot FX, as the extra dimension of relative interest rates comes into play in the pricing. The maths itself is not particularly complex but there are many ways you can trip yourself up. In modern dealing rooms both in banks and corporations there are likely to be PCs or add-ons to the main information providers that will calculate forward rates on request. All you need to do is input the far date and the near date, the two currencies in question, and the machine will do the rest. There is a danger here. It is easy to become too reliant on the PC. Understanding the background to the calculation and being able to reproduce screen forward rates will strengthen an individual's knowledge base. Should the pricing model go down, which is always an outside possibility, you will not be "blind" until it is fixed. To confirm that the rates can be calculated longhand have a try at the exercises throughout the chapter, the answers to which are below.

A final note on forward foreign exchange: things are moving very rapidly in this market and increasingly banks are looking at different ways to hedge their books, other than using loans and deposits which are very "heavy" on the banks' balance sheets. This is leading the banks to use interest rate derivatives such as FRAs and futures, to cover their risk "off-balance sheet."

I heard an interesting comment recently about trading in forward foreign exchange:

"Trading forward foreign exchange is like the elephants' graveyard. You know you have reached your sell-by date when they give you the forward book to manage."

Answers to quick fix exercises

(1)

1. The correct spot rate is 1.5402, then subtract the 11 forward points (number sequence goes high/low), making 1.5402 – 0.0011 = 1.5391.

2. The correct spot rate is 7.6590, then subtract the 622 forward points (number sequence goes high/low), making 7.6590 – 0.0622 = 7.5968 This makes a cost of FRF10,000,000 divided by 7.5968 = £1,316,343.73

3. The correct spot rate is 2.2352, then subtract the 147 forward points (number sequence goes high/low), making 2.2352 – 0.0147 = 2.2205. This makes a receipt of DEM2,000,000 divided by 2.2205 = £900,698.04.

(2)

Transaction date	Monday March 18, 1996
Spot value date	Monday March 20, 1996
Forward value date	Tuesday December 10, 1996
6-month points	68–63
12-month points	153–143
Day count – 6 months forward	184 days (December 10, 1996)
Day count – 12 months forward	365 days (March 20, 1997)
Day count – December 10, 1996	265 days

The US dollar is at a premium to sterling, so the points must be subtracted, from the left-hand side of the spot rate (as the client wishes to purchase the dollars).

Spot rate GBP/USD: 1.5392
Number of points (per day) between month 6 and month 12:

$$\frac{(0.0153 - 0.0068)}{(365 \text{ days} - 184 \text{ days})} = \frac{0.0085}{181} = 0.000047 \text{ points per day}$$

We need these extra points for a total of 81 days, making 0.000047×81 = 0.0038.

We now need to put all the components together:

Spot GBP/USD:	1.5392
6-month points:	.0068
Extra 81 days' points:	.0038
Outright	1.5286

The USD2.2 million will require £1,439,225.44 (2,200,000 divided by 1.5286).

(3)

1. The correct spot rate is 1.6456, then subtract the 28 forward points (number sequence goes high/low), making 1.6456 − 0.0028 = 1.6428, making a receipt of USD3,043,584.13.

2. The correct spot rate is 1.5322, then subtract the 20 forward points (number sequence goes high/low), making 1.5322 − 0.0020 = 1.5302, making a cost of USD1,338,925.00.

3. The correct spot rate is 1.1980, then subtract the 9-month forward points (number sequence goes high/low). Interpolate between the six- and nine-month points (385 and 206), making 29.8 points per month or 89.5 points for the extra three-month period, add on the points for the initial six-month period at 206, making a total points differential of 295.5, and subtract the total from the spot rate, making 1.1864. A total receipt of CHF2,250,000 ÷ 1.1864 = USD1,896,493.59.

(4)

Calculate the following cross rate forward outrights:

1. Spot: GBP/USD 1.5075–1.5083
3-month swap 33–31
3-month outright 1.5042–1.5052

Spot: USD/NZD 1.4968–1.4983
3-month swap 90–100
3-month outright 1.5058–1.5083

We need to multiply the same sides of the outright:

1.5042 × 1.5058 = 2.2650: how the client can sell GBP, and buy NZD.
1.5052 × 1.5083 = 2.2703: how the client can buy GBP, and sell NZD.

The bank of course will be on the other side of the price:
i.e. Forward cross rate GBP/NZD: 2.2650–2.2703.

2. Spot: USD/NZD 1.4968–1.4983
3-month swap 90–100
3-month outright 1.5058–1.5083

Spot: USD/CHF 1.2090–1.2100
3-month swap 111–106
3-month outright 1.1979–1.1994

1.5058 ÷ 1.1994 = 1.2555: how the client can buy NZD, and sell CHF.
1.5083 ÷ 1.1979 = 1.2591: how the client can sell NZD, and buy CHF.

The bank of course will be on the other side of the price:
Forward cross rate CHF/NZD: 1.2555–1.2591.

■ ■ ■

'It is better to be born lucky than beautiful.'

Ancient Japanese Rice Trader's Proverb

Spot Foreign Exchange – A Market Maker's Perspective

JOHN BANERJEE

Vice President, FX & Money Markets, Europe Citibank N.A.

Introduction

The door to a dealing room is a strange portal. It is commonly supposed that The Bank of England regulation that requires the doors to be operable only with security passes is for fraud prevention reasons. Whilst that may be true, I suspect that it is only part of the story. I think that officials at The Old Lady were concerned at whatever it is about the door of dealing rooms that transforms unassuming Dr Jekyll bankers into rabid Mr Hyde traders. . .

Spot FX Traders – Who Are They?

Successful spot FX traders have a very varied background. Until the late 1980s the vast majority were not university educated but were recruited from within the banking sector. Often the route to a trading job was and still is via being a dealer's assistant. This post within a dealing room has been described as "doing anything required to allow the trader to concentrate on trading." This involves keeping the dealer's position, taking care of "housekeeping" duties such as deal input and, at the banal end of the spectrum, collecting the trader's lunch. A dealer's assistant requires many of the same attributes as a trader in order to be successful, i.e. the ability to work under pressure, resilience, clarity of thought, numeracy, integrity and, not least, a sense of humour. Assistants are sometimes required to cover for the dealer, for instance while the dealer is in the loo. The difference between a good assistant and a potential trader is that one demonstrates the desire and determination to trade.

Nowadays, the intake of dealing rooms is predominantly graduate, with many banks putting the prospective new hire through a battery of psychometric testing. Many successful spot traders who are not graduates often pour scorn on the new employment policy of their employers, citing the many non-graduates who are at the top of the profession and the host of graduate "failures" (omitting to mention the many non-graduates who also fail to progress). A few would go as far as to say that being a graduate is actually a disadvantage in the instant world of spot foreign exchange – where two seconds taken to consider a position or price can mean an opportunity lost, or worse. The view that graduates per se are less likely or more likely to make good spot dealers is probably moot. If it were true that psychometric testing could identify potential traders, then surely it wouldn't matter whether or not the applicant were a graduate. In reality, the reason banks hire predominantly graduates is two-fold. First is the fact that today's trainee is unlikely to be trading spot FX in 25 or even 10 years time. It would be folly for banks in this day and age to employ people who were not of the utmost adaptability and of the highest educational attainment. Secondly, it can be used merely as a device to trim the level of potential applicants to a number that is more manageable – educational background is as good a filter as any. An important point to note is that the difference between a good potential trader and a top flight trader is sound judgement. This cannot be taught, but it is only through experience that sound judgement can be acquired.

What Do Market Makers Do?

A spot FX market maker is someone who makes a simultaneous buying and selling price of one currency in terms of another, usually not knowing beforehand whether the price requester is a buyer or seller. An interbank market maker is merely a market maker who is willing to quote prices to other banks as well as his own customers.

There are three reasons why a bank should want an interbank market making operation:

(1) to create or gain access to a liquidity pool to enable it to service its own customer base;

(2) to provide market information which enhances other market making activities or proprietary trading or both;

(3) to make money on the bank's account.

Of these goals, maintaining and nurturing good relations with the bank's customers are becoming increasingly important aspects of any spot FX trader's job as all banks become more "client focused." (They hope the relationship with the customer will remain and be lucrative to many other areas of the bank for a long time after any individual FX trader's retirement!) Important constraints placed on the trader include strict adherence to both the risk profile and counterparty credit limits determined by the bank.

How Do Spot Traders Make Their Money?

If you asked spot traders from the 1980s how they made money, their answer would undoubtedly mention three things: arbitrage, spread retention, and something less definable – call it "gut feel."

Triangular arbitrage between three currencies has been discussed elsewhere in the book. The other common forms of arbitrage are between centers and between brokers. This is where a market participant seeks to exploit the opportunity of simultaneously buying at one price and selling at a higher price elsewhere. For obvious reasons, these opportunities are few and far between and do not last more than seconds at most. People who, almost exclusively, habitually attempt to take advantage of such opportunities are never referred to as arbitrageurs by other market professionals, but as "snipers." Occasionally, what looks like a "free lunch" (or near-free one) appears to be available. Here is an example.

Example

In a 17–20 market, a bank wishing to sell many DEMs at mid market or above may show one broker a momentary bid for regular size at 19, while showing another broker simultaneously a 19 offer for small size. Snipers, thinking that there is greater demand than supply, will pay the 19 offer, hoping to sell the currency a tick or two higher. The broker with the "small" offer will be briefed to sell as many "smalls" as he is paid for, whilst the broker with the "regular" bid will be briefed by the bank to buy only one amount of regular size. Even though the bank may receive some DEMs if there are enough snipers in the market the ploy will often be successful. With the seemingly blind faith of some younger traders in electronic visual brokers, this is an ancient yet still effective ploy. Potential snipers take note.

The theory behind "spread retention" was that if you made prices and traded on your own rate, eventually you would retain some of your "spread" (the difference between your buying and selling rates) and make money. For instance, there follows a typical dealing conversation (with "translations," etc in brackets) between two banks on the Reuters Dealing System, which is the most commonly used medium for direct deals between banks.

From: **XYZ Bank** Tokyo   To: *CITI London*   8.17am 10/7/96

XYZ: DLR DMK 20 PL   (XYZ Bank is asking for a USD/DEM rate in 20 million USD)

CITI: 72 77   (CITI London quotes the last hundredths of a Pfennig of the price, the number of Deutsche Marks and whole Pfennigs being taken as known to both counterparties)

XYZ: YOURS   (XYZ Bank sells 20 million USD and buys the DEMs at "72")

CITI: OK   (CITI London agrees the deal as a
  I BUY 20 MILLION USD   matter of courtesy and to avoid
  AG DEM   possible misunderstandings)
  AT RATE 1.5272
  VALUE 12TH JULY 1996
  CITIBANK NYK FOR MY USD

XYZ: **CITI FFT FOR**   (XYZ Bank gives its payment
  MY DEMS   instructions)
THANKS AND BYE

END CONTACT.

In this case the USD/DEM market maker has been "given" US dollars on his price; he is now "long" in dollars and "short" in Deutsche Marks. If a market maker is given many dollars (relative to that trader's comfortable position size and broker liquidity), the market maker will make a lower price to the next inquirer (i.e. be a less competitive buyer, but a more competitive seller, of USD). In this example, if the broker market is 72–77 after being given by XYZ Bank, the market maker is likely to make a rate of 70–75 to his next inquirer. If there is not another inquiry very soon (within 30 seconds, say), the dealer will offer USD to the market through a broker, possibly at 75. If the market maker feels that "the market" is likely to be positioned in the same way (i.e. the majority of market makers are also more likely to be long in USD than short at that time), possibly because the USD that were offered through the brokers at an attractive rate were not snapped up, the market maker may decide to sell actively not only the USD he was given but also to oversell USD and "go short." This could be done by selling through the brokers. However, broker liquidity is often not enough to transact large trades. In order to transact a very large amount the trader will go to the interbank market, i.e. he will ask many other banks for their prices for USD/DEM and then sell to them directly.

In the past, there were many participants who were willing to trade on other people's spreads, even though their individual transactions would not be market–moving. Spread retention was the driving force of the interbank market. These participants may have been more willing to trade on other people's spreads because they had limited access to the market themselves. However, the world has changed dramatically since the 1980s. The spot FX market has matured, and with maturity came much greater transparency. The advent of technological advances such as EBS, Reuters direct dealing, and Reuters 2000–2 has made access to the interbank market much easier for former "outsiders." At the same time, large customers have become very much more price sensitive about their spot FX transactions. In becoming so, they have become more predatory in nature. When I asked a chief trader at a large pharmaceutical firm why, when she needs to sell 100 million Deutsche Marks, she asks many banks for a rate for 10 million instead of asking a single bank for 100 million, she replied: "Well, that's what you do when you want to shift a big amount at a good rate!"

However, the FX market is not yet a negative-sum game. There are still some banks which have built customer franchises which add revenue to those institutions, and thereby to the whole FX "system." It is in the hope of capturing some of this revenue that the multiplicity of banks set up their interbank FX operations.

A Market Maker's Typical Trading Day

The first thing to know about spot trading is that there is no such thing as a typical day – no two days are ever quite the same. At the end of a typical trading day, almost all spot FX traders square up any positions that they may be left with. It is important to note, therefore, that at the start of any day the vast majority of spot FX traders have no balances of any of the currencies which they trade in. So how does a spot trader's day begin?

London FX market makers usually start work at the same time a little after 7.00 am. The first task of the day is to find out what has happened overnight. This is done by a combination of reading the financial press (both printed and electronic) and by talking to market participants in Asia. Some larger banks have overnight desks which produce potted summaries of the night's trading activity and market-relevant news for the benefit of their clients and their in-house "day" traders. Trading between banks in Europe generally starts at 8.00 am London time (i.e. a more sedate 9.00 am Central European time!) – so woe betide the trader who isn't up to date on the night's events by then!

A spot trader may have formed an initial view on the direction of the market for the morning. This may be based on a variety of factors, including the relative movements of the other related markets such as other currency pairs, short-term and long-term interest rate movements, stock indices movements, and technical analysis of the currency pair concerned as well as expectations of upcoming economic data. The most informative clue for spot traders at larger banks is to look at the state of their bank's order books. If, for instance, a trader has more orders to buy DEM at both lower levels (take-profit orders) and higher levels (stop-loss orders) than to sell them, then (assuming that the trader's order book is likely to mirror other banks' order books) the trader is likely to take a tentative long DEM position in reflection of the view that there is likely to be greater demand than supply for DEM for the time being. If the trader has no view, the trader is most likely to acquire his or her first position for the day by making a rate to a customer or another bank.

Gut feel and – even more importantly – good luck is still, and probably always will be, an important asset to have as any kind of trader. There follows a true example of how a world class trader formed his initial view for the morning.

True story

The USD/JPY trader at a major London bank breezed into the office very early on a Friday morning. As usual he was the first person on the trading floor. He had read the *Financial Times* on the way to work and it had yielded nothing to give him a view on the market. The order book contained nothing of any particular interest, and the Tokyo session had been very quiet. The trader felt he was in for a dull day, until he spied *The Economist*. It was always worthwhile for the book reviews if nothing else. Fortunately, *The Economist* had a survey on Japan. By this time, people were drifting into the office. Suddenly the trader stood up, shouted to anyone who was walking by to please sit in a chair and call out to other banks for USD/JPY prices. "I'm selling – give every bid down to 55!" (The prevailing rate was 70–75.) The commotion caught the ear of the foreign exchange manager, a man who liked to know *precisely* what was happening in his shop at all times. He walked straight to the yen desk and calmly inquired why the trader was committing so much energy (and many hundreds of millions of the bank's capital!) into selling dollars and buying yen. The trader replied: "Have you read *The Economist*? The Japanese economy is going to increase its trade surplus with the US by another 23 percent this year. Lexus are going to sell more cars in the US than in all other export markets put together this year. The Yanks have got an increasing appetite for Japanese goods whilst the Japanese are going to do nothing about their non-tariff barriers. This currency can only go one way!" The FX manager calmly took *The Economist*. Fifteen seconds later, to a background of brokers shouting 20 offers with no bid, the FX manager tossed *The Economist* down and, with a smile, imparted these wise observations to the USD/JPY trader. "Sounds like USD/JPY is collapsing, well done – but then again, making a fortune is what I employ you for. There's just one thing old boy – do bear in mind that your *Economist* is a month old."

This true story illustrates the old Japanese rice traders' proverb: "It is better to be born lucky than beautiful."

Ordinarily, when a trader needs to execute a transaction through the interbank market, he will not be able to do this alone (even though the Reuters 2000 dealing terminal allows four simultaneous conversations with other banks, and the Telerate platform six!) Teamwork is vital to ensure efficient access to liquidity. Typically the bank's entire spot FX team will call other banks on his behalf and trade on his instructions. It is utterly imperative that all the team members act precisely on the trader's instructions and inform the trader of their actions promptly and precisely. It is often the case that there is little time for the trader to tell the rest of the desk precisely what he is trying to achieve in advance of execution, let alone the reason for his actions. Clarity of expression is absolutely vital, as is evidenced by the true story below.

Heineken "Flu"/ The Bids Get Better! – A True Tale of Miscommunication

True story The usual interbank USD/DEM trader at a large London bank was ill due to an epidemic of "Heineken" flu, which as everyone in the market knows is always most virulent on Fridays. The trader who was covering the seat was vastly experienced and had a reputation as a fiery individual, but had not traded on the major interbank desk for some time. Sadly for him, the regular USD/DEM assistant was also stricken by the same "illness" and consequently he had a rather nervous graduate trainee as an assistant. The morning's trading was uneventful as traders were unwilling to initiate fresh positions before US non-farm payroll data due at 1.30 pm London time. Before significant economic news releases, the convention is for the interbank market to continue to operate until a few minutes before the data is due for release. After this time, it is possible to transact through the broker market, but the liquidity available is very low.

At 1.25 pm the USD/DEM trader made a price to a saleswoman on an intercom for a "predatory" customer for USD100 million. It was immediately obvious to the rest of the spot desk that the customer had traded, as the USD/DEM trader stood up and screamed "Dollar/Marks everywhere!" When this sort of request is made of the spot desk at a large bank, a well-oiled machine goes into operation. Every individual stops whatever they are doing and calls those banks that are on their list for USD/DEM prices. (The idea is that no duplicated calls are to be made to the other banks so that the maximum number of banks can be asked for their quotes at precisely the same time.) As the USD/DEM assistant sits next to the USD/DEM trader, it is normal for the assistant to call the banks with whom the bank has the best relationships, in terms of speed and size of quotation. The first quote received by the bank was by the tremulous USD/DEM assistant who was shown 90–95 on USD20 million by CITI London. The USD/DEM trader, anxious not to unnerve the already jittery trainee calmly said "*Buy*." The trainee responded to this simple request by incorrectly pressing the abbreviation "S" that produced the response "Sell" on the Reuters dealing conversation.

In a large dealing room, traders have "slave" screens to one another's Reuters dealing screens, so that they can see, in real time, what prices are being made in other currencies. As USD/DEM is the largest volume currency pair traded, the USD/DEM assistant's screen is often also "slaved" to other traders' desks. Seeing that the USD/DEM assistant was selling at 90, the chief dealer who was trading cable responded to the first price he was made of 93–98 by selling also, shouting to the USD/DEM trader that he had "done 10 million dollars at 93." The cable assistant, seeing both the USD/DEM assistant and the chief dealer selling at 90 and 93, shouted out only the bid sides of the prices she received. "92?" shouted the cable assistant "*Yes!*" screamed the USD/DEM trader. At that instant, around the desk five people were being shown bids of 92 or higher. Knowing that the window of liquidity would be shutting very shortly until the "figures" were out, and also in the knowledge that the trader had already sold at 90, these bids were given first and reported to the trader next. "I've done 20 million dollars at 92!" "I've done 10 at 94!" came the shouts from around the desk. The trader, fully expecting to buy at successively higher rates, thought nothing of the fact that the rates he was being shown were higher and higher.* The chief dealer, however, thought something was wrong when, having initially sold at 90, he was shown a price of 95–00. "Careful Paul, I've got a 95 bid here!" shouted the chief dealer. Puce faced, the USD/DEM trader shouted "What do you mean? I'm buying . . ." In fact, the customer was buying from other banks at the same time.

*As a rule of thumb, if when you start a call-out to other banks you are selling at 90 and by the end of it you have the opportunity to sell higher, it is a fantastic indication that the market has greater demand than supply and the market is going to move substantially higher rather than lower.

The trader needs the feedback of what the team members have transacted both in terms of the amount and at what rates, so that he can gauge both his total exposure and how "easy" or "difficult" it was to transact at the rate of that moment.

The reason that a market maker is willing to make prices to other banks at all is that, by doing so, other banks will be obliged to do the same in return. This creates a "liquidity pool" and each bank seeks to maintain enough liquidity to exit both positions created by quoting customers in large amounts and also positions created of their own making, when they become burdensome.

All these decisions are very short term in their nature. A spot market maker is likely to be both long and short many times in one trading day.

The essential features to note about spot market making are:

(1) A great many transactions are likely to be made in any one day.

(2) The level of profit on any one trade is likely to be relatively small, as trades are entered into and exited within a relatively short time span.

(3) Flexibility of position is paramount in order to be able to quote customers in large size.

(4) It is largely reactionary rather than proactive in nature – most direct trades result in one of the counterparties being "forced" into a position.

Above all, remember that market making in spot FX is all about the creation and management of liquidity.

The Cost of Liquidity – A Salutary Story

Here is a salutary tale of a young trainee learning how the cost of liquidity can rise sharply at the end of a trading day.

The interbank market in Europe finishes for the day at around 4.00 to 4.30 pm London time. One Friday at 3.45 pm, a fresh faced spot trader at a major London bank was feeling very happy with life. He had been promoted into the coveted GBP/DEM seat a few weeks earlier, and was finishing the week an aggregate USD250,000 up. "GBP/DEM in 100 million," came a cry from a salesman from the desk that targeted other banks' business by offering a non-reciprocal pricing relationship. "Is it his full amount?" the trader inquired. The salesman handling the call knew the customer calling only by his reputation for trading large volumes. (In fact, he was a very colorful character at a large Swiss bank, known in the interbank market more for his ferocity, than his gentlemanly behavior.) "Sure it is, he's only asking you for the price," replied the salesman. A small forum of senior traders and managers gathered behind the youth, to lend support and encouragement. On the basis that the prevailing market rate was 30–40 and that the trader felt the market had more bids than offers, he quoted 33–48 in the £100 million. The client declined to trade on the price, telling the salesman that "I'm looking for a cheaper offer." The junior responded by buying a modest amount of sterling. The forum of seniors around him were full of praise for the astute youth who had quoted a quick, tight price to the client and had correctly assessed the market by making the appropriately high price.

At 4.25 pm the prevailing market rate was 40–50 and the customer called again for a price in GBP/DEM 100 million. Making a price in such an amount at that time of day is quite a tricky thing to do as the liquidity provided by European banks tapers off dramatically. The small forum of seniors had swelled by a few managers. The junior, armed with the feedback that the salesman had given him, felt quite confident that the customer was a buyer and made 50–65. Again the customer passed the rate. The gaggle of seniors eagerly advised a strategy of larger-scale sterling accumulation. As one of them put it, "If you don't take an opportunity like this for all it's worth, you'll have nothing in the tin to pay for it when it goes all horribly wrong." The junior bought some more sterling. The market moved up again, to 55–65.

At 4.50 pm the customer asked again for a price in GBP/DEM 100 million. The scrum behind the trader, sensing a large profit in the offing, eagerly volunteered advice, most of it along the lines of "us" quoting a seriously high price to what must surely be a distressed buyer, and for "us" to quote a wider price reflecting the scarcity of liquidity at that time. The junior, now loaded with £45 million in what was an illiquid New York market, decided not to pitch the rate excessively as he was quite keen to lose the sterling to the customer. He quoted 55–70, a very tight price given the time of day. "*Yours!*" came the response from the salesman. The crowd of onlookers fell silent.

The junior was stunned for an instant, but knew this was no time for indecision. Rather than bellyache to the salesman, he turned to the (rapidly thinning) crowd behind him and said, "I'm going to take all the broker offers in GBP/DEM to get the price up, plug into the direct line to our New York office, ask them to call every bank that will make a price and sell £160 million down to 40." At that instant, from the loudspeaker from the New York office, came a voice that may as well have been the Grim Reaper's as far as the ashen-faced junior was concerned. "London, watch your bid in GBP/DEM . . . we've been given an order to sell 100 million GBP/DEM down to 45. . . hang on . . . the customer wants to sell a further 100 million GBP/DEM down to 30." Unsurprisingly, the market was almost instantaneously 20–30, with considerably more on the offer than on the bid.

The junior turned to his supporters. The attractions of the weekend had suddenly overcome half the throng. However, there were still some experienced stalwarts who were willing to give constructive advice. "Why don't you sell 230 million USD/DEM, thereby making you long of

145 million GBP/USD? The effect of selling the dollars will push up the price of GBP/USD, and that will allow you to exit the position at a smaller cost," suggested a proprietary trader. A senior spot dealer suggested that what the junior should actually do was sell 300 million USD/DEM, putting him long 145 million GBP/USD and also short 70 million USD/DEM. "You will be able to repurchase the 70 million USD/DEM at lower rate once the 300 million USD/DEM filters into the market and that will improve your average rate. Don't worry, I've got a friend in New York who'll knock the dollars out for you." The junior should have known that he was in serious trouble from the moment talk had changed from "us" to "you."

The friend was called and asked to sell 300 million USD/DEM "at best." The prevailing USD/DEM rate was 70–75. After an initial depreciation as the selling went on, the rates in the broker market came back terrifyingly high. The friend reported, "The good news is that we've sold your 300 million dollars at 68 (only 2 pips of slippage). The bad news is that the market is now 85–90. A South East Asian central bank has just stepped into the market with a tremendous appetite for dollars." This meant that another loss had been incurred by becoming 70 million USD/DEM short at 68, whilst it was only possible to cover the position in the market at 90 (an increase in the aggregate loss of some DEM154,000). This induced nauseous feelings in the junior trader. What caused him blind panic, however, was the fact a higher dollar against the Deutsche Mark meant a lower pound against the dollar and he was now £145 million long against the dollar.

The chief dealer said, "Don't worry, I have a great friend in New York who will be able to get us a price in GBP/USD 145 million. I'll call them now." Unbeknown to the chief dealer the friend called the London bank's New York office for the GBP/USD rate. Over the loudspeaker from New York came the words,"A huge offer passes in 145 million GBP/USD. Watch your bid in GBP/USD, we're selling some here for ourselves." (The New York office had made a very low price because of the large buying interest for USD/DEM and the fact that they had a large interest in selling GBP/DEM.) The chief dealer's friend called back, telling him that she had guessed that he was a seller of the GBP and had been made a "ludicrously low rate" by a bank and so had passed the price. By now, the junior was truly distraught. Within an hour and a half he had gone from thinking about the shiny new sports car he was surely going to be driving by the end of the year, to wondering whether he would be a minicab driver by the end of the month.

By now, the junior trader's entire crowd of supporters had crept away. No one likes to witness the crushing of a colleague's morale. He was all alone with the FX manager. The FX manager plugged into the New York office's direct line and told them to sell 145 million GBP/USD at best. The

New York office came back with the (ugly) fill some minutes later. He turned to the junior and asked him, "How much did that little lot cost?" "About half a million dollars," replied the junior, close to tears. The FX manager, never known to waste his words, replied: "That'll teach you to trust that —— at —— bank! See you on Monday."

■ ■ ■

'Proprietary traders love to attack a weak link – history shows they offer the line of least resistance.'

Proprietary Trading

TOM ELLIOTT

Deputy General Manager
Nomura Bank International, plc

Introduction

Proprietary trading – or, to give it its more respectable title, proprietary risk management – what exactly is it? Well, proprietary trading covers a number of disciplines: not only foreign exchange but also bond, equity, commodity, and derivatives markets. It is about the ability to manage proactive risk positions. Participants on a proprietary desk will focus on a market they believe offers a positive risk/reward, having analyzed thoroughly either the economic fundamentals or the technical price activity or probably both.

The proprietary desk is the vehicle that institutions use to express their objective view on a market's products. The risk (the position) will be retained until a profit target area is achieved or an event occurs which would prompt a reassessment of the original thought process.

The risk management would normally encompass the entire spectrum of commonly traded products – all currency pairs and interest rate curves in both cash and options markets and all freely accessible futures markets. Many institutions will additionally support trading in equity and commodity markets.

Who Trades On A Proprietary Desk?

Traders responsible for proprietary risk management tend to have had practical experience in a wide range of the products under their management, for example:

- foreign exchange spot, forward, and options markets
- interest rate, cash, futures, and options markets
- equity and commodity markets.

The traders may well have had market making experience, but this is not essential. However, strong analytical skills are a must and most are familiar with both charting and fundamental techniques. They will also need to be self-starters with a patient disposition as many positions offer full gratification only after a lengthy wait.

Comparisons With Market Making

Market making is by nature responsive – traders may close many transactions with counterparties and customers without there being any substantial price change in the product concerned. Traders will attempt to secure small profits on a high percentage of the trades closed, and turnover in some transactions may show no profit at all. They will also tolerate small losses on a low percentage of their total volume of trades – building their revenue on a gradual basis. They may maintain a small core position in support of their current market view, a view which may well change several times during the course of a single trading session, but the essential ingredient is to maintain a high degree of liquidity to promote speedy and aggressive pricing of any customer inquiry.

Mental dexterity is an essential requisite in present-day market making as products have become more cross-market-driven in recent years. Self-discipline is also critical in an environment which may require the trader to reverse a long position to short and vice versa to maintain the liquidity of position referred to previously. Market making is heavily reliant on team interaction and support to promote effective execution of deals.

It would be easy to say that proprietary trading is none of the above, and essentially that is true. Proprietary trading:

- is proactive
- is a drain on market liquidity
- has low volume
- has a wide product range
- has revenue objectives which are established in terms of percentage gains, not in pips
- allows traders to choose when to enter and indeed when to exit any position.

Proprietary Trading Strategies

A rulebook on the perfect strategy or structure is, as yet, unwritten. The general rule of thumb is to trade to your own comfort level with the investment capital at your disposal, and attempt not to dilute the impact of that risk capital by running too many positions. Identify the exposure that you believe offers the best risk/reward ratio and commit yourself to that position.

Proprietary traders love to attack a weak link – history shows they offer the line of least resistance. When positioning yourself short in a weak currency, or one which you anticipate is about to weaken considerably, always secure interest rate cover by borrowing that currency for the period of time you expect to hold that position. Any central bank or government Treasury Department's last line of defence in currency protection is to impose penal short-term interest rates to discourage the speculative selling of that currency. Accurate timing of position instigation can result in profitable gratification over a relatively short time frame; nevertheless, penal interest rates imposed by central banks can damage the revenue potential of positions. Always secure interest rate cover when shorting a currency due to come under pressure. Well, almost always!

Example – Summer 1992

During the summer of 1992 sterling's floor (downside limit) within the EMS came under increasing pressure as the debate intensified surrounding the currency's true trade-related value relative to its trading partners in the Exchange Rate Mechanism. German rhetoric indicated that they had little appetite to fulfill their EMS obligation to support sterling at its floor against the Deutsche Mark – the UK authorities became more and more isolated as summer heated up in the financial markets.

Situations of this nature are an open invitation to proprietary traders. I smartly RSVP'd to the invitation and sold the sterling I had committed for this trade in exchange for Deutsche Marks (GBP/DEM). By mid-September GBP/DEM was nailed to the EMS floor at 2.7780. The reluctant support for GBP/DEM from the Bundesbank had persuaded me that the UK authorities would quickly bow to the inevitable by withdrawing sterling from the EMS and allow the currency to float – albeit downwards – rather than sacrifice huge reserve balances defending an unsustainable exchange rate. No need for interest rate cover here – it would be over quickly and without much of a fight. *Wrong!*

For days the only buyer in town was The Bank of England – both in its own name and by means of covert operations using selected commercial banks in London and Amsterdam. Day-to-day cover of short sterling balances gradually rose in cost as later respondents to the "sell GBP/DEM" invitation established their positions and sought interest rate cover.

Then came the feeding frenzy!

The second week of September and my game plan was starting to leak – whilst being short of GBP/DEM was OK, The Old Lady was fighting the good fight longer than I had anticipated and suddenly two-week cover for sterling jumped from 10–12 percent to upwards of 100 percent. Help! – "the best laid schemes o' mice an' men gang aft a-gley" sprang to mind.

Time for a strong nerve and plan B, which was to secure a stable high-yielding hedge to reduce the cost of carrying short GBP/DEM. I was aware that the Swedish Riksbank had introduced excessively high short-term interest rates – up to 500 percent for two-week money – to dissuade speculators from believing that the kroner would be decoupled from its historically stable relationship with the Deutsche Mark (DEM/SEK @

3.6600). I eliminated my DEM exposure by replacing it with Swedish kroner, creating a short GBP/SEK position – happy days – unless the SEK devalued before sterling. Strong nerve prevailed – within a week Norman Lamont announced the government's decision to withdraw sterling from the EMS, allowing the currency to float, and the reduction of official interest rates to pre-crisis levels.

GBP/SEK was 10.1700 pre-Lamont announcement.
GBP/SEK was 9.4400 two weeks later at the end of September 1992.
GBP/SEK was 8.9800 during the first week of October 1992.

The hedging activity had paid off on this occasion but the principle of securing interest rate cover when shorting weak currencies is ignored at your peril.

I would like to say that I ran short in GBP/SEK for the full trip down, but I didn't, and modesty prevents me from commenting where profits were accepted. For the record, by mid-November 1992 the Swedish Riksbank had to stand aside. The penal interest rates that had been introduced were damaging the domestic economy and speculation against the kroner continued almost unabated – GBP/SEK surged to 10.2000 – which goes to emphasize the value of timing: never overstay your welcome at any party.

Example – January 1994

No interest rate cover required!

A major policy initiative of the Clinton administration upon their election was liberalization of world trade. Access to the domestic Japanese market was of paramount importance to them in addressing the huge trade imbalance between the US and Japan. Months of intensive discussion failed to produce any cracks in the Japanese resistance to modification of their trade practices. By January 1994, the US administration adopted hardball tactics through Mickey Kantor, US Secretary for Trade, who repeatedly and publicly called for an aggressive strengthening of the yen to assist in addressing the trade imbalance between the two countries by making Japanese products more expensive.

Proprietary traders and fund managers again accepted the party invitation, which promoted an orderly appreciation of the yen from USD/JPY 113.00 to 101.00 between January 1994 and January 1995.

This was verging on stupidity! As with the UK in 1992 Japan found itself isolated in 1994. Other G-7 nations stood aside as the two economic superpowers hotly debated a relaxation of Japan's restrictive trade practices. By January 1995, the yen's strength was beginning to have a negative effect on Japanese exporters' performance, but it appeared progress in negotiations was frustratingly slow for the Americans. Again, though far less openly, Kantor et al. endorsed further yen strength. Hot money cascaded into yen, driving the exchange rate to USD/JPY 79.90 by mid-April 1995. The Bank of Japan had visited the open market many times to reduce the pace of the dollar decline during those months. Japanese industry – all sectors – began to choke; financial ruin was staring them in the face should the currency sustain these levels for a prolonged period of time. Facing a potential economic and financial abyss the Japanese government and Ministry of Finance got down to brass tacks discussions with their American counterparts.

Progress was such that following the G-7 meeting at the end of April 1995 the communiqué released referred to the US dollar as undervalued, particularly in relation to the yen. Market trends are comparable to supertankers – they are slow to change course. Your humble proprietary trader took on board – no pun – the change in American currency sentiment by jawboning for a reversal of recent yen strength, but a catalyst was needed. For three months the trading market remained skeptical of anything other than a lull in an aggressively trending market despite repeated rhetoric from both America and Japan that further yen strength would not be appropriate as Japan would be announcing details of a package which would:

(a) liberalize both its financial and industrial sectors;
(b) stimulate Japan's domestic economy;
(c) encourage overseas investment by Japanese financial institutions.

Unassumingly I set out my stall in July 1995, USD/JPY being stable in a tight range 83.00 to 85.00:

(1) Borrow yen to the extent of the proposed exposure.
(2) Sell those yen to buy USD, picking up a positive interest rate differential of 4–5 percent.
(3) Buy low-delta, out-of-the-money yen Put currency options against dollars with a three-month expiry and a strike price USD/JPY 95.00.
(4) Wait for the catalyst.

The Bank of Japan continued sporadic but heavy bouts of intervention buying USD/JPY with limited sustained impact on the spot rate until mid-August 1995, when Mr Sakakibara of the Ministry of Finance announced details of the deregulation package that had been developed. Despite the verbal forewarning over several weeks the market was wrongfooted. The Bank of Japan was joined by the US Federal Reserve Bank in aggressive FX intervention over several sessions. The Fed, buying USD/JPY in conjunction with supportive rhetoric from the US administration, acted as the final catalyst to the non-believers – Japan was no longer isolated. The dollar rally was swift and sustained as the buying frenzy gained propulsion from late arrivals to the party. Mid-September 1995 and USD/JPY was trading comfortably at 104.00 and a humble proprietary trader drew great satisfaction from responding early to the invitation.

Some years ago I was the junior partner of a proprietary team, and **True story** one day was staggered to hear my boss announce that he was going to the staff cafeteria to get his own lunch. This departure from the usual routine was presumably his subtle criticism of my selection on his behalf the preceding few days. During his absence The Bank of England unexpectedly announced a reduction of 0.5 percent in base lending rates. On his return with an armful of food he stood rooted to the spot staring in disbelief at his screens. He slumped into his chair mumbling: ...

"That was a very expensive sandwich."

"What did you have in it?" I inquired.

"Well I was long of GBP/DEM and short the gilt market and ..." he was about to regurgitate his entire sterling exposure.

"No," I interrupted, "what did you have in the sandwich?"

If only looks could kill.

■ ■ ■

'The FX broker operates within a global market with thousands of customers.'

The Role of the Forex Broker

MIKE PLANT

Managing Director, Foreign Exchange
Harlow Butler Group

The Foreign Exchange Market

Their Role As Intermediaries

Day-To-Day Operations

The Broker and Technology

Automatic Matching Systems

The Foreign Exchange Market

We can trace the first money brokers in the City of London to the early 1900s. When war broke out in 1939, there were about 35 companies involved in foreign exchange broking. The market was unregulated at this stage but this was to change when the markets reopened after the war. From 1951 The Bank of England chose to oversee the market and eventually to regulate and control the number of broking companies active in the London market.

FX broking in London is still regulated by The Bank of England. The major global broking companies today are the descendants of those companies that originated in the early 1950s. There have been many mergers of the companies. These large broking businesses have benefited from the volume of FX trading in the London market, which is still the main FX trading center in the world (see Table 10.1). However, broking today is a global business requiring a presence in all the world's major financial markets and the ability to cover a broad range of currencies.

Table 10.1

Share of global foreign exchange turnover

	Spot FX (%)	FX swaps (%)
UK	27	31
US	20	11
Japan	8	11
Singapore	7	7
Hong Kong	5	7
Switzerland	7	4
Germany	5	5
Others	21	24

Source: BIS 1995

One of the largest brokers has more than 2,300 brokers operating from 25 dealing rooms around the world. These brokers are involved in a whole range of markets including spot and forward foreign exchange. The network of broking desks covers all the time zones, starting in the Far East, with New Zealand, Sydney, Tokyo, Singapore, Hong Kong, Bahrain, London, and New York.

The role of a broker is to provide banks with access to liquidity. Liquidity is a measure of the certainty of exchange (efficiency of matching) and certainty of price (efficiency of price discovery), i.e. how easy it is to find a matching counterparty and how easy it is to deal at the quoted price. The degree of certainty is reduced to the extent that any counterparties are absent from the market. In these circumstances, exchange is not as certain as it could be and price does not include all available information.

Certainty of exchange is much more easily achieved in spot foreign exchange than certainty of price. There may be a trade-off between matching and price discovery, which means that different markets or segments of the same market may emphasize different aspects of liquidity, depending on who is in them.

Brokers also provide clear indications of market depth and information like last price, whether paid or given. Nevertheless, the intangible ability to exchange and discuss information should not be underrated in a highly price-sensitive market like foreign exchange.

Liquidity in spot foreign exchange is underwritten by market makers, i.e. banks which quote prices at which they are committed to buy and sell in reasonable size. In other words, spot foreign exchange is a quote-driven market. In a quote-driven market, the presence of market makers facilitates matching for everyone. However, price discovery becomes crucial for the market makers. This is all the more so for spot foreign exchange because of the volatility of exchange rates.

The screen-based technology of AMS (automated matching systems) mean that they are essentially limited to the order matching function. In other words, AMS are order-driven systems, i.e. there is no scope for market makers. As participants enter the system anonymously, market makers cannot be identified and there is little point therefore in being a market maker on an AMS. Instead, participants typically enter the market only if they have orders to do.

In efforts to improve efficiency, the larger brokers have automated various elements of their operations. The requirements of the bank's position keeping and risk management systems are placing pressure on brokers to produce faster confirmations and on dealing staff to input deal information quickly and accurately. The larger brokers have introduced direct deal entry (i.e. the facility to enter deal details directly into their computer systems). Collectively, brokers in the UK operate ACS (automated confirmation system), through which they can electronically dispatch confirmations to clients. Electronic confirmation of foreign exchange deals via ACS has been available for a decade and now accounts for about 75 percent of the larger brokers' spot FX transactions and more than 80 percent of forward FX. More than 220 banks now use the system, 150 in London, 25 in Europe, 25 in the US, and 20 in Singapore.

Their Role As Intermediaries

What does a broker do, and why do we use them?

Foreign exchange transactions can be conducted via three channels: either banks trade directly with an interbank counterparty by telephone or an automated dealing system, or the transaction is intermediated by a foreign exchange broker, who matches the bid and offer quotes of interbank traders. Foreign exchange brokers rely on human intermediation using voice communication over telephone lines. Client banks place orders with a broker. The broker selects the highest bid and lowest offer from the range of quotes he has received to produce a synthetic two-way quote with the narrowest dealing spread (the quote is synthetic in the sense that the bid and offer may come from different banks, which also means that it is possible to have inverted two-way quotes). The synthetic quote is broadcast back to the broker's clients.

The broker may qualify a price if it is for an amount which is considered small or large in comparison to the current market norm (for major currency pairs, this is less than 10 and more than 20 million US dollars).

It is important to recognize that brokers are not passive agents. They can actively catalyze activity in the market by encouraging clients to provide quotes. This is seen as particularly important in the period after a piece of news has hit the market.

Brokers enable prices to be dealt on before credit limits are checked. However, they also have to deal with situations where clients have to refuse counterparty names because of credit limitations. To an extent, this can be avoided by having the client warn the broker beforehand that they cannot or will not accept certain names. If, nevertheless, two counterparties are introduced who discover that there are credit obstacles between them, a broker can undertake name-switching, i.e. actively search for a mutually acceptable bank to act as an intermediary between the first two counterparties.

Brokers provide an information service to clients above and beyond the broadcasting of orders. This includes general impressions of market direction and news. More importantly brokers can give a "feel" for the market to help clients infer the short-term direction of the market

As with any competitive market, some competitors will be cheaper and some more expensive than others. If you wish to obtain competitive car insurance you go via a broker who has access to the hundreds of companies and will find the most competitive quotation.

This scenario also applies to the foreign exchange broker, who acts as a conduit to put the best bid and offer together to form the most competitive quotation. This price could involve a bank in Frankfurt against one in Singapore. The FX broker operates within a global market with thousands of customers.

Let us first look at how an international broker manages to find this best price.

How does it work?

The time is 7.15 am in London and already the spot yen desk is fully staffed with 14 brokers sitting in front of banks of open telephone lines to up to 200 banks throughout Europe. One of the team is speaking simultaneously to similar sized broking desks in Tokyo, Singapore, and Hong Kong, and from this market they combine the prices to form a competitive price, this being the best possible bid and offer which make up the quotation. In London two other companies who broke USD/JPY will also be trying to produce the most competitive quotes.

Example

Not only does the bank dealer have the choice of a best price from one broker, but in London currently has a choice of three international companies. The bank dealer also has another option: to deal inside the quoted price by either putting a "bid" or "offer" inside the broker's price, which could mean executing his business at an even better price.

The benefit to the dealer lies not only in the speed of execution of his business and in finding the best price, but very importantly the confidentiality of the process.

Day-To-Day Operations

The price mechanism that the dealer trades on is the end result of an international network of brokers working to achieve the best price – how does that price arrive?

A broker will have a dealing board which has dedicated open telephone lines to banks either in London or Europe. The combination of banks produces bids and offers which constitute the price, and this is relayed via a microphone to the broker's customers. The bank will choose to buy or sell and communicate with the broker by speaking directly into his phone which is then linked directly to the broker via a loudspeaker system.

Trades take place at a frantic pace – a second makes the difference between hitting or missing the rate.

The essence of the open line system is the speed at which deals are completed. The broker hears the dealer's instruction over a speaker system and reacts immediately to close the deal at the specified rate.

The FX broker never acts as a principal, but as an agent, where he derives a commission from each completed transaction.

The Broker and Technology

Competing alongside the brokers are the automatic matching systems (AMS) which have prompted the major FX brokers to examine ways of enhancing the service they provide. The aim is to find the optimum blend of a personal service with the advantages that information technology can provide.

Brokers already enter deals directly into computer systems so that they can be matched and processed – soon these deals will be fed electronically on the bank dealers' desks. This will remove the need for handwritten deal tickets, increase accuracy, and speed up the whole process of providing a broking service.

Automatic Matching Systems

AMS are dedicated networks connecting interactive computer terminals. Dealers in banks key in foreign exchange orders (amount, price, and a buy or sell instruction) into their terminals. Newly entered buy (sell) orders which match previously entered and still outstanding sell (buy) orders in terms of price – provided the common price is the best available in the system – are automatically offset. Orders do not have to be the same size to be matched. Several smaller orders can be matched with one larger order.

Where new orders cannot be matched with previously entered and still outstanding orders, an AMS will broadcast the price, size, and direction of the new order across the system. Other users of the AMS can accept the order directly using "mine/buy" or "yours/sell" buttons (confirmed by a transmit button). Previously entered and still outstanding orders can be withdrawn, temporarily or permanently, using other special keys. AMS will allow orders to be matched only if the counterparties have adequate credit lines available for each other.

Credit lines for deals within AMS are recorded on the systems. One of the most serious complaint against AMS is the need to keep separate limits in the system and the inconvenience of updating these limits. Dealers therefore tend to dedicate only small limits to AMSs in order to keep their room for maneuver in the interbank market.

AMS have a niche market in small orders, so it can be argued that they do not provide liquidity in the sense it is used in the wholesale market. They will find it much harder to replace brokers than is suggested by simple market share comparisons.

AMS are currently operating only in the spot markets and active trading is limited to a narrow range of currency pairs. According to the latest central banks' survey of foreign exchange the AMS accounted for 5 percent of foreign exchange turnover in London and New York and 4 percent in Tokyo.

There are currently two AMS in operation:

- Reuters Dealing 2000-2
- EBS (Electronic Broking Service).

Reuters Dealing 2000-2

2000-2 is wholly owned and operated by Reuters. It was the first AMS to begin operations, and started in April 1992. However, 2000-2 was originally scheduled for 1989.

Dealing 2000-2 is a development of Reuter's conversational direct dealing system, Dealing 2000-1, which is itself a PC-based digital enhancement of Reuter's Monitor Dealing System (RDMS).

EBS

EBS was established by the EBS Partnership, a consortium which originally included 11 London-based banks (five US, three UK, and three Swiss). There are now 14 banks involved. Operations began in September 1993.

For the bank shareholders, the principal motive behind EBS was to "reduce bank dependency on Reuters," which they believed "disadvantages banks in terms of both cost and control" (RDMS and 2000-1 had taken 94 percent of the market in conversational direct dealing systems; by 1992, such systems already controlled about one third of foreign exchange turnover in major centers and more in smaller centers).

The natural advantage of EBS is that shareholder banks are estimated to have 35 percent of the London foreign exchange market. However, EBS is seen as a club of big banks.

The most significant difference in the functionality of the systems is in the method of credit-checking. 2000-2 requires users to record credit limits on the central mainframe computer. Moreover, credit checks are performed (as in traditional broking) *after* orders have been matched. In contrast, EBS allows users to maintain their schedule of credit limits on their local node and credit checks are carried out *before* orders are matched. Moreover, local nodes will not accept and display orders from other users with whom there are inadequate credit lines (despite the fact that this withholds useful price data).

The centralization of credit limit schedules is a sensitive issue. Banks prefer to keep such information under their control, for fear that other banks may discover and be upset by the limits which have been imposed on exposures. Reuters has steadfastly refused to recognize or accommodate these fears.

Computers do not provide a broking system, but a matching system where "buy" and "sell" orders are matchable at the exact price. These machine-based systems cannot interpret customers' requests in the same way that personal service can.

As an example: you wish to buy your dream car at auction, and your bid is for £49,999. The reserve proves to be £50,000 – you would gladly pay the extra pound to buy the car. But a machine would not sell you the car as you are a pound below the offer.

That is probably a little extreme, but during a day's trading many opportunities exist where information and customer understanding can help the dealer to achieve the best deals for his bank.

■ ■ ■

'Technical analysis techniques are used for speculation and hedging. They can be used for foreign exchange, interest rates, futures, equities, and options.'

Technical Analysis

IAN WINTER

Head of Technical Analysis
ANZ Bank, London

Introduction

Definitions

Create Your Chart

Key Charting Elements

Japanese Candlesticks

Elliott Wave Techniques

Conclusion

Introduction

In early 1991 during my first attempts to forecast exchange rate movements and before I had heard of technical analysis, I thought that I had "discovered" the secret of predicting market movements. I created two moving average lines (5 days and 15 days) from historical daily USD/DEM exchange rate data and noticed that the five-day line moved above and below the 15-day line. "Buying USD" when moving above and "selling USD" when moving below the 15-day line always seemed to generate theoretical "profit."

Had I discovered the Holy Grail of technical trading?

Proudly, I revealed to my boss six months' worth of profitable "paper trading" in various currencies. He was interested but extremely skeptical that "reading tea leaves" would work.

With the benefit of hindsight the "success" was due to an ongoing trending market and not the Grail.

Moving average signals will always be good in markets that are trending in the same direction. (Figures 11.7 and 11.8 provide examples of moving average signals.)

Sideways moving markets, where the rate is moving within a narrow range and not trending in an ongoing upwards or downwards direction, will be your graveyard because many "false" moving average signals will suggest buying USD at the top or selling USD at the bottom of the market range.

In 1992 I attended a fascinating three-day seminar on technical analysis which introduced me to the real charting world. From then I was hooked. Technical analysis techniques are used for speculation and hedging. They can be used for foreign exchange, interest rates, futures, equities, and options.

My specialty is the foreign exchange markets but wherever accurate data is available charts can be created and analyzed. Charts are used by professional traders in banks, corporate customers, equity traders, analytical consultants, and private individuals who study stock markets. Knowing the "chart points" (that is, support and resistance points, Fibonacci retracement objectives, and oscillator indicators) is important to both traders and investors.

The contents of this chapter are an introduction to technical analysis and charting, and include techniques that I prefer to use on a day-to-day basis to help forecast foreign exchange rate movements.

Definitions

"Technical analysis is the study of market action, through the use of charts, for the purpose of forecasting future price trends." (J. J. Murphy).

Generally three assumptions are presumed when studying technical analysis:

(1) **The market action discounts everything.**
Anything that can affect the market price whether it be fundamental, political, or psychological information, is already reflected in the price.

(2) **Price moves in trends.**
Markets trend in a general direction and these trends continue.

(3) **History repeats itself.**
The key to understanding the future lies in the past.

Technical versus fundamental forecasting

The technician believes the three assumptions listed above and studies the effect of market movements whilst the fundamentalist (economist) studies the cause of market movements such as central bank interest rate changes.

Create Your Chart

When constructing your own chart the most important factor for good technical analysis is clean data, which is essential to produce the best quality charts. Information providers such as Reuters offer charting software that generate charts for the technical analyst to use. The studies shown in this chapter are all created using the Reuters Technical Analysis product, called RTA.

This raw data can be displayed in a variety of formats; for the purpose of illustration I have used the daily rate movements of USD/DEM for a six-month period from May 1995 to November 1995.

Different types of charts

Line charts
These use the closing price for a period, which can be hourly, daily, weekly, or even monthly (user's discretion), and display a single line. (Figure 11.1 shows the daily exchange rate movement of USD/DEM from May 1995 to November 1995.)

Point and figure charts
These display a sequence of Os and Xs. They highlight congestion areas of support and resistance points and are used to calculate price objectives. (Figure 11.2 shows the exchange rate of USD/DEM from May 1995 to November 1995.)

Bar charts
These use the high, low, and closing price for a period (user's discretion). They are built up of bars displaying a range for the period with a right hand "tick" which identifies the closing price for the period. (Figure 11.3 shows the daily exchange rate movement of USD/DEM from May 1995 to November 1995.)

Japanese candlestick charts
These use high, low, open, and closing prices for a period (user's discretion). They display the range for a period with markers for the open and

Fig 11.1

Daily line chart of USD/DEM from May 1995 to November 1995

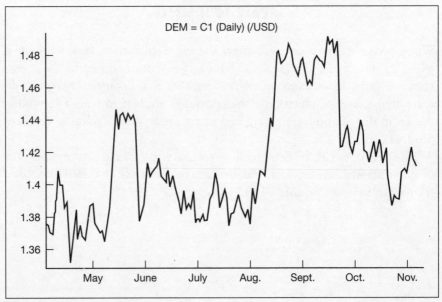

Source: Reuters Technical Analysis

close price of the period (Figure 11.4 shows the daily exchange rate movement of USD/DEM from May 1995 to November 1995.)

Daily point and figure chart of USD/DEM from May 1995 to November 1995

Fig 11.2

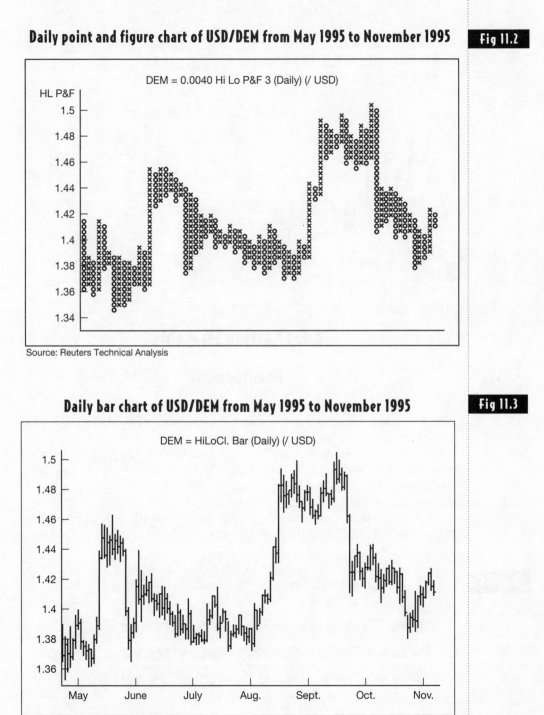

Source: Reuters Technical Analysis

Daily bar chart of USD/DEM from May 1995 to November 1995

Fig 11.3

Source: Reuters Technical Analysis

Fig 11.4 | **Daily Japanese candlestick chart of USD/DEM – May 1995 to November 1995**

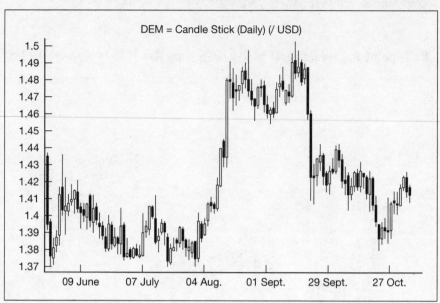

DEM = Candle Stick (Daily) (/ USD)

Source: Reuters Technical Analysis

Key Charting Elements

Fibonacci ratios

The Fibonacci series of numbers was discovered by Leonardo Fibonacci, a thirteenth-century Italian mathematician.

The series of numbers, in which each member is the sum of the two preceding numbers, is: 1, 1, 2, 3, 5, 8, 13, 21, 34, 55, 89, 144, 233, 377, and so on. The numbers are calculated by adding 1 + 2 = 3, 2 + 3 = 5, 3 + 5 = 8, 5 + 8 = 13, 8 + 13 = 21, etc.

To an analyst the importance of these numbers is the unique ratios that they generate. Excluding the first four numbers they are always the same:

Ratios

> The ratio of any number to its next highest is 0.618%
> (e.g. 89/144 = 0.618).
>
> The ratio to its lower number is 1.618% (e.g. 144/89 = 1.618).
>
> The ratio to two higher is 0.382% (e.g. 55/144 = 0.382).
>
> The ratio to two lower is 2.618% (e.g. 144/55 = 2.618).

The ratios of 38.2, 61.8, 1.618, and 2.618 percent are important for retracement and projection of rate movements.

It is suggested that the ratios are a mathematical presentation of real life. For example: the positioning of the eyes and nose on the average face is about 62 and 38 percent respectively of the distance from the chin to the forehead. The Pyramid of Gizeh built by the ancient Egyptians appears to have been designed using the 1.618 ratio. One edge is 783.3 feet long and the height is 484.4 feet (783.3 divided by 484.4 is 1.617). The height of 484.4 feet is 5,813 inches (5–8–13), numbers from the Fibonacci series.

Trend, support, and resistance lines

Figure 11.5 displays trend, support and resistance lines trends for USD/DEM from October 31, 1995 to November 5, 1995.

When chartists start analyzing the raw data they initially look for the trend and support and resistance lines.

Example of trend lines displayed on USD/DEM chart Fig 11.5

Source: Reuters Technical Analysis

Trend

Trend has three directions, namely up, down, and sideways. A sequence of higher lows would indicate an up trend whilst a series of lower highs would determine a down trend. This can be seen in Figure 11.5. Trend lines are created by joining significant peaks and troughs on the charts.

Support and resistance

Figure 11.6. shows examples of support and resistance points within an uptrending and downtrending market.

The support and resistance points identify congestion areas in rate movements where market buyers and sellers are equal. When the buyers or sellers start to dominate, the market moves in that direction until another support or resistance zone is formed.

Fig 11.6

Example of support and resistance points

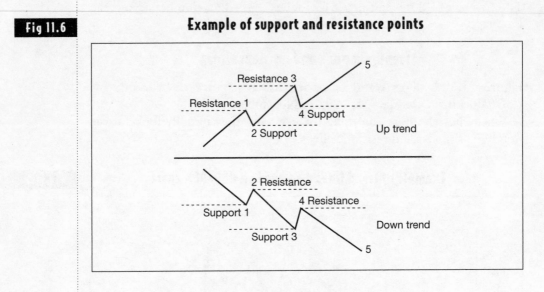

Moving averages

There are three basic moving averages:

(1) **Simple moving average** is generated from the average of a chosen number of points of data. For example, a 13-day average of closing prices is the prices for the last 13 days added up and the total divided by 13.

(2) **Weighted moving average** is generated from the average of a chosen number of data records with the most recent data weighted higher than earlier data.

(3) **Exponentially smoothed moving average** is the weighted average of total data.

Figures 11.7 and 11.8 show two weighted moving averages displayed over daily candlestick charts for USD/DEM and GBP/USD.

Buy and sell signals are created where the two lines cross.

Example of three-day and 13-day weighted moving averages displayed over a daily candlestick chart for USD/DEM

Fig 11.7

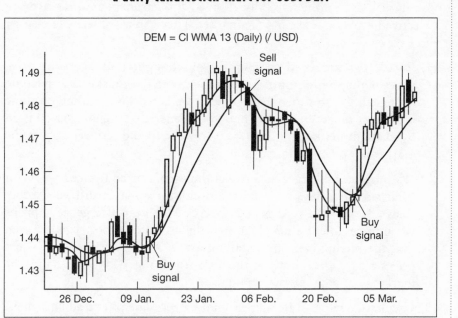

Source: Reuters Technical Analysis

Example of three-day and 13-day weighted moving averages displayed over a daily candlestick chart for GBP/USD

Fig 11.8

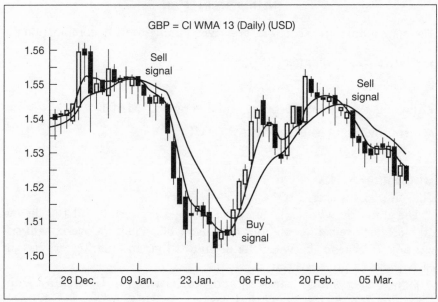

Source: Reuters Technical Analysis

Oscillators

Oscillators are mathematically derived indicators that offer a more objective means of analyzing the market. They can assist users in at least three ways:

(1) Oscillators are used to identify overbought and oversold price movements, which notify the trader that the market has become overextended and therefore subject to a correction. Scaling on these indicators ranges between 0 and 100. Generally a signal over 80 is an overbought market and below 20 is oversold and retracements in the market price can be anticipated.

(2) Warning of a divergence between the oscillator and price movement (that is, when the price and the oscillator move in different directions). There are two types of divergence. A bear divergence happens when prices are at a new high, but the oscillator is not. This is a sign that the buying pressure is falling away. A bull divergence is when prices are at a new low but the oscillator is not. This implies that the market is gaining internal strength.

(3) Oscillators with a scale plus or minus a zero line offer trading signals. Buying opportunities are signalled when the indicator crosses up through the zero line. Selling strategies are appropriate when crossing down below the zero line.

Oscillators in detail

There are numerous oscillators. However, I prefer to use a combination of:

- relative strength index (RSI)
- stochastics
- moving average convergence and divergence (MACD)
- directional movement indicator (DMI).

Relative strength index

This indicator was created by J. Welles Wilder.

The graph shows a single line which ranges between 0 and 100. Below 20 indicates oversold conditions and above 80 signals an overbought situation. Divergence between the oscillator line and market price is an early signal of price reversal.

Figure 11.9 shows the RSI and stochastics for USD/DEM from December 26, 1995 to March 5, 1996.

Stochastics

Created by George Lane, these are based on the observation that as price increases closing prices tend to be nearer the upper end of a price range. Conversely, in down trends, the closing price tends to be near the lower end of the range.

The resulting graph displays a double line within a range from 0 to 100. A line above 80 indicates an overbought condition and below 20 is oversold. Divergence with the price line warns of potential price reversal (again, see Figure 11.9).

Daily candlestick for USD/DEM with displays of relative strength index and stochastic oscillators

Fig 11.9

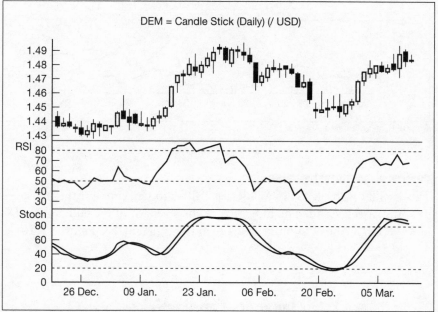

DEM = Candle Stick (Daily) (/ USD)

Source: Reuters Technical Analysis

MACD

This oscillator, by Gerald Appel, displays an exponentially smoothed moving average line of the difference between two other moving averages revolving above and below a zero line. Crossing the zero line from below is a buy signal and from above a sell. Divergence with the price line is a signal of price reversal.

Figure 11.10 shows the MACD and DMI for USD/DEM from December 26, 1995 to March 5, 1996.

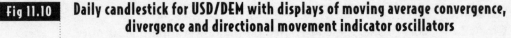

Fig 11.10 Daily candlestick for USD/DEM with displays of moving average convergence, divergence and directional movement indicator oscillators

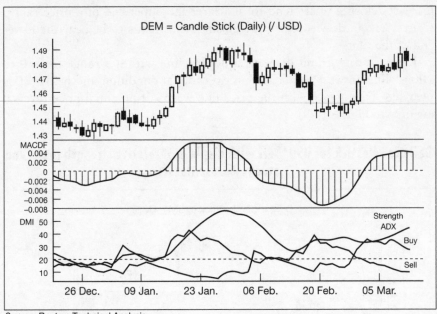

Source: Reuters Technical Analysis

Directional movement indicator

This oscillator, by J.Welles Wilder, is a filter to determine if the market is in a buy or sell trend. The indicator of the strength of a trend is the ADX line. An ADX above 20 indicates a firm trend (again, see Figure 11.10)

Japanese Candlesticks

Japanese candlesticks were invented over 350 years ago for the Japanese rice markets and are created using high, low, open, and closing rates per identified period. They offer a visual representation of market activity and produce different shaped candlestick formations depending on rate movements. Certain formations are generally good early indicators of future price movements and a candlestick analyst is constantly looking for them. This is my preferred method of analysis. Figure 11.11 shows how a candlestick is formed using the high, low, open, and closing price data for a day. Each day's activity is different – consequently the candlesticks differ.

Example of how a candlestick is created

Fig 11.11

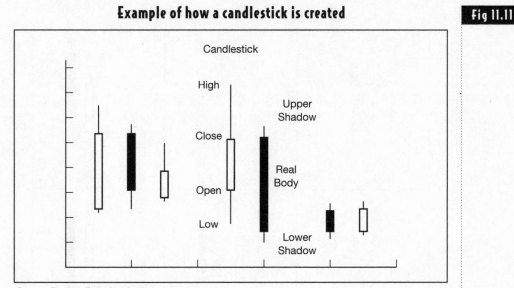

Source: Reuters Technical Analysis

Where the closing price is higher than the open the "body" is white and a closing price lower than the open creates a black "body."

Candlestick charts are indicators of market activity. The analyst is looking for formations of candles that signal future market direction. These have particular shapes and names. The most important are *reversal patterns*, shown in Figures 11.12 and 11.13. Basic bear reversal patterns (numbers 1 to 7) and bull reversal formations (numbers 8 to 12) are detailed. These formation names, translated from Japanese, are called hammer and hanging lines, harami, engulfing and piercing patterns, dark cloud cover, stars, and dojis.

Bear reversal patterns are looked for in an uptrending market. Bull reversal patterns are expected during a down trend. Both signal market retracements.

Figure 11.14 is a daily chart for USD/DEM. The initial downtrend congested around 1.4900 and the hammer pattern signaled a bull reversal which lasted for some two months. The bull rally stopped in late December where a sequence of doji patterns signaled a bear reversal.

Figure 11.15 is a daily chart for GBP/DEM which shows a down trend falling around 2.4150. A piercing pattern signaled a bull reversal which lasted nearly two weeks. Two harami patterns signaled retracements prior to the bear reversal dark cloud cover pattern of early December at 2.4650.

Fig 11.12

Examples of six bear candle patterns

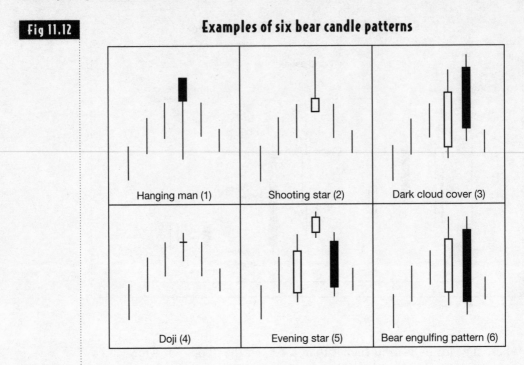

Hanging man (1) Shooting star (2) Dark cloud cover (3)

Doji (4) Evening star (5) Bear engulfing pattern (6)

Fig 11.13

Examples of one bear (number 7) and five bull (numbers 8 – 12) candle patterns

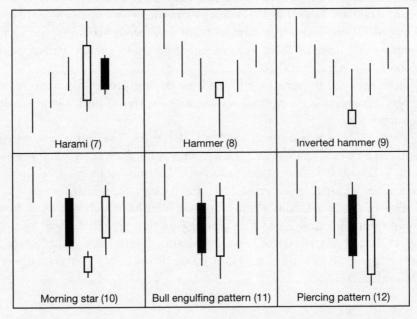

Harami (7) Hammer (8) Inverted hammer (9)

Morning star (10) Bull engulfing pattern (11) Piercing pattern (12)

Example formations displayed on daily candlesick chart for USD/DEM

Fig 11.14

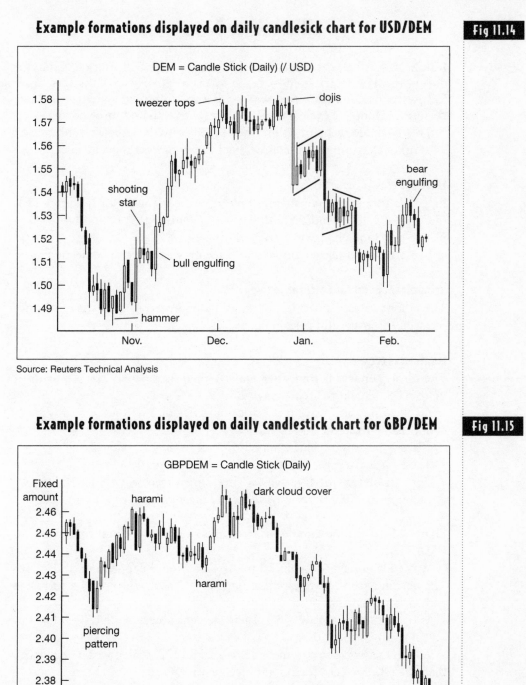

Source: Reuters Technical Analysis

Example formations displayed on daily candlestick chart for GBP/DEM

Fig 11.15

Source: Reuters Technical Analysis

Elliott Wave Techniques

Ralph Nelson Elliott developed his theory of stock market behavior during the 1920s. In its most basic form the theory says that a market follows a pattern of a five-wave advance followed by a three-wave decline. A complete cycle has eight waves – five up and three down.

This basic concept of Elliott waves can now be used in conjunction with other charting techniques when charting market movements.

Wave patterns

In a rising market analysts are looking for a sequence of five up waves (numbered 1 to 5) and three down waves (lettered A, B, and C) to complete a textbook eight-wave price movement.

In a down market five down and three up waves are the objective.

Retracement points and price objectives

The Fibonacci ratios of 38.2, 61.8, and 1.618 percent are used to identify retracement levels and price objectives.

Eight-wave cycle

The ideal scenario is that after wave 1 there is a general retracement of up to 61.8 percent to create wave 2.

A following third wave has a price objective of 1.618 percent of wave 1, commencing from the end of wave 2.

Wave 4 has a retracement target of 38.2 percent of wave 3.

The fifth wave is generally the same size as wave 1.

On completion of five waves there are three waves (A, B, and C) retracing some 50.0 percent to complete the eight-wave cycle.

Figure 11.16 is an example of a complete eight-wave bull formation, in USD/DEM.

Wave 1 commenced from a low of 1.3800 and capped out at 1.4250. The ensuing second wave pulled back to 1.3975, which was a full 61.8 percent retracement.

Wave 3 moved up towards a 1.618 percent objective of 1.4700 but ran out of steam at 1.4550.

The fourth wave retracement settled at 1.4275, which was a little more than the 38.2 percent textbook objective of 1.4320.

The final fifth wave price action moved strongly upwards and moved through the price objective of 1.4800 and capped out at 1.4925.

There followed an A, B, C retracement to 1.4410, which represented a pull back just short of the 50 percent target set at 1.4375.

Example of up trend eight-wave cycle for USD/DEM

Fig 11.16

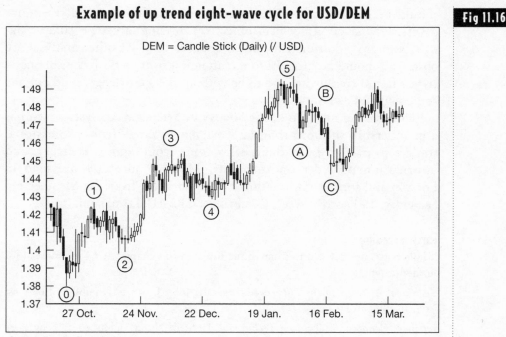

DEM = Candle Stick (Daily) (/ USD)

Source: Reuters Technical Analysis

Conclusion

My treasury trading career started in 1970. I wish that I had heard of technical analysis earlier than 1991.

Technical analysis now has an important function which adds value to a trading operation whether large or small. Traders, both in-house and corporate client, always seek the chartist's view. They want to know support and resistance points and chart price objectives.

Wherever accurate data is available charts can be created and analyzed. Consequently, products in foreign exchange markets, equity markets, money markets, and futures markets are covered.

No single method of analysis can be considered reliable. However, a combination of techniques indicating similar buying or selling signals offers confidence to the trader. For example, an up trend candlestick chart showing bear reversal formations, coupled with the RSI and stochastic oscillators in the 80 overbought area, or bear divergence signals offer retracement opportunities to the trader either to reduce a long position to lock in profit or sell looking for Fibonacci retracement objectives.

However, when positions are taken stop-loss limits should be observed to protect you. An activated stop-loss is the cost of doing business.

Some market practitioners are skeptical about the value of charts and believe them to be "self-fulfilling." My answer is that market participants should be aware of potential market action. Support and resistance points, Fibonacci retracement objectives, pricing targets, oscillator signals, and any additional technical clues as to what other analysts are observing should be brought to the attention of traders. Technical analysis is a fact of trading life and to be without this knowledge could put one at a competitive disadvantage.

I close with a mention of the Society of Technical Analysts which has a membership of more than 625. Members range from professional traders to private individuals who come from equity, Treasury, and information provider backgrounds. Monthly meetings are held in London and further information can be obtained from the Membership Secretary, 28 Panton Street, Cambridge, CB2 1DH, England.

Further reading

Whole books are devoted to some of the topics in this chapter and I recommend for further reading:

Technical Analysis of the Futures Markets, by John J. Murphy, published by New York Institute of Finance.

Japanese Candlestick Charting Techniques, by Steve Nison, published by New York Institute of Finance.

Elliott Wave Principle Applied to the Foreign Exchange Markets, by Robert Balan, published by BBS Financial Publications.

Fibonacci Applications and Strategies for Traders, by Robert Fischer, published by John Wiley & Sons Inc.

■ ■ ■

'OTC currency options continue to be very successful as more and more banks and corpora- tions seek to hedge their currency exposures with derivative products.'

Background and Development of the Currency Option Market

Introduction

The growth of the currency option market goes hand in hand with the global growth of foreign exchange and outstrips it many times. Options are one of a group of derivative instruments (the others being futures and swaps), but for those readers unfamiliar with options, let me explain what a derivative is. The expression "derivative" covers any transaction where there is no movement of principal, and where the price performance of the derivative itself is driven by the price of an underlying "asset." In the case of currency options the underlying asset is normally taken to be the outright forward foreign exchange rate. To make sense of this chapter on options I have highlighted the most important points relating to derivatives.

Basic Derivative Market Background

Definition A **derivative instrument** is one whose performance is based on (or derived from) the behavior of the price of an underlying asset (often known simply as the "underlying"). The underlying itself does not need to be bought or sold. A premium may be due.

A true derivative instrument requires no movement of principal funds. It is this characteristic that makes them such useful tools both to hedge and to take risk, and why, a few years ago, these same instruments were known as "off-balance sheet" instruments. Off-balance sheet signified that as no movement of principal occurred, there was no requirement for the transaction to appear on the company balance sheet.

There are many types of derivative product, but specifically the term includes three key products:

- options
- futures
- swaps.

Table 12.1 lists some examples, together with their respective "underlying assets."

Derivative products and their underlying assets

Table 12.1

Derivative	Underlying
Currency options	Forward FX rates
Interest rate swaps	Government bonds, (e.g. UK gilts)
Interest rate futures	Implied forward interest rates
FT-SE 100 futures	FT-SE 100 Index

Different types of derivatives

Exchange-traded vs over the counter (OTC) instruments

A derivative product can be transacted either by *exchange-traded* means, where a fixed and prespecified contract is bought or sold on a recognized exchange, or it can be transacted over the counter (OTC). An OTC instrument is written or created by a bank (or sometimes corporate and other financial institutions) and tailored to suit the exact requirements of the client, i.e. dates, amounts, currencies, etc.

An exchange-traded instrument

This is an instrument that is bought or sold directly on an exchange such as LIFFE – the London International Financial Futures Exchange – or the CBOT (the Chicago Board of Trade) or the Philadelphia Stock Exchange. There are over 30 recognized regulated exchanges worldwide each trading their own contracts as well as some that are traded globally across different exchanges

Each exchange-traded product has a "contract specification," which details precisely the characteristics of the "underlying" and who is under obligation to do what at maturity. Typical exchange-traded instruments include financial futures and listed options and traded currency options. The contracts are mostly sold by a method of trading known as "open outcry" that originated on the Chicago exchanges and entails face-to-face contact, hand signals, and loud oral agreements. The clearing house of each exchange will take the credit risk of each member, so there is no requirement to check if lines are clear in advance of a trade. For further details on how the clearing house operates refer to *Mastering Derivatives Markets*, by Francesca Taylor (Pitman Publishing, 1996).

An over the counter (OTC) instrument

An OTC instrument is one that is sold by a bank (usually) to a client (usually) and tailored to fit a specific set of requirements. Sometimes banks will purchase these products from companies or other non-banks, but each buyer and each seller must take the credit risk of their counter-party. An OTC product allows for much greater flexibility in terms of expiry date, strike, amount, underlying commodity, and vast amounts of these transactions are executed every day. An OTC instrument can be very simple in which case it is known as a "vanilla" product (named after the simplest variety of ice cream), or it can be exceedingly complex. The price of the trade will be agreed upon between the parties, is confidential, and will involve many factors.

Single vs multiple settlement

Derivatives also divide neatly into products where there is a single settle-ment at or during maturity, and those where there are multiple settlements throughout the life of transaction (see Table 12.2). Derivative products with multiple settlements, such as swaps and caps, typically cover interest rates and fall outside the scope of this book.

Table 12.2

Single and multiple settlement products

Single settlement	Multiple settlement
Financial futures/FRAs	Interest rate swaps
Interest rate options	Interest rate caps, collars, floors
Currency options	Currency swaps
Energy CFDs	Energy swaps

Premium or non-premium based

Some derivatives require the payment of a premium, others do not. Options require the payment of a premium – in fact any product, where the buyer (client or bank) has paid a premium, is an option, even if the premium is disguised. The option product allows the buyer himself to decide what course of action to take at or during the maturity. The pur-chaser (holder) of the product can "abandon" the instrument if it offers an unfavorable or worse rate than that available elsewhere in the market. The client will always choose the alternative that offers him the best out-come, either the rate on the derivative instrument or the current underlying market rate.

Any premium based instrument will guarantee for the client (holder) a worst or best case outcome, whereas a non-premium based instrument, such as an FRA or swap offers an absolute rate which cannot be improved upon.

Liquidity

Liquidity is an important concept in any tradeable instrument, especially in derivatives. It is an indicator of how likely one is to be able to sell or to buy the instrument at a particular point in time.

There is an important saying in the market: *"there is a price for buying, a price for selling and a price for selling quickly."*

Liquidity in interest rate derivatives is far greater with the exchange-traded products, and hundreds of thousands of contracts are bought and sold each day on the major exchanges. The chance therefore of finding willing buyers and willing sellers at a particular time and price is very good. With currency options and currency derivatives generally, the scale tips the other way, with a major shift towards OTC currency products rather than those that are exchange based. Liquidity in the vanilla OTC instruments is also very good, but will be spread among many types of similar but non-identical transactions. As a result of this, as deals become more complex, liquidity will start to dry up, resulting in some deals being so complex and so "structured" that there is in effect zero liquidity.

> *Liquidity needs to be monitored on a regular basis. It is affected ulti-* **Tip**
> *mately by supply and demand, but this in turn can be driven by*
> *changing credit quality, currency weakness or strength, volatility, etc.*

Credit risk

Credit risk is another important factor. It is the risk that the counterparty to the deal may go bankrupt or enter into liquidation before the contract matures, thus making them unable to fulfill their obligations. Credit risk is much lower with exchange-traded products as the clearing house (which is an affiliate of the regulated exchange) becomes counterparty to every trade, reducing exposure to individual clients. The risk on OTC products such as options is high as each party to the transaction takes the credit risk of the other. If you do not like the risk, you do not deal.

Growth of the Currency Option Market

Currency options are foreign exchange derivatives and they exhibit similar trends to those shown in the foreign exchange markets. The most thorough recent survey available is the triennial survey conducted by the Bank for International Settlements (BIS), Basle. It covered a three-year period from April 1992 to April 1995, and showed a general increase in the volume of foreign exchange traded globally to something in excess of USD1.2 trillion (USD1,200,000,000,000) per day. This figure includes spot and forward transactions, and includes all tradeable currencies.

Spot and forward foreign exchange are both traditionally OTC markets exhibiting continuous trading, 24 hours a day around the world. The FX volumes far outstrip the size of the actual trade flows. It follows therefore that if the "underlying foreign exchange asset" trades most efficiently in an OTC manner, then its derivative will also trade best in that medium.

Volumes

More recently the BIS, Basle, surveyed the derivatives markets. It is always a problem to try to estimate the size of this market as so many deals are proprietary, many are embedded in complex capital market structure, and many key players are wary of disclosing their figures. However, this new survey, with findings published in June 1996, reveals that a good guide to volume is a total outstanding notional figure of about USD47 trillion (USD47,000,000,000,000) for OTC products alone – not only OTC currency products but any customer tailored transaction. This is more than twice the size of the figures previously estimated, but still includes only 90 percent of the banks active in the market. There will also undoubtedly be an element of "double counting" where each counterparty bank has reported the same deal, although brave attempts have been made to eradicate this. Even so, this market is exceptionally large, with OTC currency and interest products accounting for the lion's share of this business. Exchange-traded currency options are available and are often used by the banking market to hedge their own positions.

OTC currency options continue to be very succesful as more and more banks and corporations seek to hedge their currency exposures with derivative products as well as traditional spot and forward foreign exchange transactions. The disciplines of currency options and foreign exchange are very close and each complements the other.

What is a Currency Option?

Definition *A **currency option** gives the buyer (holder) the right, but not the obligation, to buy or sell a specific amount of currency at a specific exchange rate (the strike), on or before a specific future date. A premium is due.*

Definition discussed

A currency option gives the client (or the bank) the chance to fix the rate of exchange that will apply to a forthcoming transaction. Everything is described from the client's, or holder's, perspective. The holder of the option need not proceed with the deal if he can find a more advantageous exchange rate elsewhere. The option instrument will let the holder choose the rate of exchange (the strike), and then the writing (or selling) bank must guarantee that rate if and when required. Because this option provides a type of optional guarantee, rather than an obligation, a premium is due. This is normally paid within two business days in either of the currencies of the option. Some banks may take the premium payment in a third currency but it is at their discretion.

In the above circumstances the client is the buyer (holder) of the option and must pay the premium. The holder has all the rights with the sole obligation to pay the premium by the due date. In contrast, the bank is the seller or writer of the option, it has all the obligations and no rights at all under the option: all it can receive is the premium paid by the purchaser yet the bank's obligations are onerous. It is the bank which must have the "underlying" foreign exchange ready in case the holder requires it. It is the bank which must also hedge the risks on the option position. The underlying in this case is the receipt or payment of one currency against another currency.

Options can be cash settled at expiry or they can be sold back at any time during the life of the transaction for residual or "fair value" (see Terminology, below). Alternatively, the currency can be physically delivered or paid to the writing bank (this is known as "exercise"). The client will then receive the counter currency at the exchange rate previously agreed under the option. It should be noted that there may not always be a positive benefit on the option, some options will expire worthless.

The currency option is a more flexible hedging instrument than traditional forward foreign exchange and gives the buyer (holder) of the option four alternatives. The choice of:

- **when** to exercise
- **whether** to exercise
- **how much** to exercise
- **the strike** (or exercise) **price**.

When?

There are two types of currency option: an American option and a European option. Under an American style currency option a greater flexibility is offered. Consider an American style option to sell US dollars and buy sterling; on exercise, the dollars can be delivered by the option holder to the bank, on any business day until expiry, for value two business days later. By comparison, under a European style option, the holder can deliver the dollars against exercise only on the actual expiry date (for value two business days later), as specified at the beginning of the option contract. A European style option operates in a similar fashion to a traditional forward foreign exchange contract. But with the forward contract the currency must be delivered on the maturity date.

With a traditional forward contract

If a client has sold forward some dollars for two months against sterling, and the dollars do not arrive in time, then the forward contract must still be honored. This may lead to the client having the expense of buying the required amount of currency from the spot market, possibly at a worse rate, and then delivering it under the forward contract.

With the European style currency option

If a client has transacted an option contract, should the dollars not arrive the option is simply abandoned, or if there is value remaining it can be sold back to the writing bank and the residual (fair) value realized (see Terminology, below)

Occasionally the underlying exposure that the option is covering may be shortened, or for some reason the option may no longer be required: then, as above, the option can be sold back to the writing bank for fair value. But if the underlying exposure is lengthened it is not possible to extend the option at the same strike, or to roll it over into a new deal, as these practices are open to fraud. If the time period on the option needs to be lengthened the most effective way to bring about this is to sell the original option back to the bank for fair value, and take out a new transaction covering the fresh maturity date at the current prevailing market conditions.

Whether?

An option will be exercised by the holder, only if it is profitable for him/her to do so. Where the spot exchange rate on maturity remains more favourable than the option strike price, the option will be allowed to lapse, and the underlying deal will be transacted in the spot market. This is known as "abandoning the option."

Note that with exotic options the reference rate may be a combination of more than one rate, see Chapter 14.

How much?

When the currency option is originally established, it is for a specific amount of a reference currency, and it is upon this figure that the premium is based. This is a notional maximum amount of currency. If the resulting currency receipt or payment turns out to be for a lesser figure, it may be possible (in some cases) for the excess cover provided by the option to be sold back for fair value to the writing bank. Should an excess amount of currency arrive there is no provision for additional cover under the original option.

Strike

The strike price of the option is chosen by the client or holder at the outset – it is sometimes known as the exercise price. The premium that is due for the option will be a function of how the strike price relates to the current market price and various other inputs into the pricing model (see Premium Determinants, below).

Terminology

The growth in currency option volumes can be traced to the beginnings of the 1970s. The first commonly used option pricing model was written in the early 1970s by Fisher Black and Myron Scholes and was published in the *Journal of Political Economy* in 1973. Their treatise contained many new descriptive words, that are now in every day usage – at least among options users and providers. This jargon can need translating and before we go any further I have detailed some of the terminology on page 176.

Terminology discussed

It is very important to specify whether you are the buyer or seller of the option and whether you are selling or buying the underlying currencies. Potentially there could be a four-way price, which is why we need the additional terms, *Puts* and *Calls*. There are also a number of different ways that people describe options. Some talk about "calling" or "putting" the foreign currency, others about calling or putting the dollar. There is added confusion when you consider cross currencies, for example, if the currencies are DEM/FFR, which one is foreign? It is always safer to specify both sides, not just to call the Deutshe Marks, but to call the Deutshe Marks and put the French francs; then there is no possibility of confusion.

Exercise is how to convert the option which at inception is simply a piece of paper into the "underlying asset." The term is also used to denote the physical movement of the underlying (the respective currencies), unless the option is to be cash settled and bought back by the writing bank or sold for its intrinsic value, (see below).

Terminology	**Currency option terminology**
Call option	The right (not the obligation) to buy foreign currency
Put option	The right (not the obligation) to sell foreign currency
Exercise	Conversion of the option into the underlying physical transaction or cash settlement
Strike price	Exchange rate chosen by the holder. Prices can be described as: At the money (ATM) In the money (ITM) Out of the money (OTM)
Expiry date	Last day on which the option may be exercised Up to 10 am New York time, two business days before the value date
Value date	The day on which the currency is delivered
Premium	The price of the option
American option	An option which can be exercised on any business day up to and including the expiry date
European option	An option which can be exercised on the expiry date only
Intrinsic value	Difference between the strike price and the current market exchange rate
Time value	Difference between the option premium and intrinsic value; including the time left until expiry, volatility, forward differentials, market expectations
Fair value	Combination of intrinsic value and time value, as calculated by an option pricing model
Volatility	Normalized annualized standard deviation of the returns of the daily underlying spot exchange rate for the rate concerned

The **strike price** or exercise price is the exchange rate chosen by the client. This can be at the same rate as the underlying commodity (in this case the forward rate) or it may be better or worse. The terms that we use are at the money (ATM), in the money (ITM), and out of the money (OTM). The pricing model itself will compare the strike with the current underlying rates.

The **expiry date** is the last date on which the option can be utilized for value two business days later. This will be the last day for both European and American style options. There is a cut off time on the expiry date and it is 10.00 hours New York time (15.00 hours London time). This is required to allow the option writers to be exercised by their clients and then they can in turn exercise their option with, perhaps, other interbank players.

The **premium** is the figure calculated by the option pricing model for the particular transaction. It is normally quoted in:

- cents per pound (sterling or other currency)
- pence per dollar (US or other currency)
- percentage of transaction amount.

The pricing model will calculate a break-even price and it will be up to the trader to spread the premium to create the bid–offer price.

An **American** option offers more flexibility to a holder who needs to deliver his dollars or his pounds physically, can be more expensive, and can be exercised on any business day up to and including the expiry date. In contrast, a **European** option can be exercised only on the expiry date for value two business days later. Both types of option can be sold back to the writing bank at any time.

The option premium calculated by the pricing model can be divided into two parts, **intrinsic** value and **time** value. The intrinsic value is measured by the present value of the amount by which it is in the money, e.g. for a European style US dollar Put, sterling Call, used to cover a dollar receivable against sterling in three months' time:

Forward outright rate for three months is $1.47
Option strike rate is $1.44
Intrinsic value is present value (PV) of $1.47 – $1.44 = PV of 3 cents.

Intrinsic value provides the minimum premium level at which the option will trade. Intrinsic value can only ever be zero or a positive number.

The **time value** component of the option expresses the risk premium in the option and is a function of several variables:

- the relationship between the strike rate and the spot rate
- the time to maturity

- the interest rate differential between the two currencies and
- the volatility of the currency pair.

The pricing model will calculate the **fair value** of an option: this is a break-even premium level. It will then be up to the trader to spread the premium to create the bid–offer price for the option.

Volatility is a measure of the degree of "scatter" of the range of possible future outcomes for the underlying commodity. A volatility input is only required for option products. If you wish to speculate on the level of volatility you will need to trade options. Its importance lies in the basic maths of the option pricing model.

Key Features of Currency Options

Insurance protection

A premium is paid by the buyer or holder of the option to the writing (selling) bank, which in turn guarantees a fixed exchange rate required by the option holder.

Profit potential

When *hedging* with an option any chance of currency loss is eliminated. The only outflow of funds relates to the premium payment. If the underlying market movement is in the holder's favor, upside potential is available, as the option will be abandoned, allowing the holder the chance to enter into a spot deal. If the underlying market movement is against the holder, the option will be "exercised" at the previously agreed rate. An option profile describes "asymmetry of risk." The most that a holder can lose is the option premium, the most he can profit is limited only by how far the market moves.

When *trading* with options, the initial up-front premium can be regarded as a stop-loss. If the market does not move in the expected direction, the option will expire worthless and the only downside will be the premium paid. Should the market move in a profitable direction, the option can be exercised or sold back to the writing bank for fair value, which will hopefully recoup more than the original premium payment.

Sell back

The option can be sold back in whole or in part, for fair value to the writing bank. The writing bank will not require an explanation for the sell back – it may be that the client has merely changed his mind. This is not a negotiable piece of paper; it can only be sold back to the writing (selling) bank, it cannot be on-sold to a third party and is not transferable.

Premium

A premium is due which is based on a series of variables that are input into an option pricing model, many of which are derived from the original Black and Scholes model. The premium figure will comprise intrinsic value and time value.

Premium Determinants

There are a number of important factors that affect the premium due on an option. Each of the following inputs is entered into the pricing model, which then calculates the option premium:

- strike price
- underlying price
- maturity
- expected currency volatility
- interest rate differentials
- American or European
- Calls or Put.

Strike price vs underlying price

The underlying benchmark against which the strike price on the currency option is measured is the appropriate forward foreign exchange rate, known in the market as the "outright forward." Strike prices are referred to as follows:

At the money (ATM)	where the strike price is equal to the current outright forward rate	**Terminology**
In the money (ITM)	where the strike price is more favorable than the outright forward rate, and the option premium is higher than that for an ATM option	
Out of the money (OTM)	where the strike rate is worse than the outright forward rate and the option premium is lower than that for an ATM option	

Table 12.2

In, at, and out of the money

Assume the current forward rate of dollars against sterling is £1 = $1.50.

Client purchases option to sell dollars against sterling		Client purchases option to buy dollars against sterling
$1.40 --------------	IN THE MONEY ------------------	$1.60
$1.50 --------------	AT THE MONEY ----------------	$1.50
$1.60 ------------	OUT OF THE MONEY ---------------	$1.40

Maturity

The longer the time to expiry or maturity, the higher the probability of large rate movements, and the higher the chance of profitable exercise by the buyer. The buyer should be prepared to pay a higher premium for a longer dated option than a short dated option. The relationship between the premium due on an option and the maturity of the transaction is not a linear relationship. As shown in Figure 12.1, the premium due for a six-month option is not double that of a three-month option, and is never likely to be.

Expected currency volatility

It is the volatility input into the pricing model that differentiates one banks' price from another. All other premium determinants are matters of fact that are available to market participants simultaneously either from current trading conditions or direct from the client. If a client purchases an option with high volatility, he has purchased an asset with a good chance of very profitable exercise.

Interest rate differentials

Forward foreign exchange rates are calculated using the interest rate differentials of the two currencies concerned. Currencies are at a premium or discount to each other, reflecting whether the forward points are added to or subtracted from the spot rate. This differential will affect the premium due on an option.

Interest rates affect option pricing in two ways:

(1) by affecting the forward price of the asset and hence the intrinsic value;
(2) by affecting the present value (PV) calculations within the option pricing model, and ultimately the (PV) of the option premium.

The non-linear relationship between maturity and premium

Fig 12.1

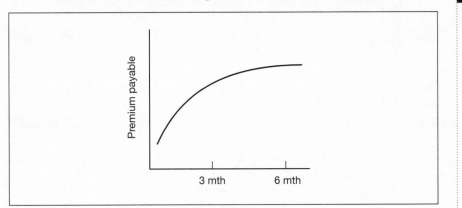

American or European?

Generally, an American style option gives the holder greater flexibility. If the client wishes to buy or call a currency with a higher interest rate (discount currency), the American style option will be more expensive. If the client wants to call a premium currency the price of the American and the European option will be the same.

Call or put?

The client needs to specify whether he or she wishes to buy or sell the foreign currency.

The Importance of Volatility

A volatility input is required for option pricing, due to certain key underlying assumptions in the pricing models. The "grandfather" option pricing model was written by Black and Scholes in 1972. This assumes that the underlying financial asset, in this case the forward foreign exchange rates, behaves in a similar fashion to a log-normal distribution. Normal distributions are typically found in nature, for example the height of trees, the weight of children, the length of snakes, etc. The volatility input into the option pricing model generates a prediction of how a particular exchange rate will move in the future. It will not necessarily predict what the exchange rate will be as a rate on a specific date in the future, but just how the exchange rate will behave; will there be a large degree of *scatter* around a theoretical average, with exchange rates all over the place, or will there be very little movement as the currency stays within a narrow range? The best way to explain this is by using an example from nature.

You have been given the job of statistically sampling a penguin population in Antarctica.

Height data is being collected from a sample representation of king penguins in Antarctica. One hundred penguins will be measured and then the data analyzed. Once we have the data we can calculate the average height of the penguins – this is known as the mean.

Many years ago a German scientist called Gauss undertook some research. He showed that if you sampled data from any population with a normal distribution, once you had calculated the mean you could calculate certain "**confidence limits**." He calculated that if you took the mean (which you have already calculated) plus or minus something called a **standard deviation** you could ensure that 66 percent of all the data readings would fall between these limits. He then further predicted that if you took the mean plus or minus two standard deviations you could then guarantee that 95 percent of all the data would fall within these wider limits.

Let's assume the penguins have been measured, the mean has been calculated at 1 metre, and the standard deviation computed from the data, giving a figure of 10 percent. This would give us a normal distribution as shown in Figure 12.2.

Once the data has been collected it is not too difficult to carry out the calculations – anyone who has studied statistics will recognize the shape of the normal distribution. But how does all this fit in with options and option pricing? Well, standard deviation and volatility are the same thing.

The statistical definition of volatility is "the normalized annualized standard deviation of the returns of the underlying commodity." The biggest problem in using volatility is trying to establish what volatility will be in the future, before there is any data to back it up.

Consider a trader trying to price a currency option in three-month USD/DEM. He has to guess the shape of the normal curve: will it be steep with low volatility, and most readings about the mean, or will it be very flat, with high volatility and many readings widely scattered? In fact the trader is trying to guess how volatile the exchange rate will be in advance. Not an easy thing to do (see Figure 12.3).

There are two different types of volatility: historic and implied.

Historic volatility

Data can be collected historically; it is possible to analyze the spread of movements of the underlying commodity by recording, for example, the

Projected analysis of the height of king penguins

Fig 12.2

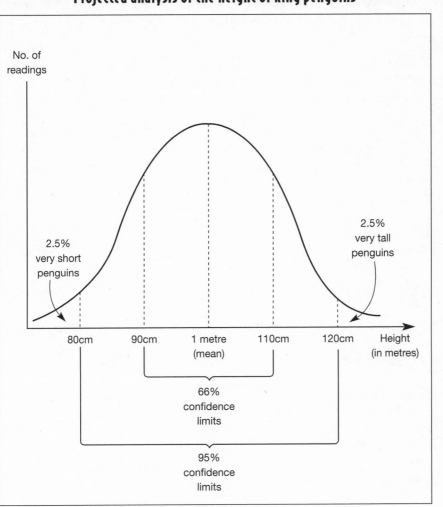

No. of
readings

2.5%
very short
penguins

2.5%
very tall
penguins

80cm   90cm   1 metre   110cm   120cm   Height
                   (mean)   (in metres)

66%
confidence
limits

95%
confidence
limits

daily closing prices of USD/DEM. If these prices were plotted on a graph a type of scatter pattern would emerge. Volatility is in effect the definition of this scatter. Whilst this type of analysis allows historical data to be examined, it can only ever indicate future prices, it will not be able to predict them but, rather, give an idea of where they might be, taking into account how the commodity has moved in the past. This is assuming you believe that history repeats itself.

Implied volatility

What the trader will actually input into his option pricing model is implied volatility. This is the current volatility level implicit in today's option prices. It can be derived from prices in both exchange-traded and

Fig 12.3   **The effect of different volatility levels on the shape of the normal curve**

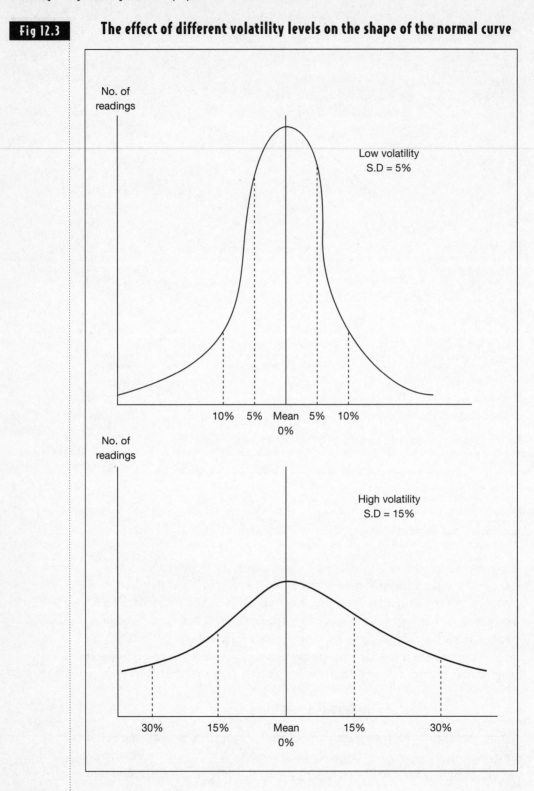

OTC options – you may wonder how. Firstly, find a premium that is already quoted and trading in the market, with a similar expiry date and the same currency pair, and then get the model to work backwards to deduce the volatility. This is illustrated in Figure 12.4.

Volatility itself has a spread. It is quoted as an annual percentage. For example, it may be quoted as 10.3–10.1 percent. If the client wants to buy the option, use 10.3 percent; if he is trying to sell it to you, use 10.1 percent.

There are a number of different option pricing models and they are mostly PC based. A number of inputs are requested by the model, which then calculates the premium. Whichever single input you do not give the model it will take the data from the other inputs and work backwards.

In conclusion, we saw earlier in the section that the premium/maturity profile was non-linear, but the profile of premium/volatility is linear, as shown in Figure 12.5, i.e. the higher the perceived volatility, the higher the premium. Higher volatility implies a greater possible dispersion of prices at expiry, and logically the option holder has an asset with a greater chance of more profitable exercise.

Comparisons Between OTC Currency Options and Forward Foreign Exchange

Both traders and hedgers can use currency options and forward foreign exchange. The easiest way to compare the two products is to consider the similarities and differences from the user's or holder's point of view.

Table 12.3 summarizes the main differences between OTC currency options and traditional forward foreign exchange. A forward contract is fine as a hedging product if complete information is available; the amount is known, the currencies, and when – to the day – the currency will be paid/received ("the end of the month" is not acceptable, it is too vague). In everyday business the luxury of complete information is not always available, dates and amounts have to be estimated, and some clients simply pay late. In those circumstances an option is the perfect alternative. It is not a zero cost alternative like a forward transaction but it is immensely flexible, and some options can be designed to have very low or even zero premiums.

Fig 12.4

Variable inputs for option premium calculation

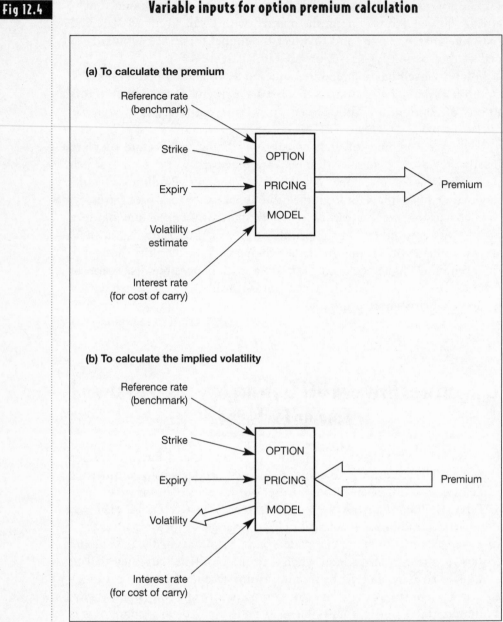

(a) To calculate the premium

Reference rate (benchmark)

Strike

Expiry

Volatility estimate

Interest rate (for cost of carry)

OPTION PRICING MODEL

Premium

(b) To calculate the implied volatility

Reference rate (benchmark)

Strike

Expiry

Volatility

Interest rate (for cost of carry)

OPTION PRICING MODEL

Premium

Using a Currency Option to Hedge a Currency Receivable

Example

October 2

A major British company has won an export order in the Far East. Delivery and payment will be in six months' time and will be in dollars.

The linear relationship between premium and volatility

Fig 12.5

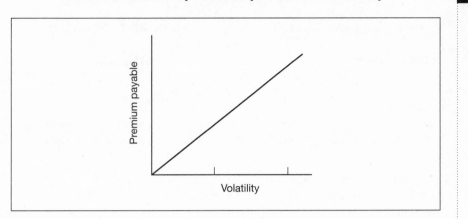

The treasurer is unsure on which day the money will be available in his account, and is worried that the value of the dollar may fall (depreciate) before he receives his invoice amount of US$2,250,000. If he does nothing and the value of the dollar falls, he will not realize sufficient sterling from the resulting foreign exchange conversion to cover his costs and the profit margin. But if the value of the dollar increases he will be very happy. He is not sure in which direction the dollar will move, but under his company policy he is not allowed to do nothing, because of the possible risk of losing money. If he transacts a forward contract with one of his bankers, he must give up any windfall profits should the currency move in his favor, but if he transacts an option he has insurance if things go wrong and profit opportunities if things go right.

Action – October 2

The treasurer will ask for an indication level on a dollar Put, sterling Call option, American style, strike = at the money, and an expiry date in three months (January 2) for value two business days later.

The current financial information available is:
GBP/USD
Spot rate: 1.5100
Six-month outright forward rate: 1.5050

The option strike will be at the money forward (ATMF), at $1.5050. The premium due for this option is, say, 1.9 percent of the dollar amount. The total premium is 1.9 percent of US$2,250,000, which is US$42,750, and must be paid to the option writer two business days after the deal is struck. The option can now be filed or put in a drawer for six months until expiry, or until the dollars arrive, whichever is earlier.

Table 12.3

Comparison between OTC currency options and forward foreign exchange

CURRENCY OPTIONS	FORWARD CONTRACTS
Right to buy or sell	Obligation to buy or sell
No obligation to deliver or receive currency	Must deliver currency on/before maturity date
No loss possible except the premium, which can be considerable	Unlimited opportunity loss possible, as the forward ties the client into a fixed rate
Eliminates downside risk whilst retaining unlimited profit potential	Eliminates all downside risk but allows no upside potential at all
Perfect hedge for variable exposures, but can be expensive	Rigid hedge for variable exposures

Action – April 2

The dollars arrive by the due date. The treasurer calls his bank to check the current level of the spot rate. If the dollar has strengthened (appreciated) to, say, US$1.4550=£1, then the option will be worthless and will be abandoned and the transaction will be effected in the spot market. If the dollar has depreciated to, say, US$1.5550=£1, the treasurer will exercise the option at the agreed rate of US$1.5050. The company will need to call the bank to confirm that it wishes to exercise its option, as exercise is not automatic. It is the holder's responsibility to exercise the option. The bank has no obligation to remind the client to exercise. If the company exercises the option, the treasurer must deliver US$2,250,000 and will receive sterling at US$1.5050, giving a sterling out-turn of £1,495,016.61. Technically the option premium should be deducted to work out the break-even rate (to be absolutely correct the NPV of the premium). This would give a net sterling out-turn of £1,495,016.61 less the amount of the option premium in sterling (for premium conversion purposes the spot rate is always used, US$42,750 divided by 1.5100 = £28,311.26): a total figure of £1,466,705.35.

Under the terms of this currency option it does not matter when the dollars arrive as the treasurer has purchased an American style option, allowing delivery of the currency on any business day in the period (for value two business days later). If originally the company had purchased a European style option, there would be a restriction and the dollars would need to be placed on deposit until the expiry date, when they could be delivered under the option.

Best and worst case outcomes for the example

Fig 12.6

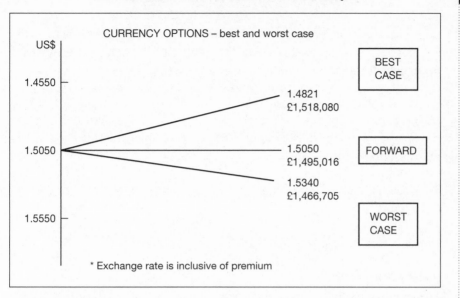

As Figure 12.6 shows, there is always a best and worst case – indeed the nature of FX means that no one knows how far or how fast a currency will move. A 5 cent move in the six-month period has been used for the purposes of illustration.

If the client had chosen a traditional forward contract and been lucky with the receipt of the dollars on the correct date, he would have achieved at best (worst) a rate of US$1.5100 – an out-turn of £1,495,016.61.

In hindsight, the option will always be the second best alternative. If the client knew with 100 percent certainty that the dollar was going to depreciate, he would sell forward, a hedging alternative that would cost nothing and allow no profit. But if he was not expecting to profit he has given up nothing. If the client had known with 100 percent certainty that the dollar would appreciate, he would do nothing and simply sell the dollars at the better rate when they arrived in three month's time. The option allows you to get the best possible outcome, the "insured" rate when required, or the profit when the market moves favorably, but a premium is required. In effect, the option allows you to be wrong without it costing the holder too much money. The interesting point is a client would be more than happy to abandon an option – it implies the underlying transaction is showing a profit.

Using Currency Options to Speculate

Example A private client believes that the Japanese yen will appreciate against the dollar over the next two weeks. He is prepared to put on a position equivalent to US$10 million. He has no desire physically to hold either currency and no requirement for flexibility on the date, so he will purchase a two-week European style option that he can sell back, but will not need to exercise. By selling the option back to the option writer the currency gain, if there is one, will be factored into the sell-back price. This negates the need for physical foreign exchange transactions.

Current financial information:
USD/JPY
Spot rate: 105.00
Outright forward rate: 104.00

Strategy

The client will purchase a European style yen Call, US dollar Put in US$10 million for expiry in two weeks. The option premium is calculated at 0.6 percent, which is US$60,000 or yen 6.3 million, payable within two business days of the transaction date. This option will run for two weeks. The client must decide when he believes he has the maximum profit on the deal. Let us assume that, ten days after inception, the option trade is showing a healthy profit. The strike on the ATMF option was originally set at USD/JPY 104.00, the spot rate is now 100.50 and the client does not think there will be much more movement, so he wants to close out his position and take his profit. As this is a European option, he must contact the writing bank and ask them to "buy-back" the option. They will calculate the buy-back premium (fair value) through the option pricing model. The buy-back premium will incorporate the foreign exchange gain (intrinsic value) and will also incorporate any residual time value.

Early exercise

If the private client had purchased a more expensive American style option, he could still have sold it back at any time. But why pay for exercise flexibility if you never want to exercise? In this case the client had no requirement for either of the currencies, so the ability to exercise the option into its underlying currencies is superfluous. This client simply wants to profit from his view on exchange rates.

The other problem with exercising an option early is that all the client or trader would receive is the intrinsic value; that is, the amount by which the option is in the money, the amount by which the option is better than the underlying market rate. If there was any time value left it would be lost. Instead of early exercise it is always better to sell back an option. This ensures that the time value component is always included in the sell back premium.

Another consideration for using European options and selling them back, is that if the client chose to exercise the option it would be necessary for him to take delivery of the physical yen and pay for them with physical dollars, simultaneously needing to sell the yen back into the market to crystallize the profit. In that case the transaction costs on the foreign exchange deals may be significant on their own.

For further insights into how to trade currency options see Chapter 15.

Basic Workings of Currency Options

Whether the market participants use American or European options, whether they buy them or sell them, will depend upon a number of factors acting either in isolation or simultaneously, but the following rules apply:

(1) The option is exercised only when it is advantageous for the holder.

(2) If the ruling spot rate is more favorable, the option will be abandoned.

(3) The downside risk is protected, with a one-for-one gain if the market moves favorably.

(4) The writer of the option is obliged to deliver the "underlying" if the option is exercised.

■ ■ ■

'The fair value of an option at expiry is the sum of every possible value it could achieve, multiplied by the probability of that value occurring.'

Mechanics of Currency Options

Introduction

Most option pricing models have evolved from the model written by Professors Fisher Black and Myron Scholes in the early 1970s. There has been a fair amount of tinkering with the basic Black and Scholes formula to make it work with interest rates and currency, but the essential element within the model confirms that exchange rates move in the same way as nature, and that a normal distribution is a fair way of considering the data. Option pricing is actually based on a log-normal distribution, which is very different from a straight normal distribution to a statistician, but for our purposes it is close enough to be viewed similarly. It would be dangerous to assume that exchange rates moved in a normal fashion, but while the prices are not normally distributed, the returns mostly are. An investor holding dollars is just as likely to see the value of the dollar increase as decrease.

The Black and Scholes Option Pricing Model

In 1973 Fisher Black and Myron Scholes published their paper on option pricing. The mathematics needed to derive the complete formula are awesome, and I do not intend to develop them in this book.

But, generally speaking, Black and Scholes proved that the fair price for any financial asset is its expected value. If the gold price had a 35 percent chance of achieving USD419, and a 65 percent chance of achieving USD450, the fair value of gold at that time would be:

$$(0.35 \times \$419) + (0.65 \times \$450) = \$439.15 \text{ per ounce}$$

The same principle applies to options: the fair value of an option at expiry is the sum of every possible value it could achieve, multiplied by the probability of that value occurring. In the example above there were only two discrete outcomes, but options can take on almost any value, so continuous rather than discrete probability distributions are required.

The discussion of the B–S formula that I find most helpful is that developed by Lawrence Galitz in his book *Financial Engineering*, (Pitman Publishing, 1994). For those readers who wish to follow the math a little more closely this is reproduced in Appendix Three.

It is important to bear in mind that pricing models are exactly that, *models* of reality, rather than reality itself. The Black and Scholes model makes other assumptions apart from normally distributed returns. These are shown below:

Basic assumptions of the Black and Scholes model

Table 13.1

- The option is European style, and cannot be exercised before expiry.
- There are no taxes, transaction costs, or margin requirements.
- Lending and borrowing are possible at the same riskless rate, which accrues continuously in time.
- The underlying asset can be bought or sold freely, even in fractional units.
- The underlying asset can be sold short, and the proceeds are available to the short seller.
- The underlying asset pays no dividends or other distributions before maturity.
- The underlying price is continuous in time, with no jumps or discontinuities.
- The variability of underlying asset prices and interest rates remains constant.

Source: L Galitz. Financial Engineering, Pitman Publishing

Whilst many of the assumptions are not strictly true, the basic model can be adjusted. For example, in a currency option the foreign currency does pay a *distribution* as when the currency is placed on deposit it will accrue interest; when this is factored into the formula you have the Garman–Kohlhagen model for currency options.

The reason the B–S model (and its derivatives) has been so successful is due to its reliability, robustness, and consistent pricing. There are other option pricing models, some of them complex or more up to date, and every practitioner will have his or her own favorites.

Expiry or Profit and Loss Profiles

Options can be Puts and Calls, both of which can be bought or sold. These four basic structures are long Call, short Call, long Put, short Put. In fact, the right to buy or sell the underlying and the right to buy or sell the option itself. Each type of option has a particular "signature." The easiest way to understand how options work is to construct the profit and loss (P/L) profile of the transaction at expiry. Some people know these as expiry profiles.

Consider the currency pair USD/DEM: if a trader bought cash DEM today in the expectation of the DEM strengthening, the P/L profile would be as shown in Figure 13.1.

Fig 13.1

Expiry profile of an unhedged position

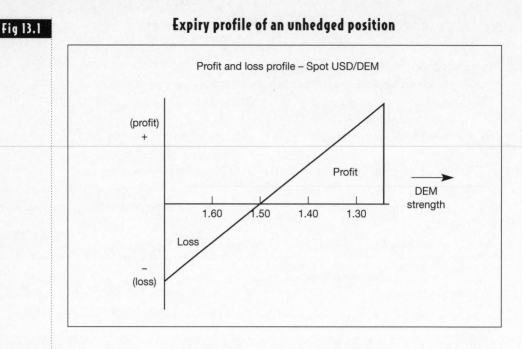

The trader buys the DEM at 1.50 and then, as the Deutsche Mark appreciates, and the dollar weakens (towards 1.40), the position will start moving into profit. In contrast, if the DEM depreciates and the dollar strengthens (towards 1.60), the same position would move into loss. This is equivalent to an unhedged position, with an equal probability of profit or loss.

Instead of running a spot risk with an equal chance of gain or loss the trader could purchase an option with the same strike of 1.5000. This would allow a similar 1:1 profit opportunity, but where the potential downside is now limited to the premium paid. The upside is limited only by the extent of the positive market movement. The trader will buy a DEM Call, USD Put option, he would be "long" the call. The P/L profile is shown in Figure 13.2.

The profile of the DEM Call option mirrors that of the unhedged position, except that it starts from a negative position reflecting the premium paid. One must take into account the premium on the option and any associated interest rate costs. An option purchaser may need to fund (borrow) the option premium, or if the trader does not need to fund the position he may be forgoing extra interest on a potential deposit. Other associated opportunity costs should be also recognized.

The bank writing the DEM Call option against USD, as shown in Figure 13.2, would have a mirror image of the position. It will receive the premium, yet its potential for losses is high, unless the position is hedged. This is shown in Figure 13.3.

Expiry profile of a long Call option

Fig 13.2

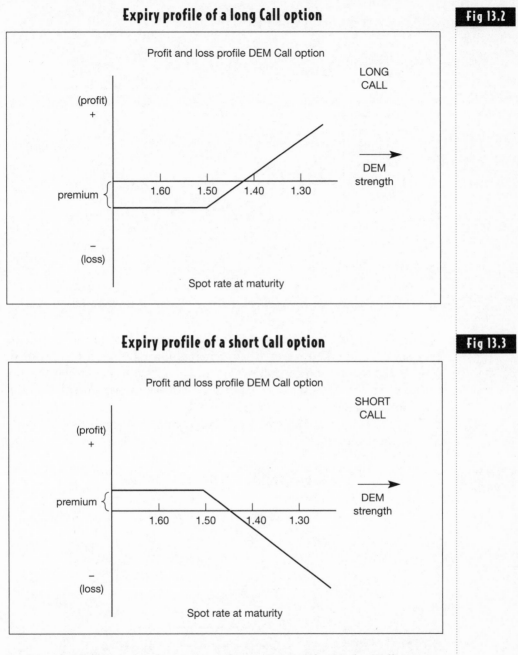

Expiry profile of a short Call option

Fig 13.3

In this case the bank that has written the option is "short" the Call option.

Assume that the trader has now changed his mind about the direction of the Deutsche Mark. He feels the DEM is about to weaken, so with his new trade he needs to buy a DEM Put, USD Call option, (see Figure 13.4). The trader is hoping to profit from a fall in the value of the DEM so wishes to profit towards the right-hand side of Figure 13.4 – this is why the diagram appears the other way around.

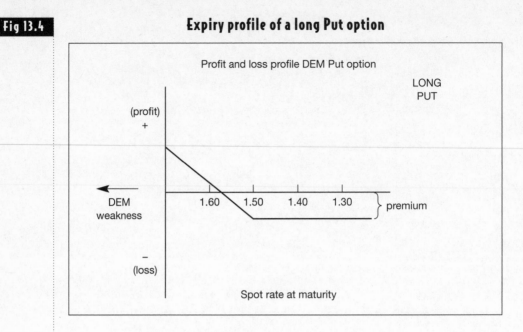

Fig 13.4

Expiry profile of a long Put option

This P/L profile shows that the holder of this option can lose only his premium, should the exchange rate remain above 1.50, but can profit as long as the market moves in his favor (towards 1.60). In comparison the writer of this option, who is "short" the DEM Put option, could lose a considerable amount, as shown in Figure 13.5.

The four key strategies – the long Call, long Put, short Call, short Put – are shown together in Figure 13.6.

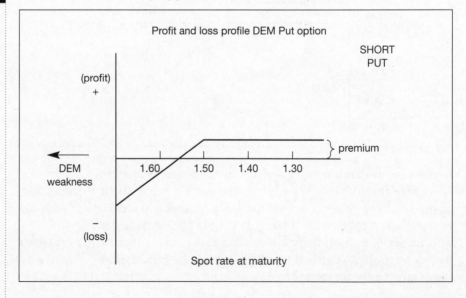

Fig 13.5

Expiry profile of a short Put option

The four basic option strategies

Fig 13.6

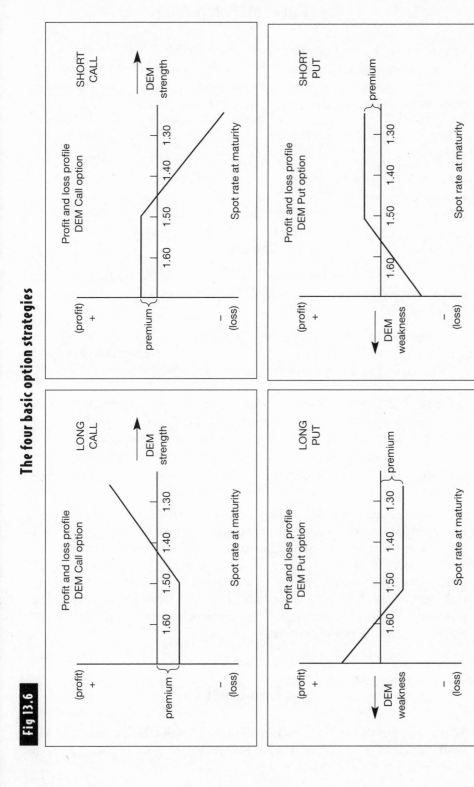

Put–Call Parity

You may have noticed in our discussion on the Black and Scholes model for option pricing that we have concentrated on calculating the value of a Call option. Well, what about Put options – surely, they are equally important? Luckily the price of a Call option and the price of a Put option are linked through a relationship known as the Put–Call parity theorem.

Imagine you had to transact the following deals simultaneously:

- sell a Call option, with strike ATM and expiry three months
- buy a Put option, with strike ATM and expiry three months
- buy the underlying asset
- borrow money to fund the purchase of the asset for three months.

Outcome

In three months' time the borrowing will need to be repaid. The Call option will either be in the money (ITM), at the money (ATM), or out of the money (OTM) at expiry:

(1) If the Call option is in the money at expiry it will be exercised against the seller, who must deliver the asset at the agreed strike price, and this will repay the borrowing. The Put will expire worthless. Net cash flow zero.

(2) If the Call option is out of the money at expiry, the Put can be exercised, giving the buyer the right to sell the underlying at the agreed strike price, and this can then repay the borrowing. Net cash flow zero.

(3) If the Call option is exactly at the money at expiry, both options are worthless, and the underlying asset can be sold at the market price, and can repay the original borrowing.

This set of transactions will *always* produce a zero cash flow, and allows for pricing a Put option from the price of a Call option. For those readers who prefer to think in diagrammatic form, Figure 13.7 describes the profit and loss profile of an unhedged forward contract. It superimposes the profiles of a European style long Put option and European style short Call option upon the forward purchase of the DEM. Creating forward positions through the simultaneous purchase and sale of options gives rise to *synthetic* forward positions.

Option Greeks

When a traditional option reaches maturity its value is determined solely by the price of the underlying asset and the strike price of the option, in

Put–Call parity

Fig 13.7

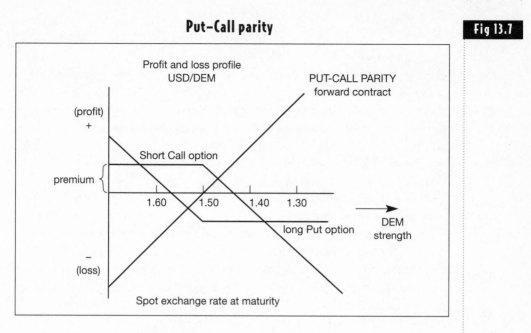

effect its intrinsic value. But prior to maturity the value of the option will depend upon a number of factors:

- strike price
- underlying price
- maturity
- expected currency volatility
- interest rates.

The option pricing model needs the above inputs in order to calculate the option premium. Only the strike price will remain fixed; all the other variables will change with the market or with the passage of time. Each variable changes the option premium in a distinct way. The manner of the change in movement is described by the "option Greeks." They define how the single variable changes while the others remain the same. The most important option Greeks are:

- delta
- gamma
- theta
- vega
- phi/rho.

Those of you with a classical education may recognize that vega is not a Greek letter. It probably came from *Star Trek*!

Delta

The definition of delta is "The change in the option premium for a unit change in the underlying exchange rate." This is an important measure as it shows how the price of the option will change as the underlying market moves. The value of delta can range from zero to one. An option which is deeply out of the money (OTM), with no chance of profitable exercise, will have a delta of 0.00. An option which is deeply in the money (ITM) will behave like the underlying cash market because there is a 100 percent certainty that the option will be exercised – in this case the delta will be 1.00. An option which is at the money (ATM) will have a delta of 0.5. The deltas of ITM options increase as expiry nears and exercise becomes more certain. Deltas of OTM options decrease as expiry nears and the option looks like being abandoned. There are two interpretations of delta: firstly, that delta describes the slope of the premium/underlying asset curve: and, secondly, that delta is the *hedge ratio*. Using delta as a hedge ratio means that the delta on a particular option can meaningfully help hedge the position.

Consider a trader who has bought an ATM DEM Call, USD Put option in DEM10 million, with one month to expiry. As the underlying spot rate moves so the option will become worth more or less, it will not stay ATM. If the option goes into the money the trader will exercise the option, and the writing bank must have the DEM10 million ready for him. If the option at expiry is OTM the trader will not exercise the option and the writing bank needs to hold zero DEM.

On the day of purchase when the option is ATM the chance of profitable exercise is deemed to be 50 percent, i.e. there is an equal chance that the currency could strengthen or weaken and the delta is 0.5. The option writer therefore needs to hold 50 percent of the underlying DEM ready for the buyer, should he require it at expiry. The option writer will buy in 50 percent of DEM 10 million. A week later the spot market has moved in the option's favor and the delta on the position is now 60 percent or 0.6; the option writer needs to buy in another 10 percent of cover. The next day the market moves back to 55 percent or 0.55, the option writer needs to sell 5 percent if the cover, and so on. Every time the position is re-hedged the trader will pay away the bid–offer spread, and will incur a loss.

This procedure is known as delta hedging: it is time consuming and costly. If the position is delta neutral, or delta hedged, the spot component has been locked in, at that point. Option portfolios that are not exposed to small movements in the underlying exchange rate are said to be delta hedged or delta neutral (see Figure 13.8).

Fig 13.8

Delta of a Call option at various points

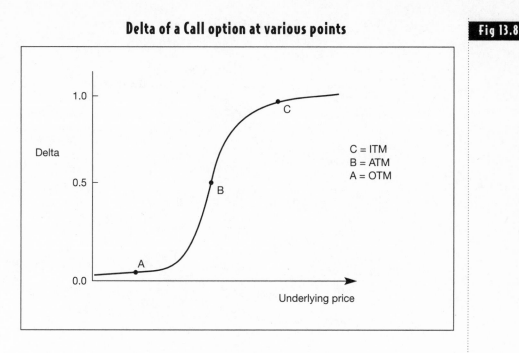

Gamma

This is the only option Greek that does not measure the sensitivity of the option premium. Instead gamma measures how the option's delta changes when the underlying asset moves. The definition of gamma is "The rate of change of delta for a unit change in the underlying exchange rate." The more frequently an option portfolio needs to be re-hedged the higher will be the gamma, for a given movement in the underlying asset. It reflects how much and how fast the hedge ratio changes. Options with a small gamma are relatively easy to hedge, because the hedge ratio will not change much as the spot rate moves. Options with a high gamma such as short dated ATM options can be treacherous to manage and very costly.

Imagine the last day of an option's maturity; it is still ATM, a very small move in the underlying spot rate, say + 0.0005, may swing the option ITM. In that case the option writer needs to have 100 percent of the underlying ready for the option holder not if, but *when*, he exercises. Twenty minutes later the spot rate has moved back − 0.0007, the option is now OTM. The option writer now needs to hold 0 percent cover. Every time the market moves, even in very small amounts, the delta may swing from zero to one; with nothing in between, this is the classic high gamma position (see Figure 13.9).

Fig 13.9

Gamma of a Call option

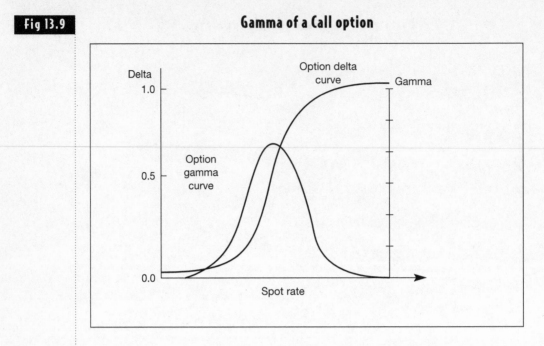

Theta

The definition of theta is "The change in the option premium for a given change in the period to expiry (usually the passage of a day)."

The time value component of the option expresses the risk premium in the option and is a function of several variables:

- the relationship between the strike rate and the spot rate
- the time to maturity
- the interest rate differential between the two currencies and
- the volatility of the currency pair.

To the option writer this risk premium is highest when the option is at the money, because at this point there is the greatest uncertainty over whether the option will expire worthless or have some value at maturity.

If the option moves into the money, the writer can be more sure the option will be exercised, if it moves out of the money the opposite applies. The more deeply in or out of the money the option moves the greater the confidence of the option writer in the final outcome: will it or won't it be exercised?

In simple terms the longer the time to expiry the more an option is worth. As time passes, the option writer can define the risk more accurately, and in the last few days before expiry the time value diminishes rapidly. The time value of an option decays as expiry approaches.

Long dated options have more time value than short dated options; as an option ages, so its time value will decay. Theta describes exactly how much time value is lost from day to day, and is a precise measure of time decay. At inception an option will have 100 percent of its time value. Consider a 90-day ATM option. How much time value has been lost after one day? Answer: one nineteenth. The next day the option loses one eightyninth, and so on. So in the early part of an option's maturity it retains most of its time value. Time decay is almost constant for the first two thirds of the option's life, and 70 percent through the life of an option it still retains around half of its original value. The decay increases in the last third, and in the last week it loses progressively one seventh, then one sixth, then one fifth, etc of the time value that is left. Theta is highest in ATM options close to expiry. Time decay is highest with ATM options and is shown in Figure 13.10.

Vega

The definition of vega is "The change in the option premium for a 1 percent change in volatility." This is a straight-line relationship. As volatility increases so does uncertainty and so does the premium. An option with a high volatility gives the holder a greater chance of more profitable exercise than an option with low volatility (see Figure 13.11).

Graph of time value decay

Fig 13.10

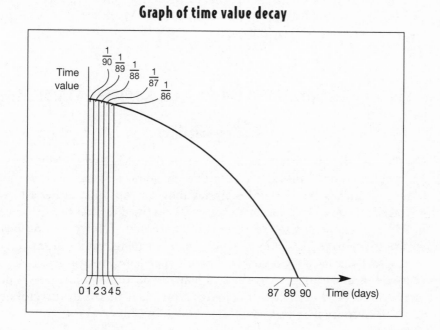

Fig 13.11

Volatility of an ATM Call option

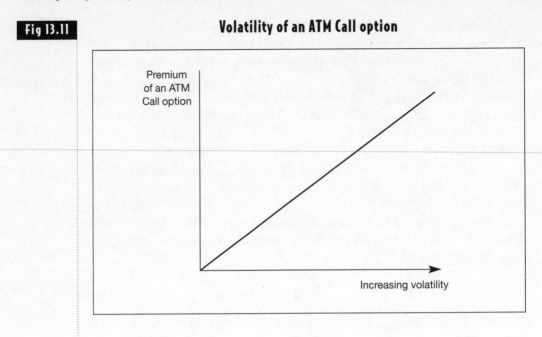

Premium of an ATM Call option

Increasing volatility

Phi /rho

This is one of the lesser used sensitivity ratios, but for completeness I will define it here. Phi is the change in premium for a unit change in interest rates. In the case of a USD/DEM option, phi is the change in premium for a unit change in the US dollar interest rate (the base currency). Rho is the change in the Deutsche Mark interest rate (the "foreign" or "quoted" currency).

Combining Options to Create More Complex Strategies

Trading volatility

Options are the only product, derivative or otherwise, where volatility is an input. We have discussed volatility at some length, and we have looked at how a hedger and a trader may use options, either to risk manage a currency position or to speculate on the direction of a currency. It is also possible to trade or speculate on volatility. This does not mean we are trying to forecast the direction on an exchange rate; rather, we are trying to forecast a "slowdown" or a "speed up," or an increase or decrease in uncertainty. Mostly it is banks who trade volatility, corporates would need very clear mandates from their board of directors to allow them to trade in this way.

Volatility strategies

The long straddle

A trader takes the view that volatility will increase; it often does at the beginning of a new financial year when everyone is back in the market "bright eyed and bushy tailed." The direction of the market is unknown, but he feels definitely that it will move. If he thought the currency would strengthen he would buy a Call option, if he thought the currency were going to weaken he would buy a Put option. In fact he will buy both the Call option and the Put option. This will entail paying two premiums. But if the market moves far enough, one of the options will be heavily in the money (ITM), and when it is sold back it will more than cover the cost of the two original option premiums, and allow for some profit (see Figure 13.12).

If the market strengthens the Call option goes ITM. If the market weakens the Put option goes ITM. Whichever option goes in the money you sell it back, hoping that the profit on the one option will cover the cost of the two premiums. As long as the market moves you make profits with this strategy. You will make most money if there is a big swing in one direction quickly – then when you sell the option back you can recover some time value. You will lose most money – both your premiums – if the market does not move at all.

The short straddle

It is early December. In the run up to Christmas and New Year many banks' trading operations tend to calm down, staff go on holiday, and it is rare for big trading positions to be put on at this time. If a speculative

The long straddle

Fig 13.12

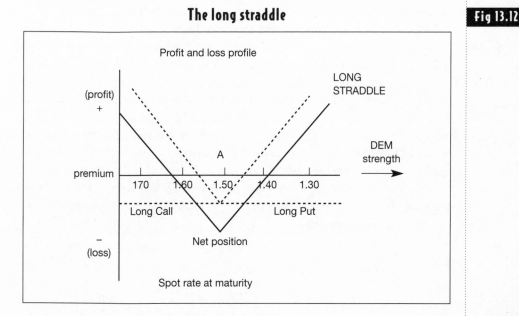

Profit and loss profile

Fig 13.13

The short straddle

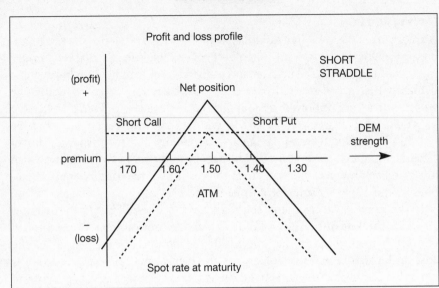

position goes wrong, it may be hard to trade out of as liquidity will be lower. A bad position may affect the dealer's bonus, which he has hopefully earned, and which is paid annually, based on profits up to December 31; the last thing he wants to do is something risky that may lose him money. Bearing this in mind you would expect volatility to decrease; less players in the market, smaller positions. But should you sell the Call or a Put? Your view on volatility will not give you a guide as to the direction of the currency. The answer is that you sell both the Call and the Put, ATM, receiving two option premiums (see Figure 13.13).

This is a high risk strategy. In this example you have taken in two expensive premiums, but if the view on the market is wrong and volatility increases not decreases, there is a possibility of serious loss. In effect you will have sold options at, say, a volatility of 9 percent and may have to buy them back to close out the positions at 12 percent, making a loss. You will make most profit if the volatility decreases or remains the same, and you will lose if the market exchange rate moves by even a small amount in either direction. The amount of the loss will be realized only at expiry or sell back – potentially it could be very big indeed; it will be limited only by how far the market moves (in either direction). For further background on trading currency options see Chapter 15 on *practicalities of trading foreign currency options*.

Availability

The OTC currency option is very liquid and most commercial banks will have an option service that they offer to clients. The large international banks will offer a service in many currencies, whilst some smaller banks will concentrate on niche markets. The minimum transaction size for a currency option will vary from bank to bank, but is likely to be in the region of USD250,000 or equivalent. To be assured of a competitive price the size of the transaction will ideally be in excess of USD250,000.

■ ■ ■

'Exotic options continue to be developed and, together with the more traditional varieties, can be found singly or in groups and often embedded in capital market type structures.'

Exotic Options

Introduction

Options are very versatile instruments and over the last few years a whole new range of option products has grown up – these are known as exotic options (not to be confused with exotic currencies). Some of these new option types definitely fall in the category, "Have I got a solution for you!" – their relevance to everyday business is somewhat limited. Others have fanciful if not gimmicky structures but the seasoned option trader and option user may well find applications for them.

Definition

> An **exotic option** breaks at least one of the standard contract terms of a traditional option, notably concerning the expiry, price, strike, or underlying asset(s).

Definition discussed

An option will be valuable to the holder if it is in-the-money. How this is determined is by reference to an "underlying" rate. An exotic option payoff may be linked to the average underlying exchange rate over a pre-specified period rather than the rate on a specific date. In contrast, the payoff may be contingent upon the price performance of a second asset, not the one on which the option is struck. In some cases the strike may be set after the option has been set up. There are a number of ways that a traditional option structure can be manipulated to behave in a different way. Essentially, exotic options fall into one of these categories:

- contract variation
- path-dependent options
- limit-dependent options
- multi-factor options.

I shall discuss each of these options briefly, but as new uses for these options are being discovered all the time, I will leave it to the reader to consider appropriate applications. A more exhaustive list of currently available exotic options can be found in Appendix Four, courtesy Chappel Ltd.

Contract Variation

Bermudan options

Also known as semi-American style options, these options are halfway between a traditional American and European option. Exercise is allowed on specific dates rather than on any business day or only on the expiry date.

Digital or binary options

Normally the option payoff of an in the money option is dependent upon how much it is in the money at expiry. With a digital or binary option the amount it is in the money is irrelevant – the payoff is either the predetermined amount or nothing. These can come in two variations; the *all-or-nothing* and the *one-touch*.

- All-or-nothing pays out if it is in the money at expiry.
- One-touch will pay out if it was in the money at any stage, at any time during the maturity. The one-touch is also path dependent.

Pay later or contingent options

The premium is payable only if the option is exercised, but it must be exercised if it is in the money. To the option holder the advantage is that no premium is payable if the option expires out of the money, but the disadvantage is that these options are very expensive.

Chooser option

The holder is allowed to choose on some specific future date whether the option is a Call or a Put. It is quite similar to a "long straddle" except that, with the straddle, the trader is long both Call and Put options.

Path-Dependent Options

Asian options

These are also known as average rate options. With a traditional option the payoff at expiry is a function of the difference between the strike price of the option and the underlying asset price at expiry – the spot foreign exchange rate. With an average rate option the strike on the option is compared to the average rate over the period. This may be the average of daily, weekly, or monthly rates. By averaging out the data the volatility effect is smoothed. Average rate options are cheaper than standard options, the more frequent the averaging the lower the premium. The whole life of the option can be averaged or just the exchange rates between two specific dates. An arithmetic (rather than a geometric) average is used.

Lookback options

A lookback option is a European option where the strike is set at maturity. The holder can choose the best price achieved in the option's lifetime. For a lookback Call option the strike price will be the cheapest rate achieved over the period, and for a lookback Put option, the highest price achieved during the period. The lookback will always be exercised at the best possible price and it is impossible for the option to expire out of the money. Because the payoff for this type of option will always be greater than that for a standard option they can be expensive. It is quite common for them to be at least twice the price of a standard option.

Limit-Dependent Options

Barrier type options

These options have a mechanism that activates or inactivates (knock-ins and knock-outs) the option, when a particular trigger is reached. When the trigger level is touched certain things happen. With a knock-out option, the option starts like a traditional option but is knocked out or terminated at the trigger level. With a knock-in option, the option is activated only when the barrier is reached. This gives rise to down-and-out Calls, and down-and-in Calls, as well as up-and-out Puts and up-and-in Puts.

Example

A knock-out option

A UK exporter has sold some manufactured goods to the US. Delivery and payment are due in three months' time. The company is concerned at the weakness of the dollar and wishes to safeguard its sterling revenues.

Consider the following market information:

GBP/USD:
Spot rate: 1. 5600
3-month forward outright: 1.5500

To purchase a standard European style dollar Put, sterling Call option with a strike at USD1.55, and three-month expiry will cost, say, 1.7 per-cent of the US dollar amount.

A knock-out option, dollar Put, sterling Call with a strike at USD1.55 and a three-month expiry, *and* with a drop-out level of USD1.51 will cost 1.05 percent of the sterling amount.

(1) If the spot rate remains above USD1.51 (numerically higher) for the life of the option, and at expiry the strike of USD1.55 is in the money, the option will be exercised in the usual way. If the option is out of the money on expiry, but the USD1.51 level has not been breached, the option will be abandoned.

(2) If the spot rate falls to or below the drop-out level of USD1.51, the option will terminate, and no exercise will be possible.

In this example the company needs protection in case the dollar weakens, so will exercise the option to provide it with a guaranteed rate no worse than 1.55. But should the dollar strengthen and move to, say, 1.5100 the company wishes to take advantage of this gain and lock it in through the simultaneous transaction of a forward contract. Once the forward has been executed the option is no longer required.

Multi-Factor Options

These options involve a payoff based on the relationship between multiple assets rather than their price, and include rainbow options and quanto options.

Rainbow options

These are most frequently used in relation to equities and more importantly equity indexes. A rainbow Call option can offer the holder the chance to receive a return equal to the maximum gain from either the FT-SE 100, DAX, or the S&P 500.

Quanto options

The quanto involves an option on an uncertain amount of the underlying asset (in fact a quantity adjusting option). Quite often you will find quantos quoted in one currency upon an underlying asset denominated in another currency: for example, a Put option on the Nikkei with a strike in US dollars. If the option is in the money, the yen proceeds need to be converted to dollars at the original spot rate through exercise of a yen put. But the amount of the yen Put option will not be known at the outset of the transaction.

Exotic options continue to be developed and, together with the more traditional varieties, can be found singly or in groups and, often embedded in capital market type structures. Any banking or investment product that gives you the "right" to something in the future is going to have an option product in it somewhere.

Conclusion

There are many options market practitioners who are conscious that their margins are being squeezed, primarily due to the fact that nearly every bank now has a degree of options trading capability. The traditional vanilla option is a mature product. The quest for increased profitability has led to the exotic option, a less "transparent" product, where price levels are harder to compare and where less interbank competition exists.

■ ■ ■

'What is important
to the options
professional is the
actual volatility level
of different options
contracts, and the
relative value of one
contract to another.'

Practicalities of Trading Foreign Currency Options

DAVID LI. JONES

Deputy Head of Currency Options
Royal Bank of Scotland, London

Introduction

Over the years I have found very little written about the "hands-on" practicalities of trading currency options; the texts have been full of the theory, the payoff diagrams, the strategies, but nothing to help prepare the individual sitting for the first time on the trading desk. The theory must always underpin the practicality, but as we all know real life is not learnt in books (except, I hope, this one!).

There is no "secret" to trading options, no one way that is correct; as with all trading it's what works for you and hopefully makes you money! I do, however, hope to illustrate that there are a number of basic ingredients to put into the options recipe, but the proportions are up to the individual. The trader has a number of unavoidable parameters and variables when trading options – it is how these are "juggled" in response to market conditions that will make the difference between a profit and a loss.

In this chapter I will be giving very few definitions and no complex theory, on the assumption that the reader has read and understood the other chapters in this book on option theory. Consequently this chapter will bring the theoretical strands together, but the reader must bear in mind that it is difficult totally to isolate individual elements; all of them must be borne in mind so that at the end the "whole" can be seen.

Background

The currency options market is as global and unbroken as the spot FX market; the banks which operate in this market, like the spot market, range from the small to the very large. There are the banks with small treasury operations which do not run active options books. They might require options for customers or for their own positions. These banks will ask another bank for a "live" price: the "spot" price of an option at any one moment. Generally a trade like this covers just customer business. This is not really an options trading strategy, it is a static options scenario.

Next there are the banks with treasury departments which trade from one geographic center, and above them the very large global banks which by definition run global books on a 24-hour basis. These two trade in a similar way, the difference being size, risk appetite, and turnover.

In the marketplace the professional options players trade "volatility;" that element which is unique to options.

Volatility

The volatility that banks trade is expected future volatility, expressed as an annualized percentage. There is no magic formula for future volatility – it is simply what the market-making banks think it will be. This is where brokers are very important: brokers obtain volatility levels for different periods from the market-making banks and disseminate this information to the market; making it aware of where trading is possible.

Figure 15.1 shows volatility levels which are tradeable with the broker (in this example, the Exco Group). These are "at the money forward volatility;" the simplest to quote, and the basis of all option volatility levels. The brokers, via their knowledge of market activity, can advise banks of what might be good levels for non-standard options (here I mean options other than those with 50 percent deltas), and also for expiry dates that are not frequently traded. Also, the broker can approach a market maker with a request for a specific option price, thus facilitating trade and increasing the markets' knowledge of price levels.

What is important to the options professional is the actual volatility level of different options contracts, and the relative value of one contract to another. This volatility number can be considered as a "commodity" in its own right, irrespective of the option contract in which it is embedded.

Let us assume that the option being priced is a USD Call, DEM Put with expiry of three months, and a strike at the outright forward.

Volatility levels

Fig 15.1

	[EXCO GROUP] [CURRENCY OPTIONS]		4720 24/06/96 08.08 GMT		
	GBP/USD	USD/DEM	USD/FRF	USD/JPY	DEM/JPY	AUD/USD
R/R	–	0.0 – 0.3	–	0.35 – 0.65	–	0.0 – 0.3
1WK	–	–	–	–	–	5.7 – 6.2
2WK	–	–	–	–	–	5.9 – 6.3
1M	5.5 – 5.9	7.2 – 7.45	6.3 – 6.6	7.8 – 7.95	7.25 – 7.65	6.25 – 6.35
2M	5.6 – 6.0	7.7 – 8.0	6.65 – 6.95	8.3 – 8.6	7.6 – 8.0	6.45 – 6.65
3M	5.65 – 6.05	8.1 – 8.35	6.9 – 7.2	8.85 – 9.05	8.0 – 8.35	6.65 – 6.9
6M	6.0 – 6.4	8.7 – 9.0	–	9.75 – 9.95	8.65 – 8.95	6.7 – 7.0
1YR	6.7 – 7.0	9.05 – 9.3	–	10.3 – 10.5	9.2 – 9.4	6.75 – 7.0

Source: Exco Group plc
Courtesy: Dow Jones Telerate

Fig 15.2 **Pricing an option on a "Live" basis**

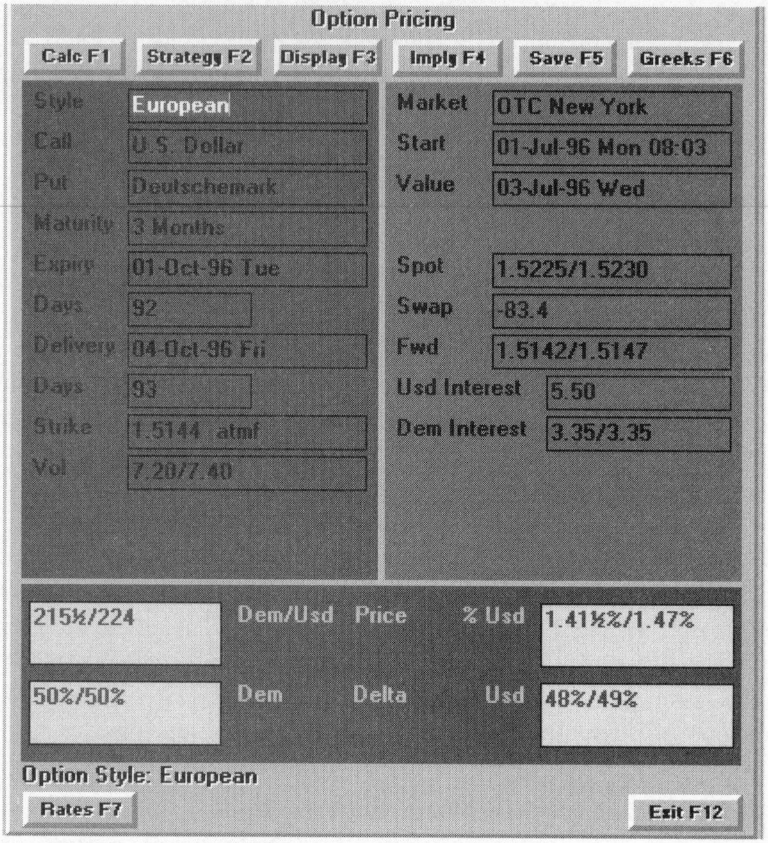

When quoting "Live" option prices, all that is important is the real cost (i.e. how much is it) since "live" options are generally dealt by those who are not trading options on a day-to-day basis (specifically those wishing to hedge an existing position, or those wishing to express a directional view through options). This is taken from the "SWAN" option pricing model (see Figure 15.2), and you will find that the elements here are common to all pricing models (see Chapter 13 on *option mechanics*). This example shows the pricing of a "live" option: the price is 1.415–1.47 percent of principal USD amount: you will notice there is a volatility price spread, since we don't know if the option being quoted will be bought or sold. Also there is a spot spread, since as soon as the option is traded then the option dealer must cover the position in the underlying cash market with an amount equivalent to the delta (to be delta neutral) i.e. if you buy a USD Call must sell the cash at spot or, if you sell the USD Call, must buy the cash at spot.

If you are quoting an option as the spot rate changes, the change must be reflected in the pricing model, so that the price of the option reflects the true option value at any one time. If the spot rate that you deal at is the same as that in the pricing model, then the level of volatility traded is fixed at the level the trader inputs into the model. If you are unable to trade at the desired spot level, the option may result in being traded at a better or worse level of volatility, e.g. if the trader sells the USD Call but, instead of buying the USD cash in the spot market at 1.5230 (see Figure 15.3), it is bought at 1.5220. Then the option has been sold at a higher level of volatility than was intended (the converse is true if the spot rises before completing the cash hedge). This option has been sold at 1.47 percent of dollar principal amount, and the lower level of spot means the price should be cheaper because the option is further out of the money by 0.03 percent in actual price terms. By executing the delta hedge at a lower level of spot where the option should be worth 1.44 percent, you can see that there is a windfall benefit which is translated into a real volatility level gain, which is 7.56 volatility, whilst the intended offer level of volatility was 7.4 (see Figure 15.4). You can also see in Figure 15.3 that if spot had risen to 1.5240 then the price should be 1.50 percent, 0.03 percent more expensive than the option was sold for; in the same way this translates to a real volatility loss.

To summarize, the matrix (Figure 15.3) simply illustrates the sensitivity of the price to spot movement, while Figure 15.4 shows via the pricing model the true volatility level of the option. The price of 1.47 percent has been dealt on, so that cannot be changed; the parameter which has moved is spot, and this reveals the true volatility level as 7.56 and not 7.4 as intended. This is a windfall volatility gain to the option seller.

To the option professional all elements of an option's price (spot, forward, and deposit rates) are known. The only unknown is the volatility – hence, when trading, professionals outline the specific contract specifications (put/call, strike, expiry, etc) and request a volatility price level for

Matrix showing price sensitivity to spot changes

Fig 15.3

Premium % Usd			
Spot \ Vol	6.20/6.40	7.20/7.40	8.20/8.40
1.5220	1.20%/1.24%	1.40%/1.44%	1.59½%/1.63½%
1.5230	1.23½%/1.27%	1.43%/1.47%	1.63%/1.66½%
1.5240	1.26½%/1.30½%	1.46%/1.50%	1.66%/1.70%

Option Style: European

Rates F7   Exit F12

Fig 15.4

Example of the actual traded volatility

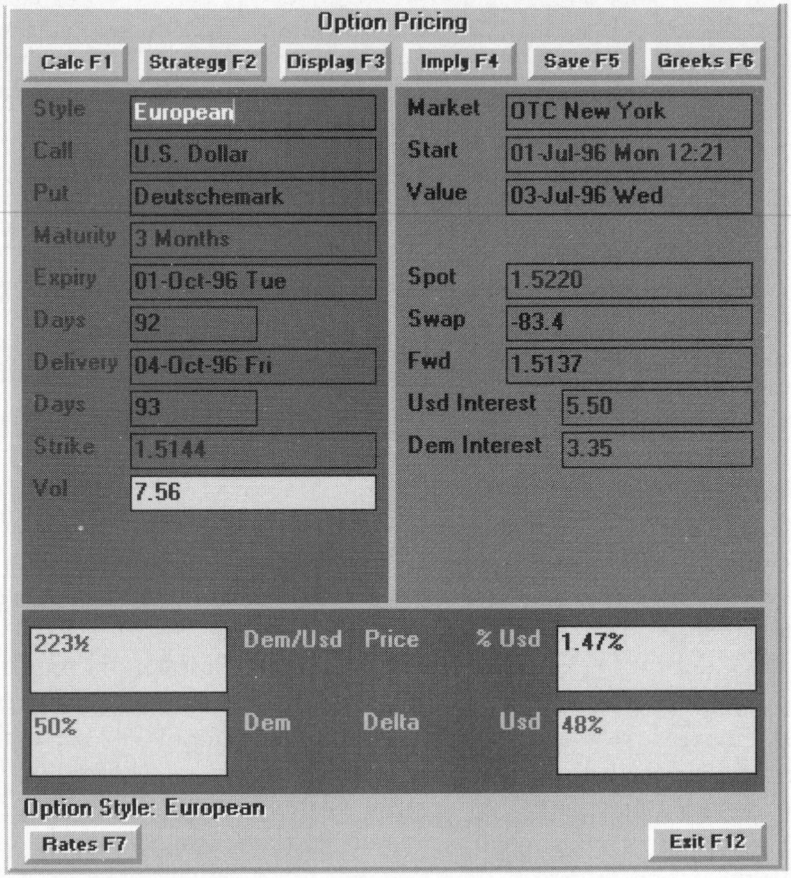

Option Pricing					
Calc F1	Strategy F2	Display F3	Imply F4	Save F5	Greeks F6

Style	European	Market	OTC New York	
Call	U.S. Dollar	Start	01-Jul-96 Mon 12:21	
Put	Deutschemark	Value	03-Jul-96 Wed	
Maturity	3 Months			
Expiry	01-Oct-96 Tue	Spot	1.5220	
Days	92	Swap	-83.4	
Delivery	04-Oct-96 Fri	Fwd	1.5137	
Days	93	Usd Interest	5.50	
Strike	1.5144	Dem Interest	3.35	
Vol	7.56			

223½	Dem/Usd Price	% Usd	1.47%
50%	Dem Delta	Usd	48%

Option Style: European

Rates F7   Exit F12

the contract. If a trade occurs (in this case the option is sold), the two counterparties will agree on a "spot" level to put into their pricing models; in this example 1.5230. The option will be priced off this "spot;" also the agreed volatility level is input: the price was 7.2/7.4 in volatility, thus 7.4 is input. The price will be agreed between the two parties and the delta hedge exchanged. You will notice that the price spread is narrower than for the "live" price (Figure 15.2). This is because there is no spot risk on the delta (spot moving, as explained above), the counterparties exchanging the delta between themselves, consequently fixing the level of volatility. This is shown in Figure 15.5.

The main difference between the two trading methods is that for volatility trading deltas are transacted, i.e. the cash hedge of the option is exchanged with the counterparty, and for the "live" method no delta hedge is transacted between the two counterparties.

Pricing an option traded on a "volatility" basis

Fig 15.5

Option Pricing					
Calc F1	Strategy F2	Display F3	Imply F4	Save F5	Greeks F6

Style	European	Market	OTC New York
Call	U.S. Dollar	Start	01-Jul-96 Mon 12:13
Put	Deutschemark	Value	03-Jul-96 Wed
Maturity	3 Months		
Expiry	01-Oct-96 Tue	Spot	1.5230
Days	92	Swap	-83.4
Delivery	04-Oct-96 Fri	Fwd	1.5147
Days	93	Usd Interest	5.50
Strike	1.5144	Dem Interest	3.35
Vol	7.20/7.40		

218/224	Dem/Usd	Price	% Usd	1.43%/1.47%	
50%/50%	Dem	Delta	Usd	49%/49%	

Option Style: European

Rates F7		Exit F12

Groundwork – The "Greeks"

Figure 15.6 shows the main theoretical "Greeks" generated from our example of the three-month USD Call.

The Greeks (vega, theta, gamma, etc) must never be far from the option trader's mind; all these are interconnected and can never be considered separately, since they are all trade-offs. The three Greeks, theta, vega and gamma are the most important to the options trader; however, rho must always be borne in mind. With a portfolio of many Puts and Calls, the rho effect may be small, but if there is a majority of one or the other (Puts or Calls) this could give a substantial interest rate position, which, if unhedged, could lead to considerable losses (or gains).

Let us compare our option example at two different time periods. The two following tables compare the Greeks at three months (see Figure 15.6) and on the day of expiry (see Figure 15.7). Here I assume that the spot is the same as the strike. You will notice that the only Greeks showing any significant numbers are the delta and gamma, which is what you would expect on the final day with the market spot level close to the option strike. At 10.00 am New York time – the official expiry time for options – the delta will be either 100 or 0, i.e. in the money, or out of the money, and consequently be exercised or not exercised.

If the reader requires further information on the Greeks, see Chapter 13 on *option mechanics*.

An option is a wasting asset, losing some of its value each day: the time decay. Figure 15.7 is a continuation of 15.6. Continuing the assumption that the spot on expiry is the same as the strike, i.e. the forward is the approximation of where spot will be in three months, consequently the value of the option is nothing, i.e out of the money and unexercisable. This represents a real loss to the option trader – the premium – if the option was purchased. It will be a gain if the option was sold. The intuitive logic of buying an option often called buying volatility is that the trader believes it will be volatile, and if actual volatility annualized in percentage terms over the three months is higher than the volatility at which the option was purchased, then, over the life of the

Fig 15.6

The Greeks of a three-month option

	Forward Hedge	49%/49%
51%/51%		49%/49%
-0.7/-0.7	Theta	-0.005%/-0.005%
30.1/30.1	Vega	0.20%/0.20%
10.74%/10.46% Gamma	Breakeven	1.5361/1.5370
-18.7/-18.9 Phi	Rho	19.4/19.5

Option Style: European

Rates F7   Exit F12

Fig 15.7

The Greeks on the day of expiry

	Forward Hedge	50%/50%
50%/50%		50%/50%
0.0	Theta	0.000%
0.1	Vega	0.001%/0.001%
50.00% Gamma	Breakeven	1.5143
0.0 Phi	Rho	0.0

Option Style: European

Rates F7   Exit F12

option, the trader should make back more than the cost of the option, i.e. he makes money, provided that the option gamma is actively traded.

You will recognize Figure 15.8 as the classic "hockey-stick" payoff diagram of an option on the day of expiry. Theoretically the delta is either 0 or 1, i.e. in the money (spot above the strike) or out of the money (spot below the strike). However, I will assume here that the option is not at expiry. Consider for the analysis that the option has just been traded (the expiry date is not important), it is a USD Call, DEM Put with a strike of 1.5244 in an amount of USD10 million.

The spot level when the transaction occurred is 1.5044; the cash delta hedge is executed. If we have bought the USD Call, then the delta is sold.

For this analysis, at a spot of 1.5044 ((1) on Figure 15.8) the option delta is 20 percent, so the delta hedge is to sell USD2 million (cash line A). The position is now delta neutral (all other things being equal, which I am assuming for clarity). Now spot rises to 1.5244 ((2) on Figure 15.8) the option delta is 50 percent. Previously USD2 million was sold, so at point (2) the position is now long USD3 million (long USD5 million from the option and short USD2 million cash). The option delta has increased from 20 percent to 50 percent between (1) and (2) so the trader has become long of USD3 million and spot has been rising. This will be a profit, but only if the trader crystallizes this profit by selling USD3 million in the cash market (cash line B), his position is now delta neutral. Spot continues to rise to 1.5444 ((3) on Figure 15.8). The option delta is now 70 percent, the position the trader has is long USD2 million (option delta position is long USD7 million, but previously USD5 million cash has been sold: resulting in a net position of long USD2 million).

If USD2 million is now sold in the cash market (cash line C) delta neutrality will once again be obtained and the profit from the position crystallized.

Simplistic analysis of the mechanics of gamma trading

Fig 15.8

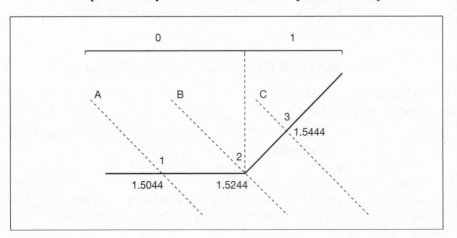

Spot now declines to 1.5044 (1). The option delta is now 20 percent, but the trader's position is short USD5 million since over the option's life USD7 million has been sold. The trader now buys USD5 million in the cash market, delta neutrality is once again obtained, and a profit is again realized.

By actively cash hedging the trader is attempting to recoup time value, and generate a profit. You will notice that trading this way is exactly the same as being long or short of a "straddle".

These are the mechanics of gamma trading. In reality things are not quite that straightforward: time plays a very important role, since the longer dated the option, the less the gamma, and the most gamma is at expiry where the delta can flip from 0 to 1 each side of the strike.

Figure 15.8 is not totally accurate mathematically but its simplicity does illustrate the points I wish to make about gamma trading – or, more clearly, how the trader makes money by being long of volatility, or can lose money by being short. As spot moves the trader trades cash against the movement, "locking in" the profits. If the spot rises and the trader doesn't trade the underlying, then spot falls, an opportunity loss has occurred, no profit has been crystallized, and every day the option is losing value. So you can see that a static spot, or very tight ranges, and inability to trade the underlying form the worst scenario for an option trader who is long options. Remember that every day costs time decay, especially since if this persists the market will look to sell volatility, preferring to be short options and earn time value in quiet markets. The opposite argument is true if you are short options.

Consequently, if the trader is long options, the underlying must be traded as much as possible; if short options the trader must trade the underlying as little as possible. Thus by logical extension if the gamma of the option can be actively traded the market must be volatile, as a result the traders will mark "volatility" higher, and the option that you have bought will be worth more. If the trader so wishes the option (volatility) can now be sold back to the market at the higher market volatility level, and a volatility profit realized.

How movement in volatility affects the option price

Using Figure 15.3 again I wish to illustrate the vega of an option: again using the example of the three-month option, the figure shows how the price changes as the levels of volatility used to price the options change. At any one level of spot, if implied volatilities (volatility put into the pricing model) are changed it will have an impact on the option price. If we look at Figure 15.6 the matrix shows the option as having a vega of 0.20 percent (this is an absolute price effect) – hence for a 1 percent change in volatility, e.g. from 6.4 to 7.4, the price will change by 0.20 percent.

Strike Risk

On the day of expiry the spot can be in the money, out of the money or at the money. If the option is in the money the option trader will have totally hedged the option with the underlying (see Figure 15.8). Thus, when the option is exercised no position will result; the cash hedge will offset the exercise. If the option is out of the money there will be no cash hedge and no exercise.

Now examine a situation where the spot is near to the strike but out of the money. If we continue with our previous example, the option is a Call so as spot rises through the strike a position is created equal to the principal amount of the option; thus this rise above the strike (Figure 15.8) gives the opportunity to trade the gamma and make money. If the spot on the day of expiry is above the strike the trader will have sold the principal amount in the cash market and the intrinsic value is locked in. If the spot rate now goes below the strike, the trader is just short of the cash which can now be bought back for profit. On the day of expiry the more times the spot moves through the strike, the more the opportunity to generate profits. However, if the trader was short the option every cash trade would be a loss, i.e. buying high and selling low to hedge the short option position. This is said to be a situation of infinite gamma where the delta of the option changes from 0 to 1 at one level of spot, i.e. around the strike.

This needs to be clearly understood as the point must be made that traders trade ATMF (at the money forward) options purely for volatility, since ATMF options are the most liquid and are the easiest prices to make. You will have noticed that the USD Call which is cash hedged has exactly the same payoff profile as a "straddle," that is, where a Put and Call are both either bought or sold with the same strike. Thus, when trading volatility, professionals prefer to trade ATMF straddles, both options having 50 percent delta since the strike is at the forward, but by using both puts and calls there is no need for a cash hedge since the deltas negate each other so there is no initial forward risk. However, you will find that the vast majority of option requests are for options with deltas other than 50 percent.

Making the Price

First of all traders aim to be consistent in their quotes (depending on currency pairs and market conditions). In Figure 15.9 a one-month ATMF option is used as a benchmark (row 6). This we compare with a 25-delta option over three time periods. The price spread for a 25-delta option is narrower than for ATMF options when using the same volatility so it becomes necessary to widen the price spread – this is the result of wider volatility price, but still much cheaper than the ATMF. But, if you sell the 25-delta option this might be too cheap since over the month the spot could certainly reach or surpass the strike. The trader must consider "risk/reward" on a subjective basis, and also how the market is pricing such options.

Thus option traders have a tendency to bid up low delta options since the chances of a low delta option ending up in the money on the day of expiry is more likely to occur than the model would suggest; they have to ask themselves what is the true value of that risk. This is known as the "smile effect," and the degree of "smile" is market dependent.

Row 6 in Figure 15.9 shows the price of an ATMF option for one month, showing the volatility used and the resultant prices. I have included all the Greeks for comparison purposes in Figure 15.10. As expiry is approached you will see that the gamma is increasing as well as the theta, but the vega is declining. This is what theory suggests should happen, and the example illustrates this even though it uses 25-delta options (not as sensitive as 50-delta options).

Looking at the two-week and one-week option examples, the volatility spread may seem wide when compared to the one-month, but when the actual price is considered it is not that wide at all (Figure 15.9). These volatility and price spreads are for illustrative purposes only. In the market these prices will tend to be a lot wider, especially the one-week and two-week.

Fig 15.9

Comparison of option deltas over different maturities

	Call/Buy	Put/Sell	Maturity	Strike/Rate	Delta % Usd	Volatility	Premium % Usd
1	Usd	Dem	1 Week	1.5395	24%/25%	7.10/7.50	0.14½%/0.16%
2	Usd	Dem	1 Week	1.5395	25%/25%	7.20/7.40	0.14½%/0.15½%
3	Usd	Dem	2 Weeks	1.5430	25%/26%	7.15/7.45	0.21%/0.22½%
4	Usd	Dem	2 Weeks	1.5430	25%/25%	7.20/7.40	0.21%/0.22½%
5	Usd	Dem	1 Month	1.5495	25%/25%	7.20/7.40	0.32%/0.34%
6	Usd	Dem	1 Month	1.5268 atmf	49%/49%	7.20/7.40	0.86%/0.88½%

Fig 15.10

The Greeks associated with the maturities and deltas in Figure 15.9

	Theta % Usd	Vega % Usd	Gamma % Dem amnt	Phi Dem/Usd	Rho Dem/Usd
1	0.021%/-0.023%	0.045%/0.046%	28.87%/28.10%	-0.7/-0.8	0.7/0.8
2	0.021%/-0.022%	0.045%/0.046%	28.68%/28.30%	-0.7/-0.7	0.7/0.8
3	0.015%/-0.015%	0.064%/0.065%	21.49%/21.03%	-1.5/-1.5	1.5/1.5
4	0.015%/-0.015%	0.064%/0.065%	21.41%/21.11%	-1.5/-1.5	1.5/1.5
5	0.009%/-0.009%	0.098%/0.099%	14.33%/14.12%	-3.2/-3.3	3.3/3.4
6	0.010%/-0.011%	0.12%/0.12%	17.68%/17.23%	-6.5/-6.5	6.6/6.6

Since the market trades volatility the professional interbank players will quote all prices as a volatility spread. It must be remembered, however, that volatility has increasingly less effect on option pricing as expiry approaches, so for very short dated options where there is no specific price in the market the trader will look at the risk reward of the real cash price, and allocate a volatility price based on this.

To continue our example, if we have a 25-delta USD Call (ATMF volatility 7.2/7.4), and we quote the volatility on this as 7.3/7.6, the mirror image of this option, the 75-delta USD Put, should be quoted the same – this is because of Put–Call parity. The behavior of these two options is exactly the same, but only when each has its resultant delta in place, i.e. if long 75-delta USD Put buy 75 percent of the underlying in cash. As spot rises the delta of the option declines, and the cash stays constant (assuming no gamma trading). If long the 25-delta USD Call sell 25 percent of the underlying; as spot rises the delta of the option increases. Thus the net result of both options is the same.

Risk reversals

This whole idea of low delta options takes us a step further from "smile" curves to "risk reversals (R/R)." The smile curve illustrates how much low delta options are bid up relative to the ATMF volatility. The risk reversal is the market professional's name for a "collar;" a structure whereby a Call option is sold and a Put is bought, or vice versa, for the same expiry day, but both tend to have out of the money strikes. For a corporate it is a cheap hedging tool, for the option trader it is a way of taking a directional position, e.g. if the USD Call is bought and USD Put sold the view is that USD will go up.

So the smile shows "mark up" and the risk reversal shows "bias", i.e. for Calls or Puts. We know that in terms of volatility a trader is not bothered whether an ATM Call or an ATM Put is traded since both have 50 delta, the same vega sensitivity, and same gamma sensitivity. There is no direction bias, i.e. if the dollar goes up or down it is not important. We can now call ATMF volatility "par."

The trader thinks that the dollar will rise so he wants to buy a cheap option; a 25-delta USD Call, out of the money. This option has a directional bias, and at time of dealing vega and gamma sensitivity is low compared to the ATMF.

The low delta is given a "smile" to reflect the risk reversal. If the person selling the options thinks to himself that although the delta is low there is always the chance of spot getting to the strike level – and besides it is a cheap option to have as protection – the option price maker will mark the volatility higher to give himself a greater comfort level of risk reward.

If there is no bias in the market at all to the dollar rising or falling then a 25-delta Put will be marked up as well. Thus a situation might be as follows: ATMF vol 7.2/7.4 while the option with a delta of 25 on the dollar Call with the volatility at 7.4/7.8 and the same for dollar Puts. We have adjusted the price by 0.2 to reflect cheapness and risk; the price is widened in an attempt to maintain consistency of spread.

Risk reversals (R/R) are very commonly traded, normally having deltas of 25. Since both options are vega neutral at instigation, the important question is the directional bias of the market. If there is no bias the bank making the market in the risk reversal could show "0.2 around par" as the price. The bank asking the price would know that if it wanted to buy or sell the Puts in the risk reversal it would have to pay away 0.2 as a volatility spread in either case.

If the market now believes the dollar is more likely to go up, the price of the risk reversal would be better bid in favor of USD Calls, e.g. "flat /0.3 bid for USD Calls." This would mean that the bank making the price would buy the USD Call and sell the USD Put for the same volatility, but would sell the USD Call and buy the USD Put only if it could earn 0.3 in volatility.

If it becomes increasingly certain that the dollar will rise the risk reversal might well be quoted: "0.2/0.6 bid for USD Calls." Here, the price maker is prepared to pay away 0.2 in volatility to buy the dollar Call, but wants to earn 0.6 to sell the dollar Call.

These levels and spreads are determined by the market and the degree of bias of the risk reversal. The level that the risk reversal is trading will have a strong influence on where the volatility level is for single low delta options. What volatility price the dealer makes is down to his skill and judgement but the risk reversal gives an idea of how much to mark the price up. If the ATMF volatility is 7.2/7.4, then the price for an R/R is flat /0.3 bid for USD calls. It is then reasonable to make the USD Call single option with a 25-delta a volatility of 7.3/7.6. If the R/R is quoted at 0.2/0.6 for USD calls, then the 25 delta sterling Put would have a volatility of 7.4/7.8.

This is not a science. The risk reversal gives only an indication of what the mark up should be – you don't know if you're right until you make the price. The 25-delta USD Puts move down towards the ATMF volatilities and sometimes even go to discount. This can happen when the market is so convinced that the dollar is going up that it doesn't want any dollar Puts and sells them at any price. The result is that oversupply of Puts forces them to discount. When this happens, and since spot never moves in a straight line, the Puts begin to look attractive on a risk reward basis.

If the risk reversal is traded between interbank counterparties, the volatility levels must be agreed. The dealer who has made the price will generally suggest the actual volatilities upon which the options will be priced, and these will be close to the ATMF volatility since with both options having the same delta, they have the same vega sensitivity: at the time of trading the dealer will have no vega sensitivity resulting from the two options. If the deltas are different, the vega is different, and the volatility levels chosen to price the options will become more important. A pricing screen for a risk reversal is shown in Figure 15.11.

The pricing of a risk reversal

Fig 15.11

Option Pricing						Strategies	
Calc F1	Strategy F2	Display F3	Imply F4	Save F5	Greeks F6	Option 1	Option 2

			Market	OTC New York	European	European
	U.S. Dollar	Start	01-Jul-96 Mon 12:56	1.00	Usd	1.00	Usd
	Deutschemark	Value	03-Jul-96 Wed	Buy		Sell	
Maturity	1 Month						
Expiry	01-Aug-96 Thu 15:00	Spot	1.5142	Call	Usd	Put	Usd
Days	31.09	Swap	-26.0	Put	Dem	Call	Dem
Delivery	05-Aug-96 Mon	Fwd	1.5116	1.5329		1.4901	
Days	33	Usd Interest	5.58	7.10/7.40			
		Dem Interest	3.58				

| 3 | Dem/Usd | Price | % Usd | 0.02% | 46½ | 49½ |
| 50% | Dem | Delta | Usd | 50% | 25% | -25% |

Deutschemark interest rate

| Rates F7 | | Exit F12 | Dem/Usd |

Banks in the market quote the risk reversal as stated for simplicity. Market professionals trade volatility so that is what they want to see; a volatility price level. If the trade goes ahead the option is then priced. Dealing a "live" risk reversal is very difficult since there are very few pricing systems that can manage it, so if quoting a customer most banks ask what option is being sold.

Spreads

Banks are often asked to quote spreads, the simplest being Put/Call spreads and calendar spreads. Market convention is to quote a spread on one price and make the other "choice" – the client can buy or sell at the same price. Since you are selling one and buying another it is thought that risk is reduced and therefore the spread needs to be tighter than for single options. So, for example, the trader is requested to quote a two-month 40-delta dollar Call versus a 20-delta dollar Call. If it is a spread we know that one option will be sold. Generally the price with the spread on will be the one that is most vega sensitive, 40-delta: in this case, e.g, 7.25/7.45.

If in this case dollar Calls are bid and the 25-delta risk reversal is quoted for the period "flat 0.3 USD Calls bid" the 20-delta could be made 7.55 choice (if it was 25-delta should make 7.45 choice). So the trader making the price pays away 0.1 for the low delta dollar Call and receives 0.3 for selling the low delta dollar Call. So, if you want to sell the low delta option (in this example), you get a much better price than asking for the low delta option on its own.

Simple calendar spreads are, for example, two-month vs four-month ATMF $20 million per period. This is a request for ATMF straddles in USD10 million a leg; the far date being more vega sensitive would be spread, and the near date made a "choice price." The trader will mark the price up or down to reflect any interest that he may have.

If, however, in the case of the calendar spread the amounts of each period were ratioed, e.g. 3:1, near to far date, then it is possible that the vega sensitivity of two months might be greater than the four months, hence the two-month would have a spread and the four-month choice.

What Does All This Mean?

Hopefully, this chapter has given you an idea of what goes into pricing an option and what considerations a trader must make. It is important to quote the option correctly; around your book, or the market. But once the option is in the portfolio it is lost; and the option trader must risk manage the whole portfolio, juggling all these elements: vega, gamma, and theta.

What moves volatilities, or the trader's perception of future volatilities? Firstly, unexpected news, economic or political – any uncertainty and traders will rush to buy volatility. If the spot breaks out of trading ranges, demand and supply of Puts and Calls may change: a situation may occur where the market is short of Puts and spot is moving slowly down, it is not volatile at all, yet volatilities keep going up because the market doesn't want to be shorter. If the market is short of Puts and that is the favored side (i.e. better bid in terms of the risk reversal), and spot declines, the options that traders are short of will increase in vega sensitivity, as they become more in the money, and as volatility rises their losses will increase. Also, for the option trader the cost of buying options to cover this risk will increase as volatility rises and the risk reversal becomes increasingly bid in favor of USD Puts.

Conversely, in quiet markets or tight ranges perceived volatility will be sold to earn the time decay and income from declining levels of volatility.

Brokers

Unlike the spot market the options market is not transparent. Every option is different: two-month 50-delta Calls are traded differently from three-month 20-delta Puts. There are many markets within the overall options market, and the brokers have a lot of information. They facilitate trading and advise of levels used on trades that they have seen or heard about. Brokers will obtain support levels in volatility from market makers and will get prices in specific interests. Obviously banks can call other banks for prices, but the broker can generally get tighter prices – then negotiation can begin.

Conclusion

Hopefully I have given some insight into trading options, Not everything has been covered, and, indeed, some aspects have been touched on only superficially. It is important to be aware that relative levels of implied volatility are important for all options, and since the majority of business in options is less than two months the demand and supply for Puts and calls have just as much bearing on implied volatility prices as do actual volatility perceptions in the market. The one important point is this: there is no "correct" answer. Science doesn't help with the trading: there is subjectivity in making a price, but the market will not allow this to become too extreme, what is important is that you are aware of the risks and if the way you manage that risk makes money then you can be said to be doing it right!

■ ■ ■

'Foreign exchange risk is dangerous; it is expensive and should not be ignored.'

Hedging Foreign Exchange Risk

Introduction

The management of foreign exchange risk is critical in today's ever changing financial markets. But what is currency risk? In terms of volumes, with something in excess of USD1.2 trillion changing hands every day on the foreign exchanges, only a very small percentage is accounted for by corporates hedging their positions – between 5 percent and 10 percent of the total figure. The balance consists of global interbank business. Currency risk can initially be subdivided by the two groups of people who are most active in the markets: hedgers and traders.

A *hedger* is a company or individual who has an actual exposure to a particular currency: they need to pay away a foreign currency or receive a foreign currency, and wish to manage (avoid) the risk of an adverse exchange rate movement. The risk to a hedger is either of receiving a smaller amount of the base (or domestic) currency than expected, or of paying out more of the base currency to purchase a required amount of foreign currency.

A *trader*, on the other hand, has no requirement to pay or receive the currency but simply wants to speculate on the future direction of the currency movement for profit. It can be argued however, that most interbank foreign exchange trading is hedging, as each bank seeks to get out of positions that it has just received as a result of business from customers or other banks. The risk to a trader is that his view on the market is wrong, it may lose him money, or not make him as much as he thought, or the timing is wrong.

Example

Example of Currency Risk

November 19

A UK company, Brain Tools plc, has sold some machine parts to the US. The company's base currency is sterling, but it has agreed to receive payment in US dollars in three months' time, on February 19. Brain needs to recover the sterling price (including profit margin) of £250,000; it will then convert this amount to US dollars for invoicing purposes. Let us assume that Brain chooses to use today's spot exchange rate – which is, say, GBP/USD: 1.60.

When Brain sends its invoice to the US buyer, it will state that the buyer is due to pay the seller USD400,000 (1.60 × 250,000) in three months' time. If Brain does not hedge its currency exposure on this invoice it could make an exchange rate profit or a loss on the transaction, i.e. the rate could go in Brain's favor or may move against it. A profit is unlikely to cause a problem (but in some companies it may), but a loss will certainly be unwelcome.

If Brain decides not to hedge its position on the foreign exchanges, it is running a risk. It is impossible to predict the direction of an exchange rate with confidence, so we must assume one of two things can happen: the rate can increase or decrease (weaken or strengthen) against the base currency. In a three-month period it is not impossible for the FX rate to move 5 cents in either direction.

February 19

The original spot rate of exchange (the rate quoted on November 19 for value two business days later) could have moved by the end of this three-month period as shown below:

- USD increases (strengthens) to: GBP/USD 1. 5500
- USD decreases (weakens) to: GBP/USD 1.6500

The treasurer of Brain has already calculated that she needs to receive £250,000 for the transaction. If she does not hedge her position, she will be compelled to accept the exchange rate on the day the dollars actually arrive, i.e:

- If the dollar has strengthened to GBP/USD 1.5500, the company will receive £258,064.
- If the dollar has weakened to GBP/USD 1.6500, the company will receive only £242,424.

In the first instance the company has made a windfall profit, in the second it has not received what it requires for the goods. Brain may end up selling the machine parts at a loss. Yet the client has paid what he was asked to, and the company quoted the dollar equivalent on the day. No one is to blame, but worldwide events have changed either the value of sterling or the value of the US dollar. This is why currency risk is accepted as a way of life for companies who both export and import goods.

In the case of an importer, he may need to buy Deutsche Marks to pay a supplier, and budgets on the piece of equipment costing, say, £175,000. But when it comes to payment date, if he has taken out no hedging transactions, when he buys the Deutsche Marks on the foreign exchanges they may cost as much as £195,000.

Company Attitudes to Risk

The corporate culture inherent in a company will influence the way that foreign exchange hedging is taken out. Different companies view foreign exchange risk in different ways. There are two extreme views. Firstly, the company whose view is that "we make widgets, we do not speculate on the foreign exchanges." This company would almost certainly hedge every single transaction denominated in foreign currency, usually by using traditional forward foreign exchange contracts.

Secondly, there is the company that believes that the flows of currency through the treasury department should be "managed" and the return maximized. Inevitably, this will involve decisions where a view on a particular currency is taken in anticipation of a receipt or payment. In some cases it may actually entail opening up currency positions for gain. Naturally enough – and especially with imperfect information – the trades that are undertaken to maximize profit may end up as loss-making positions.

Although there are some companies which do hold these extreme positions, most corporations will generally fall somewhere in the middle, although there will be a greater concentration towards the conservative end.

Hedging Guidelines

There are a number of steps to be taken after the original currency risk has been identified.

Step 1

The *identification* of the currency risk is vital. Currency risk can vary from the "staring you in the face risk" to the "I feel uncomfortable about this price risk." Once the risk has been identified there are other steps to follow before leaping on the phone to call your bank's dealers. Ideally, the whole process should look like Figure 16.1.

Hedging comes last although most clients will readily admit that they often skip the middle steps. We will arrive at the hedging soon, but I've always found it important to set the terms of reference. We know now that we have the exposure, so what should we do next?

The hedging process

Fig 16.1

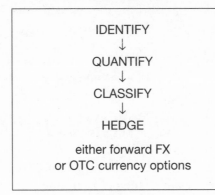

IDENTIFY
↓
QUANTIFY
↓
CLASSIFY
↓
HEDGE

either forward FX
or OTC currency options

Step 2

This is where we must *quantify* the risk. Each company and client will have a different threshold where they begin to feel pain. For a small company it may be USD5,000, for a larger multinational institution it may be USD100,000. There comes a point where the exposure may well exist but was regarded as not material enough to worry about. Ideally, the board of directors will have decided the level of cover and what constitutes a material exposure. If it is a material exposure we will need to ascertain the exact size as far as is possible.

Step 3

Now we must *classify* the type of risk to give us the best chance of hedging correctly. There are a range of currency risks that look similar but are in fact quite different. The terms relating to currency exposure that many readers, especially corporates, will recognize are:

- transaction
- translation
- economic.

Unfortunately, these terms lead to a certain amount of confusion. Transaction and translation risk are not so hard to understand. But what is economic exposure? Does it mean that if it isn't transaction or translation it must be economic? This was usually cited as a reason for not covering the exposure. It is now possible to subdivide currency risks still further, and I suggest a classification as follows.

Transaction exposures

(1) **Standard**: the risk that exchange rates will move between the time an invoice is raised and payment is made.

(2) **Recurring**: the exposure to movements in currency rates that the company knows it will enter into at some time in the future, but cannot be certain as to the exact value or timing. Most exports and imports fall into this category.

(3) **Contingent**: tender to contract (TTC) exposure. Where the company has tendered or bid for business in a foreign currency, and must keep the currency rate fixed, but where there is no certainty that the company will win the business and it may well be three to six months before the result of the bid is known.

Trading exposures

(1) **Liquidity exposure**: arising from deliberate treasury management action to change the currency of debt or cash with the specific aim of optimizing interest levels.

(2) **Speculative exposures**: deliberate management action to open foreign exchange positions which are not to manage commercial exposures but instead to take speculative positions.

Competitive exposures

(1) **Direct**: as a result of the company's home currency strengthening, its competitors, because production costs will reduce in lower terms, will be able to undercut the sales price in both the domestic and the export markets.

(2) **Indirect**: adverse currency movements will change a company's competitive position even though the currency may not be one that the company trades in directly, e.g. a UK company trading woodpulp in USD is at risk to Scandinavian currencies, because of the location of the world woodpulp manufacturers.

Translation exposures

(1) **Balance sheet**: when an asset is translated at year end, and due to an exchange rate move, the asset value will fluctuate with the FX markets, giving rise to possible profits or losses later, e.g. Dutch company, NLG balance sheet, with a French subsidiary to be revalued.

(2) **Consolidated P/L**: the risk that currency movements during the year will adversely impact on the profits of the group, and thus on the earnings per share of an international group of companies. This could be due to a fall in the value of the currency in which one or more of the subsidiary's accounts are prepared, relative to the parent company.

Quantifying and hedging foreign exchange risk

Table 16.1

Exposure	Method of quantification	Cover method
Transaction exposures		
Standard	Books of account	Forwards or currency options
Recurring	Estimate turnover for a given period	Include with standard exposures – use forwards or currency options
Contingent	Avoid – or forecast likelihood	Include with standard exposures or use currency options
Trading exposures		
Liquidity	Books of account adjusted for positions	Forward market
Speculative	Dealing positions	Spot or forward market
Competitive exposures		
Direct	Competitor analysis	None in short term – relevant to new investments
Indirect	Project analysis	None in short term – relevant to new investments
Translation exposures		
Balance sheet	Books of account	Match fund assets
Profit and loss	Profit forecasts	Forwards or currency options

Table 16.1 shows the suggested methods of quantifying and covering these risks.

Step 4

The last step is to *hedge* the position. Some companies will use forward contracts and others will benefit from currency options. Essentially, the main choices facing a hedger are:

- do nothing
- fix the FX rate by means of an option type product, where a premium is due
- fix the FX rate by means of a zero premium product, such as a traditional forward FX deal.

There is a complication with managing currency risks: not only can both sides of the equation move (both currencies in the pair can strengthen or weaken) but to cover longer-term foreign exchange exposures (over, say, five years) a different product is required – the currency swap. In simple terms a currency swap has a closer relationship with long-term forward foreign exchange than with other types of swaps. However, conventional classification places it firmly in the derivative category and outside the scope of this book, but further details can be found in *Mastering Derivatives Markets*, by Francesca Taylor (Pitman Publishing, 1996).

Compare and Contrast Traditional FX Forwards and OTC Options

If the client chooses to use traditional forward FX for his hedge he will achieve a zero cost transaction, but may forgo profit opportunities later. An option will cost the client a premium but may in the end achieve a more favorable outcome (see Table 16.2).

The real deal breaker as far as most companies are concerned is the cost of the option. If options were available free of charge then, almost without exception, every single piece of forward hedging would be taken out using options. It is clear they are a far superior product, but they have to be paid for, and it has to be admitted that sometimes they are expensive. Forward foreign exchange contracts are available free of charge as long as the client has sufficient room on an available credit line.

The real choice for many companies will be finely balanced, taking into account the extra benefits available under the option – but where a premium is payable for the product – against a foreign exchange deal, which costs nothing but which allows no chance of profit at all as it obligates both parties to convert the currency at the predetermined rate.

Some companies will wish to profit from their currency transactions and may well deliberately not hedge existing currency exposures. Some companies, as we have discussed, may also actively seek foreign exchange risk as a means of enhancing their income. The danger here is that the commercial side of the business, which may be profitable in its own right, could be overshadowed by foreign exchange losses if some irresponsible or unlucky decisions on currency are taken.

The corporate culture of the company can be situated at either end of our decision bracket in Figure 16.2.

Comparison of OTC currency options and forward contracts

Table 16.2

CURRENCY OPTIONS	FORWARD CONTRACTS
Right to buy or sell	Obligation to buy or sell, or pay away the currency
No obligation to deliver or pay the underlying currency	Must deliver on/before maturity
No loss possible excluding the option premium	Unlimited opportunity loss possible, with respect to the forward rate
Eliminates downside risk and retains unlimited profit potential	Eliminates downside risk and upside potential
Perfect hedge for variable exposures	Imperfect currency hedge for variable exposures

True hedgers in the corporate world are comparatively rare. Let me explain what I mean by a true hedger – a company or individual who sells forward even if they believe that the currency may move in their favor. They wish to make no windfall profits or windfall losses, all they require of their hedging transaction is the ability to know in advance what the rate of exchange will be for their transaction. Typically, this type of company is risk averse, and no conscious thought is required of their dealers: they know they must sell or buy the currency forward, all that remains is to get the best deal on the day at the best rate. This generally is known as a *cost center* treasury.

Corporate speculators do exist: companies such as the big multinationals which have their own treasury functions where they can actively open up speculative positions for profit. This is classified as a *profit*

Hedging decisions

Fig 16.2

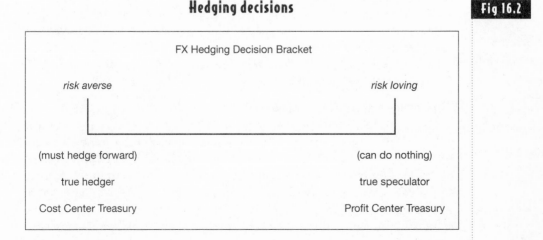

FX Hedging Decision Bracket

risk averse — risk loving

(must hedge forward) — (can do nothing)

true hedger — true speculator

Cost Center Treasury — Profit Center Treasury

center treasury. They will be allowed to run unhedged positions as part of their mandate.

Decision Rules

Are there any guidelines as to when a particular product should be used ?

Once the risk identification/hedging process has been followed, and the risk has been classified, some risks can still be hedged with either an option or a forward. Assuming the company has the mandate to use either product, the final decision should come down to the circumstances on the day. Some days a traditional forward will be the right choice, on others the option. The decision will entail the company taking a "view on the market." This is nothing to be frightened of.

Example

Consider a receiver of dollars in three months' time:
The company is not allowed to do nothing because that could be speculative.

(1) If the company felt the value of the dollar was going to weaken. In this case the traditional forward contract would be the right choice – it costs nothing and covers the downside.
(2) If the company felt the value of the dollar was going to strengthen then it would hope to realize more sterling. Here a traditional forward would be a questionable choice. (By selling the currency forward the client would be saying he does not want to realize the extra sterling.) The correct choice would be an OTC currency option. It will cost a premium but this can be more than offset by the sterling gain.
(3) If the company felt the dollar was going nowhere, the traditional forward would again be the right choice – it costs nothing and covers the downside, and no upside is expected.
(4) If the company felt the GBP/USD exchange rate would be volatile, the option would be the right choice because with a volatile market there is always the chance that the currency will suddenly improve, realizing more sterling. The danger here is that if the market is already volatile the option will be expensive.

These rules can be summarized as in Table 16.3.

One cautionary note: it is easy for a company with a risk management policy to feel "smug" – especially if it sells or buys all its currency forward. But ask yourself a question: if no one knows in which direction the US dollar (or any other currency for that matter) is going to move tomorrow or the next day, and if you believe every single piece of known information is in the exchange rate already, what is the probability of that hedge being successful? Answer: 50:50. So every company which hedges its exposures

Hedging guidelines

Table 16.3

View on the target currency	Risk management instrument
Weakens	Forward contract
Strengthens	Currency option
Goes nowhere	Forward contract
Highly volatile	Currency option

using forwards will be right half the time, and the companies which have a rather more cavalier attitude to risk and don't hedge because they think it is all a "mug's game" will also be right half the time. A sobering thought!

Trading Risk

A true speculator will be a bank. But any institution that makes some or all of its profits by taking "views" on currency or other commodities for profit is trading. These speculative positions may be live for a matter of a few minutes or a few months. There is rarely any underlying transaction.

Trading example

A foreign exchange trader in a bank or in a large corporate wishes to take risk by buying and selling currency for a profit. He may have a short-term view on the direction of the US dollar, or a long-term view on some other currency. He will position himself accordingly, by either buying or selling the currency now, in order to reverse out of the deal at a later date – hopefully, making money in the process.

May 10

A proprietary trader in a financial institution feels that the dollar is show-ing signs of strength and wishes to take a position that will make him money in the near future. He decides to hold dollars for a week.

Action – May 10

First he must choose which currency pair to trade in. Let us assume it is USD/JPY. He will buy the dollars on the market either spot – in which case he must fund the position from two days' time – or he can swap them forward for, say, a week. He decides to buy the dollars forward (value May 19) and is able to buy in at a rate of USD/JPY 100.50.

Action – May 17

In a week's time the dollar has strengthened to USD/JPY 103.50, so he sells the yen back (value May 19) without taking delivery of them, and makes a profit. If the position had been taken in USD10 million the profit would be:

Dollars	USD/JPY		Yen	Transaction
10,000,000 × 100.50		=	1,005,000,000	(Sell yen and buy dollars)
10,000,000 × 103.50		=	1,035,000,000	(Sell dollars and buy yen)
Profit			30,000,000	

At the current spot rate the profit in dollars is USD289,855.

If the view had been wrong it would have been just as easy to lose the same amount of money.

Conclusion

I have addressed the concept of foreign exchange risk management in isolation. I have deliberately not tried to imply that if you hedge your foreign exchange risk you must be achieving a better deal for the company than if you weren't hedging the risks. The *McKinsey Quarterly* (1996, Vol. 1) has two interesting articles: "Why derivatives don't reduce FX risk" by Thomas Copeland and Yash Loshi, and "Are you taking the wrong FX risk?" by Bruno Coppe, Michael Graham, and Timothy M. Koller. These articles consider hedging part of an overall strategy and they arrive at some interesting conclusions.

Foreign exchange risk is dangerous; it is expensive and should not be ignored. The "do nothing" alternative is an option only if it is a conscious decision, rather than "I thought someone else was going to do it" or the regular dealer was off sick that day. There are many and various techniques to use and a working knowledge of these will always be beneficial, even if the company has not yet got a mandate to use them. Remember the saying: "time spent in reconnaissance is never lost."

■ ■ ■

*'The power of a
computer occupying
a large room in 1960
was contained within
a 386 PC by 1990.'*

Technology and the Markets

DAVID JOYCE

Applications Marketing Manager
UK and Ireland, Reuters plc

Introduction

The Position Today

The Instruments Traded

Systems Arbitrage

Internet

Conclusion

Introduction

Technology and the markets have always gone hand in hand. The process began in the 1850s, with the laying of the first cross-channel telegraph cable to the continent. Paul Julius Reuter used this to transmit share prices between London and Paris. Previously he had used carrier pigeons. Embracing this new technology began a trend of inseparable involvement between the financial markets and technology.

Since then markets have always been quick to take advantage of advances in technology, and particularly information technology. And the pace of change has never been faster than in the past few years. Occasionally, of course, changes in government policy and regulations have also lent a hand to change. To give some feel for this recent increase in the rate of change, the following potted history may help.

1964   Reuters launched Stockmaster, the world's first computerized financial information retrieval system. The user typed in a short code for a stock and its price appeared, glowing on the end of three light bulbs. It looks extremely primitive now.

1971   The Bretton Woods agreement signaled the end of the fixed exchange rate mechanisms for the major industrialized nations. Floating exchange rates meant competing dealers quoting prices for various currencies: the birth of the foreign exchange markets.

1973   Reuters launched the Monitor service, the first desktop screen-based information service for the FX and money markets, displaying news and information contributed by the same dealers watching the data: a major advance in market transparency.

1986   Big Bang. Electronic trading arrived in London, with shares traded via computers away from the Stock Exchange floor.

Photographs of FX dealing rooms prior to 1973 and the introduction of Monitor show a tangle of telephones and cables – the only means by which dealers could keep in touch with one another's prices. After 1973 dealing rooms took on a slightly more orderly appearance, as the excessive reliance on telephones diminished.

After Monitor's launch, there was a proliferation of companies offering screen-based information services: Telerate, Knight Ridder, Bloomberg, Quick, ADP, and many others around the world.

The Position Today

Between and around the dates mentioned above, technology has developed dramatically. The power of a computer occupying a large room in

1960 sat within a 386 PC in 1990. And the shift in emphasis from mainframe computing to personal computers has been inexorable since the first IBM PC in the early 1980s. Since 1990, PCs have roughly doubled in computing power every two years, while their storage capacity has increased by 60 percent a year. The rapid increase in cheap computing power has brought computers to almost every desk in the City of London and other office environments.

Modern dealing rooms rely heavily on the most up-to-date information technology. Dealing rooms the size of football pitches, with perhaps 1,000 dealers, could not be built without massive investment in technology. This (more or less integrated) technology allows dealers to watch markets, perform analytical calculations, contribute prices, and, most important of all, execute profitable trades (it is to be hoped). There are also secure electronic dealing services operated by the likes of EBS and Reuters, offering dealing networks, where FX and money market deals can be agreed through electronic conversations rather than over the phone. This has been extended to electronic broking, in both the money markets and soon the UK equity market, with the introduction of Sequence 6. Counterparties enter their bids and offers into these systems, and when prices match deals are executed automatically.

The Instruments Traded

The range of financial instruments has grown dramatically, too. In the early 1970s the choice was somewhat limited: foreign exchange, shares, bonds, commodity futures. Now we have a bewildering range of instruments: futures, options, FRAs, caps, floors, swaps, etc on every conceivable market. It is in derivatives particularly, then, where there has been huge growth, in both the number of types of derivatives traded and their traded volumes. Figure 17.1 shows the explosive growth in interest rate swap trading since 1988. This growth seems unlikely to slow greatly in the foreseeable future, with figures for the first half of 1995 showing a 22 percent increase over 1994. Possibly the only dampener on this phenomenal growth rate is the prospect of a widely adopted single European currency, which seems somewhat remote at present.

The increasing power of computers has pushed out the boundaries of what is possible in the markets, in terms of both trading methods and the types of instruments traded. In April 1973 the first traded options were dealt on the Chicago Board Options Exchange (CBOE) in the US. Shortly after, Fisher Black and Myron Scholes developed their seminal option pricing model. Few people then had ready access to the computing power to perform these calculations for traded options. Now, the most basic of PCs

Fig 17.1 **Outstanding notional principal in interest rate swaps (all currencies), US dollar equivalent (billions).**

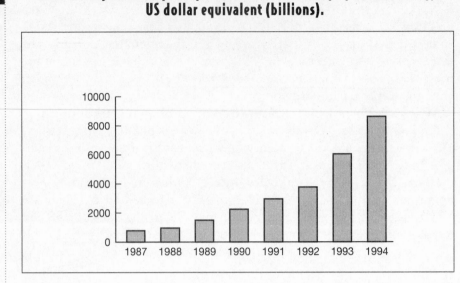

Source: ISDA

can perform many such calculations each second. Mathematical models have increased in sophistication, with a consequent demand for more computer power. With each advance in one comes an advance in the other.

And just as advances in computing power have enabled financial engineers to create and price ever more exotic financial instruments, the need to measure the values of these instruments has grown. And their riskiness as well. It's all very well trading a wide range of instruments and holding them in a portfolio, but it is essential (and increasingly these days compulsory) to have a clear idea of the *risk* the portfolio contains. In recent years this has fueled the spread of technology not just into the front office (dealing room) and back office (settlements area), but the relatively new *middle office*. This is where much risk management takes place. This involves the identification of risk, its measurement, and identifying the actions needed to reduce risk.

Futures and options are the commonest exchange-traded derivatives and, as well as being risky instruments in their own right, in certain cases they are also used to reduce risk. They undoubtedly represent a double-edged sword, however, especially when combined with powerful computers. Take the case of the crash in 1987. Briefly, the US share market started to decline. Many fund managers holding large quantities of shares employed *program trades*, automatic computer-generated trades triggered by changes in share indices, such as the Dow Jones Industrial Average. The fall in the index triggered short selling of index futures in order to hedge the risk of further falls. This drove down the price of the futures. The relationship between the index and the index futures being highly correlated, this drove down the prices of the shares in the equity market still further. The effect of this was to trigger more program trades to short the futures, causing futures prices to fall again, and equities to follow suit. And so it continued, creating a downward spiral which became the crash. Technology took the blame, of course. Although "circuit breakers" now exist on the floors of the derivatives exchanges to prevent another such occurrence, the fear remains that it could happen again.

Systems Arbitrage

The pinnacle of this reliance on technology is reached in so-called systems arbitrage. There are many models and systems offered in the financial software marketplace to price the myriad of different instruments in existence. Although probably apocryphal, there are rumors of the bigger trading houses having many of these systems working side by side, producing theoretical prices. From time to time the systems may throw out radically different results for the price of the same instrument. If the house knows that Bank A uses such a model and Bank B another, the potential exists to buy the instrument from one of these banks and sell it to the other, the result being instant arbitrage profits.

Internet

Finally, no discussion of technology and the markets would be complete without mention of the Internet, the worldwide linking of computers, databases, and networks. This cheap but simple and extremely popular method of distributing information is proving very useful. Many financial organizations use it as a marketing tool; others to distribute real-time market rates, competing with the networks and display applications of the traditional data vendors, such as Reuters and Telerate. The vendors themselves, however, are not lagging in embracing this new technology, either. They all have their "Web sites," advertising products and new initiatives. The future looks even brighter for Web crawlers with the introduction of Java, which offers the facility for Internet users to download software as well as data. The only fly in the ointment seems to be Internet security. Financial information, such as credit card numbers, is notoriously difficult to protect against fraud, particularly in such an open environment as the Internet. And viruses are easily spread, as users download files by the million around the world, assisting in the spread of the viruses, which can destroy data and software. Despite these drawbacks, however, it is certain that the financial markets will take full advantage of this latest technology, too.

Conclusion

The future looks very interesting, then, as technology like the Internet and PCs themselves become cheaper, more powerful, and more common in the home as well as the office and trading room.

APPENDIX ONE

Central Bank Contributors to the 1992–1995 BIS Survey

The following is a list of the official monetary institutions which conducted national exchange market surveys, and to which requests for copies of the BIS report should be addressed, rather than to the BIS. Queries about the contents of the survey may be made to the BIS. The telephone numbers are prefaced by the relevant country and area codes.

Australia	Reserve Bank of Australia	(+61 2) 5518402
Austria	Österreichische Nationalbank	(+43 1) 40420-3006
Bahrain	Bahrain Monetary Agency	(+973) 535535
Belgium	Banque Nationale de Belgique	(+32 2) 2212057
Canada	Bank of Canada	(+1613) 7828168
Denmark	Danmarks Nationalbank	(+45 33) 141411-3110
Finland	Suomen Pankki – Finlands Bank	(+358 0) 183 2324
France	Banque de France	(+33 1) 42923168
Germany	Deutsche Bundesbank	(+49 69) 9566-2334
Greece	Bank of Greece	(+30 1) 3232042
Hong Kong	Hong Kong Monetary Authority	(+852) 28781657
Ireland	Central Bank of Ireland	(+353 1) 6716666-341
Italy	Ufficio Italiano dei Cambi	(+39 6) 46631
Japan	Bank of Japan	(+81 3) 32791111
Luxembourg	Institut Monétaire Luxembourgeois	(+352 1) 402929
Netherlands	De Nederlandsche Bank	(+31 20) 5243500
New Zealand	Reserve Bank of New Zealand	(+64 4) 4722029
Norway	Norges Bank	(+47 22) 316173
Portugal	Banco de Portugal	(+351 1) 3462931
Singapore	Monetary Authority of Singapore	(+65) 2299626
South Africa	South African Reserve Bank	(+27 12) 3133641
Spain	Banco de España	(+34 1) 3385000
Sweden	Sveriges Riksbank	(+46 8) 7870131
Switzerland	Schweizerische Nationalbank	(+41 1) 6313311
United Kingdom	Bank of England	(+44 171) 6014444
United States	Federal Reserve Bank of New York	(+ 1 212) 7205000

Bank for International Settlements		(+41 61) 2808080

Source: BIS

APPENDIX TWO
SWIFT Currency Codes

SWIFT is the bank-owned cooperative supplying secure messaging services and interface software to over 5,200 financial institutions in 135 countries. Over 600 million messages were carried on the SWIFT network in 1995, with an average daily value for the combined payment messages on the network estimated at over USD2 trillion.

Currency codes from Afghanistan to Zimbabwe
This list shows the codes for the representation of currencies and funds by ALPHABETICAL ORDER OF THE COUNTRY NAME.

Country	Currency	Code
Afghanistan	Afghani	AFA
Albania	Lek	ALL
Algeria	Algerian dinar	DZD
American Samoa	US dollar	USD
Andorra	Andorran peseta	ADP
Andorra	Spanish peseta	ESP
Andorra	French franc	FRF
Angola	New kwanza	AON
Angola	Kwanza reajustado	AOR
Anguilla	East Caribbean dollar	XCD
Antigua and Barbuda	East Caribbean dollar	XCD
Argentina	Argentine peso	ARS
Armenia	Armenian dram	AMD
Aruba	Aruban guilder	AWG
Australia	Australian dollar	AUD
Austria	Schilling	ATS
Azerbaijan	Azerbaijanian manat	AZM
Bahamas	Bahamian dollar	BSD
Bahrain	Bahraini dinar	BHD
Bangladesh	Taka	BDT
Barbados	Barbados dollar	BBD
Belarus	Belarussian ruble	BYB
Belgium	Belgian franc	BEF
Belize	Belize dollar	BZD
Benin	CFA franc BCEAO	XOF
Bermuda	Bermudian dollar	BMD
Bhutan	Ngultrum	BTN
Bhutan	Indian rupee	INR
Boliva	Boliviano	BOB
Boliva	Mvdol	BOV
Bosnia-Herzegovina	Dinar	BAD
Botswana	Pula	BWP
Bouvet Island	Norwegian krone	NOK
Brazil	Brazilian real	BRL

British Indian Ocean Territory	US dollar	USD
Brunei Darussalam	Brunei dollar	BND
Bulgaria	Lev	BGL
Burkina Faso	CFA franc BCEAO	XOF
Burundi	Burundi franc	BIF
Cambodia	Riel	KHR
Cameroon	CFA franc BEAC	XAF
Canada	Canadian dollar	CAD
Cape Verde	Cape Verde escudo	CVE
Cayman Islands	Cayman Islands dollar	KYD
Central African Republic	CFA franc BEAC	XAF
Chad	CFA franc BEAC	XAF
Chile	Unidades De Formento	CLF
Chile	Chilean peso	CLP
China	Yuan renminbi	CNY
Christmas Island	Australian dollar	AUD
Cocos (Keeling) Islands	Australian dollar	AUD
Colombia	Colombian peso	COP
Comoros	Comoro franc	KMF
Congo	CFA franc BEAC	XAF
Cook Islands	New Zealand dollar	NZD
Costa Rica	Costa Rican colon	CRC
Côte d'Ivoire	CFA franc BCEAO	XOF
Croatia	Kuna	HRK
Cuba	Cuban peso	CUP
Cyprus	Cyprus pound	CYP
Czech Republic	Czech koruna	CZK
Denmark	Danish krone	DKK
Djibouti	Djibouti franc	DJF
Dominica	East Caribbean dollar	XCD
Dominican Republic	Dominican peso	DOP
East Timor	Rupiah	IDR
East Timor	Timor escudo	TPE
Ecuador	Sucre	ECS
Ecuador	Unidad de valor constante (UVC)	ECV
Egypt	Egyptian pound	EGP
El Salvador	El Salvador colon	SVC
Equatorial Guinea	CFA franc BEAC	XAF
Estonia	Kroon	EEK
Ethiopia	Ethiopian birr	ETB
Faeroe Islands	Danish krone	DKK
Falkland Islands (Malvinas)	Falkland Islands pound	FKP
Fiji	Fiji dollar	FJD
Finland	Markka	FIM
France	French franc	FRF
French Guiana	French franc	FRF
French Polynesia	CFP franc	XPF
French Southern Territories	French franc	FRF
Gabon	CFA franc BEAC	XAF
Gambia	Dalasi	GMD
Georgia	Lari	GEL
Germany	Deutsche Mark	DEM
Ghana	Cedi	GHC
Gibraltar	Gibraltar pound	GIP
Greece	Drachma	GRD
Greenland	Danish krone	DKK
Grenada	East Caribbean dollar	XCD

Guadeloupe	French franc	FRF
Guam	US dollar	USD
Guatemala	Quetzal	GTQ
Guernsey, C I	Pound sterling	GBP
Guinea	Guinea franc	GNF
Guinea-Bissau	Guinea-Bissau peso	GWP
Guyana	Guyana dollar	GYD
Haiti	Gourde	HTG
Haiti	US dollar	USD
Heard and McDonald Islands	Australian dollar	AUD
Honduras	Lempira	HNL
Hong Kong	Hong Kong dollar	HKD
Hungary	Forint	HUF
Iceland	Iceland krona	ISK
India	Indian rupee	INR
Indonesia	Rupiah	IDR
Iran (Islamic Republic of)	Iranian rial	IRR
Iraq	Iraqi dinar	IQD
Ireland	Irish pound	IEP
Isle of Man	Pound sterling	GBP
Israel	Shekel	ILS
Italy	Italian lira	ITL
Jamaica	Jamaican dollar	JMD
Japan	Yen	JPY
Jersey, C I	Pound sterling	GBP
Jordan	Jordanian dollar	JOD
Kazakhstan	Tenge	KZT
Kenya	Kenyan shilling	KES
Kiribati	Australian dollar	AUD
Korea, Democratic People's Rep of	North Korean won	KPW
Korea, Republic of	Won	KRW
Kuwait	Kuwaiti dinar	KWD
Kyrgyzstan	Som	KGS
Lao People's Democratic Republic	Kip	LAK
Latvia	Latvian lats	LVL
Lebanon	Lebanese pound	LBP
Lesotho	Loti	LSL
Lesotho	Rand	ZAR
Liberia	Liberian dollar	LRD
Libyan Arab Jamahiriya	Libyan dinar	LYD
Liechtenstein	Swiss franc	CHF
Lithuania	Lithuanian litas	LTL
Luxembourg	Belgian franc	BEF
Luxembourg	Luxembourg franc	LUF
Macau	Pataca	MOP
Macedonia, the Former Yugoslav Republ. of	Denar	MKD
Madagascar	Malagasy franc	MG F
Malawi	Kwacha	MWK
Malayia	Malaysian Ringgit	MYR
Maldives	Rufiyaa	MVR
Mali	CFA franc BCEAO	XOF
Malta	Maltese lira	MTL
Marshall Islands	US dollar	U S D
Martinique	French franc	F R F
Mauritania	Ouguiya	M R O
Mauritius	Mauritus Rupee	MUR

Mexico	Mexican nuevo peso	UXN
Micronesia (Federated States of)	US dollar	USD
Moldova, Republic of	Moldovan leu	MDL
Monaco	French franc	FRF
Mongolia	Iugrik	MNT
Montserrat	East Caribbean dollar	XCD
Morocco	Moroccan dirham	MAD
Mozambique	Metical	MZM
Myanmar	Kyat	MMK
Namibia	Namibian dollar	NAD
Namibia	Rand	ZAR
Nauru	Australian dollar	AUD
Nepal	Nepalese rupee	NPR
Netherlands Antilles	Netherlands Antillean guilder	ANG
Netherlands	Netherlands guilder	NLG
New Caledonia	CFP franc	XPF
New Zealand	New Zealand dollar	NZD
Nicaragua	Cordoba oro	NI0
Niger	CFA franc BCEAO	XOF
Nigeria	Naira	NGN
Niue	New Zealnd dollar	NZD
Norfolk Islands	Australian dollar	AUD
Northern Mariana Islands	US dollar	U S D
Norway	Norwegian krone	NOK
Oman	Rial Omani	OMR
Pakistan	Pakistan rupee	PKR
Palau	US dollar	USD
Panama	Balboa	PAB
Panama	US dollar	USD
Papua New Guinea	Kina	PGK
Paraguay	Guarani	PYG
Peru	Nuevo sol	PEN
Philippines	Philipine peso	PHP
Pitcairn	New Zealand dollar	NZD
Poland	Zloty	PLN
Poland	Zloty	PLZ
Portugal	Portugese Escudo	PTE
Puerto Rico	US dollar	USD
Qatar	Qatari rial	QAR
Reunion	French franc	FRF
Romania	Leu	ROL
Russian Federation	Russian ruble	RUR
Rwanda	Rwanda franc	RWF
Saint Kitts and Nevis	East Caribbean dollar	XCD
Saint Lucia	East Caribbean dollar	XCD
Saint Vincent and the Grenadines	East Caribbean dollar	XCD
Samoa	Tala	WST
San Marino	Italian lira	ITL
Sao Tome and Principe	Dobra	STD
Saudi Arabia	Saudi Riyal	SAR
Senegal	CFA franc BCEAO	XOF
Seychelles	Seychelles rupee	SCR
Sierra Leone	Leone	SLL
Singapore	Singapore dollar	SGD
Slovakia	Slovak koruna	SKK
Slovenia	Tolar	SIT
Solomon Islands	Solomon Islands dollar	SBD

Somalia	Somali shilling	SOS
South Africa	Rand	ZAR
Spain	Spanish peseta	ESP
Sri Lanka	Sri Lanka rupee	LKR
St Helena	St Helena pound	S H P
St Pierre and Miquelon	French franc	FRF
Sudan	Sudanese guilder	S DD
Suriname	Surinam guilder	S RG
Svalbard and Jan Mayen Islands	Norwegian krone	NOK
Swaziland	Lilangen	S Z L
Sweden	Swedish krona	S EK
Switzerland	Swiss franc	CH F
Syrian Arab Republic	Syrian pound	S Y P
Taiwan	New Taiwan dollar	TWD
Tajikistan	Tajik ruble	TJR
Tanzania, United Republic of	Tanzanian shilling	TZS
Thailand	Baht	TH B
Togo	CFA franc BCEAO	XOF
Tokelau	New Zealand dollar	NZD
Tonga	Pa'anga	TOP
Trinidad and Tobago	Trinidad and Tobago dollar	TTD
Tunisia	Tunisian diner	TND
Turkey	Turkish lira	TRL
Turkmenistan	Manat	TMM
Turks and Caicos Islands	US dollar	USD
Tuvalu	Australian dollar	AUD
U.A.E	U.A.E dirham	AED
Uganda	Uganda shilling	UGX
Ukraine	Karbovanet	UAK
United Kingdom	Pound sterling	GBP
United States	US dollar	USD
Uniter States	US dollar, next day funds	USN
United States minor outlying islands	US dollar	USD
Uruguay	Peso Uruguayo	UYU
Uzbekistan	Uzbekistan sum	UZS
Vanuatu	Vatu	VUV
Vatican City State	Italian lira	ITL
Venezuela	Bolivar	VEB
Vietnam	Dong	VND
Virgin Islands (British)	US dollar	USD
Virgin Islands (US)	US dollar	USD
Wallis and Futuna Islands	CFP franc	XPF
Western Sahara	Moroccan Dirham	MAD
Yemen	Yemeni Rial	YER
Yugoslavia	New dinar	YUM
Zaire	New Zaire	ZRN
Zambia	Kwacha	ZMK
Zimbabwe	Zimbabwe dollar	ZWD

APPENDIX THREE

The Black–Scholes Option Pricing Formula

The fair price for any financial asset is its expected value. For example, if a share had a 30% chance of achieving a price of 40, and a 70% chance of achieving a price of 50, the fair value at that time would be:

$$(0.30 \times 40) + (0.70 \times 50) = 47$$

The same principle applies to options. The fair value of an option at expiry is the sum of every possible value it could achieve multiplied by the probability of that value occurring. In the simple example given above, there were just two discrete outcomes. Options, however, can take on almost any value, so it is necessary to use continuous rather than discrete probability distributions. With a discrete distribution, the probability of a particular outcome can be measured directly from the height of the bar. For continuous distributions, the probability of a particular range of outcomes is measured by taking the area beneath that section of the curve.

From the definition of a Call option, the expected value of the option at maturity is:

$$E[C_T] = E[max\ (S_T{-}X,\ o)] \tag{A}$$

where:
$E[C_T]$ is the expected value of the Call option at maturity
S_T is the price of the underlying asset at maturity
X is the strike price of the option

There are two possible situations that can arise at maturity. If $S_T > X$, the Call option expires in the money, and $max(S_T{-}X,o,) = S_T{-}X$. If $S_T < X$, the option expires out of the money, and $max(S_T{-}X,o) = o$. If p is defined as the probability that $S_T > X$, equation (A) can be rewritten:

$$E[C_T] = p \times (E[S_T 1 S_T > X]{-}X) + (I - p) \times o$$
$$= p \times (E[S_T 1 S_T > X]{-}X) \tag{B}$$

where:

p is the probability that $S_T > X$
$E[S_T 1 S_T > X]$ is the expected value of S_T given that $S_T > X$

Equation (B) gives us an expression for the expected value of the Call at maturity. To obtain the fair price at the inception of the contract, the expression must be discounted back to its present value to obtain the following:

$$C = p \times e^{-rt} \times E[S_T 1 S_T > X]{-}X) \tag{C}$$

where:

C is the fair price for the option at inception
r is the continuously compounded riskless rate of interest
t is the length of time until maturity

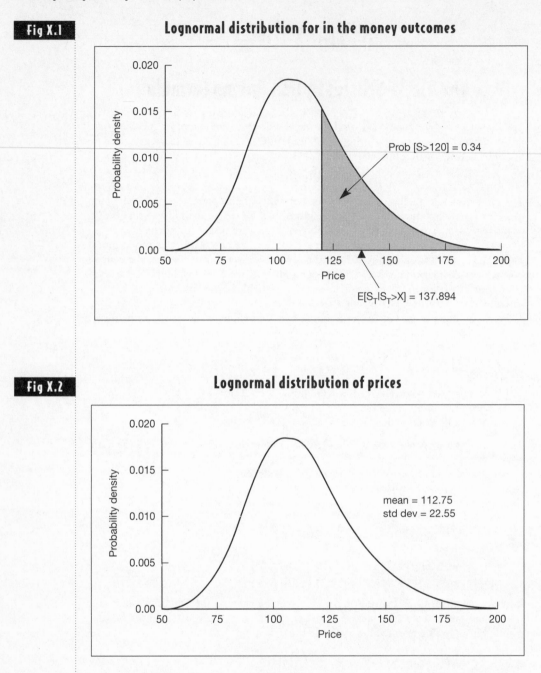

Fig X.1

Lognormal distribution for in the money outcomes

Prob [S>120] = 0.34

$E[S_T|S_T>X] = 137.894$

Fig X.2

Lognormal distribution of prices

mean = 112.75
std dev = 22.55

The problem of pricing an option has been reduced to two slightly simpler problems:

(a) determine p – the probability that the option ends in the money such that $S_T > X$

(b) determine $E[S_T 1 S_T > X]$ – the expected value of the underlying asset given that the option ends in the money

The solution for both of these problems can be found in the lognormal distribution of financial prices. Figure X.1 shows the same lognormal price distribution as that of Figure X.2, but highlights the part of the distribution for which the price exceeds 120. This will be of interest if we wish to price an option whose strike price was set at 120.

The area of the shaded part is 34% of the area under the graph as a whole, so the probability that the final price will exceed 120 is 0.34. The expected value of the shaded part is 137.894. If continuously compounded interest rates are 12%, the fair price for the option struck at 120 is:

$$C = 0.34 \times e^{-0.12} \times (137.894 - 120) = 5.40$$

This is, in fact, exactly the value of the option as suggested by the B–S model.

How were the values of 0.34 and 137.894 calculated? It is relatively straightforward to derive an expression for the probability p, but rather more difficult to do so for the expectation expression $E[S_T 1 S_T > X]$. We therefore will show here how the probability can be calculated, but not how the expectation can be derived; for the latter we will merely state the end result. Combining the two expressions will give us the formula for the B–S model itself.

Finding the probability p that the underlying price at maturity S_T will exceed some critical price X is the same as finding the probability that the return over the period will exceed some critical value r_x This is an easier problem to solve, because returns follow a normal distribution, and normal distributions are easier to work with than lognormal distributions. Remembering that returns are defined as the logarithm of the price relatives means that we must find the probability p such that:

$$p = Prob \; [S_T > X] = Prob \left[return > \ln \left(\frac{X}{S_0} \right) \right] \qquad (D)$$

where S_0 is the underlying price at the outset.

In general, the probability that a normally distributed variable x will exceed some critical value x_{crit} is given by:

$$Prob \; [x > x_{crit}] = I - N \left(\frac{x_{crit} - \mu^*}{\sigma^*} \right) \qquad (E)$$

where:

μ^* is the mean of x
σ^* is the standard deviation of x
$N(.)$ is the cumulative normal distribution

In the context of equation (D), we need to find expressions for μ^* and σ^*, the mean and standard deviation of returns. We have an expression for the expected value of the price relative S_T/S_0. This is:

$$E \left[\frac{S_t}{S_0} \right] = e^{\mu t} + \frac{\sigma^2 t}{2}$$

If we define r such that:

$$r = \mu + \frac{\sigma^2}{2} \qquad (F)$$

we can then rewrite equation 10.7 in a simpler way:

$$E \left[\frac{S_T}{S_0} \right] = e^{rt} \qquad (G)$$

The new variable r is not only a convenient shorthand for the expression $\mu + \sigma^2/2$, it is actually the continuously compounded riskless rate of interest. It may seem surprising that this is the relevant interest rate to use when valuing risky investments like options, but the answer to this conundrum lies in the risk neutrality argument.

The basis for the risk neutrality argument is the possibility of constructing a riskless portfolio combining an option with some proportion of the underlying asset. In fact, this approach is the foundation of the binomial method for option valuation. A riskless portfolio is one that has the same financial outcome regardless of events, and therefore future cash flows should be discounted at the riskless interest rate. With such a portfolio, investors' risk preferences are irrelevant, and the portfolio should be worth the same whether being valued by risk-averse or by risk-neutral investors. Since it is easier to value the portfolio at the riskless rate used by risk-neutral investors, we may as well choose the riskless rate.

Note that the risk neutrality argument does not imply that all financial assets actually do grow at the riskless rate implied by equation (G). What the argument says is that the same answer for the price of an option will be obtained whether we choose the riskless rate or some higher interest rate. If a higher rate were selected, the underlying asset would grow at a faster rate, but the payoffs from an option on this asset would also have to be discounted back at a higher rate, and the two effects cancel out.

Another way to consider this is to remember that the option price is determined in proportion to the price of the underlying asset; double both the underlying asset price and the strike price, and the option price will also double. If the underlying asset price happens to be depressed because risk-averse investors are discounting future cash flows at a particularly high rate, the price of the option will also be depressed since it is calculated in proportion, but this is just as it should be. To be consistent, the same investors should discount future cash flows from the option at the same high rate.

We now have:

$$E\left[1n\left(\frac{S_t}{S_0}\right)\right] = \mu t = \left(r - \frac{\sigma^2}{2}\right)t = \mu^* \tag{H}$$

which gives an expression for μ^*, the mean return. The standard deviation of returns is defined as $\sigma\sqrt{t}$. Combining equations (D) and (E) we now have:

$$Prob\,[S_T > X] = Prob\left[return > 1n\left(\frac{X}{S_0}\right)\right] = I - N\left(\frac{1n\left(\frac{X}{S_0}\right) - \left(r - \frac{\sigma^2}{2}\right)t}{\sigma\sqrt{t}}\right) \tag{I}$$

The symmetry of the normal distribution means that $I-N(d) = N(-d)$, so:

$$p = Prob\,[S_T > X] = N\left(\frac{1n\left(\frac{S_0}{X}\right) + \left(r - \frac{\sigma^2}{2}\right)t}{\sigma\sqrt{t}}\right) \tag{J}$$

Substituting the values in the previous example, we have:

$$Prob[S_T > X] = N\left(\frac{1n\left(\frac{100}{120}\right) + \left(0.12 - \frac{0.20^2}{2}\right) \times 1}{0.20\sqrt{I}}\right) = N(-0.4116) = 0.34$$

and this is the value for the probability p obtained before.

Finding a formula for the expression $E[S_T 1 S_T > X]$ involves integrating the normal distribution curve over the range X to ∞. When this is done, the result is:

$$E[S_T 1 S_T > X] = S_0 e^{rt} \frac{N(d_1)}{N(d_2)} \tag{K}$$

where:

$$d_1 = \frac{1n\left(\frac{S_0}{X}\right) + \left(r + \frac{\sigma^2}{2}\right)t}{\sigma\sqrt{t}} \text{ and } d_2 = \frac{1n\left(\frac{S_0}{X}\right) + \left(r - \frac{\sigma^2}{2}\right)t}{\sigma\sqrt{t}} = d_1 - \sigma\sqrt{t} \tag{L}$$

Now we have expressions for p (equation (J)) and $E[S_T 1 S_T > X]$ (equation (K)), and can insert these into equation (C) to obtain the complete formula for a Call option:

$$C = N(d_2) \times e\text{–rt} \times \left(S_0 e^{rt} \frac{N(d_1)}{N(d_2)} - X\right)$$

$$\therefore C = S_0 N(d_1) - Xe^{-rt}N(d_2) \tag{M}$$

This is the famous Black-Scholes model. It provides a single formula, which enables the fair price for a Call option to be calculated. As the foregoing derivation has demonstrated, the formula can be interpreted as measuring the expected present value of the option based on the key assumption that prices follow a lognormal distribution.

As an illustration of this, Figures X.3 and X.4 show the results of a Monte Carlo simulation. The behavior of a financial asset was simulated by a computer over 10,000 trials. In each trial, the return was sampled at random from a normal distribution with mean $\mu = 10\%$ and standard deviation $\sigma = 20\%$. If the return in a given trial turned out to be p, the price S_t after a period of time t would be given by $S_t = S_0 e^{pt}$, and the present value of the option would be $(S_t–X)/e^{-rt}$ if $S_t > X$, and 0 otherwise.

Starting always with an initial price of 100, this experiment gave rise to the distribution of prices after one year illustrated in Figure X.3. This has a mean equation 112.75 and a standard deviation of 22.77, almost exactly that predicted by equation

Distribution of underlying asset prices

Fig X.3

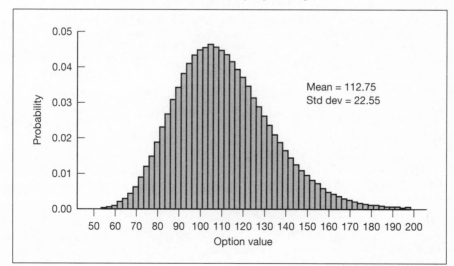

Mean = 112.75
Std dev = 22.55

Fig X.4

Distribution of option values

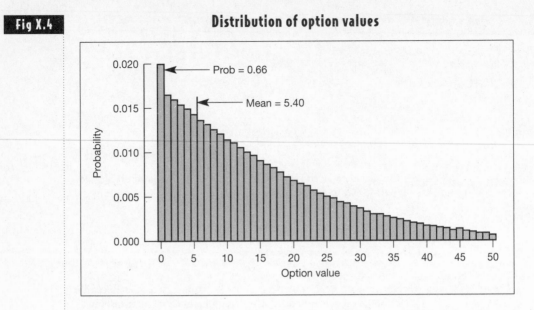

10.7 and illustrated in the theoretical distribution of Figure X.2. The probability of the underlying price being below 120 was 0.66, the same as the theoretical figure of 0.66 (1.00-0.34) predicted by equation (J).

The corresponding distribution of option prices is illustrated in Figure X.4. The option expired out of the money in 66% of the trials, while in the remainder of cases it expired in the money with values ranging from just above zero to as high as 110. The mean of this wide distribution was 5.40, exactly the price calculated using the B-S model in equation (M).

Thus, starting only with an assumption of returns which are normally distributed, and using nothing other than very simple arithmetic, the Monte Carlo simulation arrives at the same answer for the expected value of the option as the B-S model.

APPENDIX FOUR

Range of Exotic Options

Barrier type options

1. Knock-out options

The standard knock-out type option has the barrier below the spot in the case of a Call option and above in the case of a Put option.

The knock-out rate for a knock-out option is the level at which the option ceases to exist if the spot market breaches the rate during the option's life. Therefore the closer this level is placed to current spot, the cheaper the option becomes.

This gives the option some peculiar characteristics, in particular the tendency for it to have negative vega when the knock-out rate is placed close to spot, i.e. the option premium will decrease with an increase in volatility. The reason for this is that, with an increase in volatility, the probability that the option will cease to exist prematurely increases, thereby lessening its value.

Another point of interest is that the spot delta can be far in excess of 100 percent. To appreciate this consider the concept of delta. The delta is the amount of the underlying required to replicate the change in value of an option over a small move in the underlying spot market. The payoff of a knock-out option is identical with that of the European option if the barrier is not breached. Therefore if the barrier option increases in value, its characteristics will eventually become identical with the European. If the barrier knocks-out, the delta will cover the loss of premium, all other factors being equal. This characteristic is most obvious when the barrier has a longer maturity, with a large interest rate differential between the two currencies and the option is a Call on the currency with the lower interest rate.

Finally, the long-dated barrier options can have awkward interest rate sensitivities. As the spot moves close to the barrier, the sensitivity to interest rates will disappear and this can lead to difficult re-hedging conditions when taking into account transaction costs, i.e. spreads.

2. Knock-in options

This option type has a payoff identical with a combined position of a long European option and a short knock-out option with the same parameters. The net result is that there is no payout from the option unless the barrier level is breached. The closer the barrier rate is to the spot rate, the closer the premium will be to the European premium, as the likelihood of the option knocking in and becoming a European option is increased.

3. Reverse knock-out options

The reverse knock-out option is similar in mechanism to a plain knock-out option except that the barrier is set at a rate where the underlying contract would have intrinsic value when it was knocked-out. Its characteristics are such that hedging the contract becomes a very difficult proposition when it approaches its boundaries.

4. Reverse knock-in options

The reverse knock-in option is similar in mechanism to a plain knock-in option except that the barrier is set at a rate where the underlying contract would have intrinsic value when it was knocked-in. Its characteristics are such that hedging the contract becomes a very difficult proposition when it approaches its boundaries.

5. Knock-in with rebate

These option types are valid only if the strike was already in the money at inception. This rebate is paid two business days after expiry if the option does not knock-in during its life. If the option does knock-in during its life the payout will be the same as the European at expiry.

6. Knock-out with rebate

These option types are valid only if the strike was already in the money at inception. This rebate is paid two business days after expiry if the option does knock-out during its life. If the option does not knock-out during its life, the payout will be the same as the European.

7. Reverse knock-in with rebate

The rebate is paid two business days after expiry if the option does not knock-in during its life; otherwise it behaves like a reverse knock-in option.

8. Reverse knock-out with rebate

The rebate is paid two business days after expiry if the option does knock-out during its life; otherwise it behaves like a reverse knock-out option.

Average rate options

The average rate option payoff is the difference between the strike and the average spot over the period of the option. The average spot is dependent on the fixing intervals selected. These can be daily, weekly, monthly, or a specific number of days, e.g. two days. Forward start average rate options are also available. For comparison purposes the European option strip is suggested.

Digital type options

The digital option is an option that pays out a predetermined amount at expiry if the option is in the money; therefore there is a payout field. As there is no principal amount the option price is given as a premium amount rather than in currency terms (DEM/USD) or percentage (% USD).

1. One touch digital

This is a digital type option where the purchaser receives the payout two business days after expiry of the option, if the barrier is reached by the spot rate during the life of the option. Therefore there is no strike associated with this option, and up and down is displayed rather than Put/Call.

2. Instant one touch

Similar to the one touch except the payout is received two business days after the barrier has been reached by the spot rate.

3. No touch

The payout is received if the spot rate does not touch the barrier rate during the life of the option.

4. Digital knock-in

This option is a combination of a digital and a knock-out option. Therefore the payoff is the same as the digital, i.e. the payout amount is paid if the option is in the money at expiry and the barrier has been touched by the spot rate during the option's life.

5. Digital knock-out

This option is a combination of a digital and a knock-out option. Therefore the payoff is the same as the digital, i.e. the payout amount is paid if the option is in the money at expiry and the barrier has not been touched by the spot rate during the option's life.

6. Digital reverse knock-in

The reverse knock-in option is an option that pays out if at expiry the spot has reached the barrier during its life and the option is in the money. In the case of the digital reverse knock-in option, therefore, the payout amount is received or paid under the above conditions

7. Digital reverse knock-out

The reverse knock-out option is an option that pays out if at expiry the spot has not reached the barrier during its life and the option is in the money. In the case of the digital reverse knock-out option, therefore, the payout amount is received or paid under the above conditions

8. Double knock-out

This option has two barriers. If either is reached during the life of the option it ceases to exist. If the barriers are not reached the payoff is the same as a European option.

9. Double knock-in

This option has two barriers. If either is reached during the life of the option, the option exists. If the barriers are reached the payoff is the same as a European option.

10. Digital double knock-out

This option type has a fixed payout which is received if the spot rate does not breach either of the barriers during its life and the option is in the money at expiry.

11. Digital double knock-in

This option type has a fixed payout which is received if the spot rate breaches either of the barriers during its life and the option is in the money at expiry.

12. Double one touch

There is no strike associated with this option but two barriers. If either is breached during its life the payout is received two business days after expiry. As there is no strike, and spot can go in either direction to breach a barrier, there is no Put/Call or up/down described.

13. Double no touch

There is no strike associated with this option but two barriers. If either is breached during its life the option ceases to exist. If this does not happen the payout is received two business days after expiry. As there is no strike, and spot can go in either direction to breach a barrier, there is no Put/Call or up/down described.

14. Double instant one touch

There is no strike associated with this option but two barriers. If either is breached during its life the payout is received two business days after the breach has occurred. As there is no strike, and spot can go in either direction to breach a barrier, there is no Put/Call or up/down described.

APPENDIX FIVE

Codes of Conduct

Introduction

The first published code of conduct in the wholesale financial markets was written by the Committee for Professionalism of the ACI (Association Cambiste Internationale – the Financial Markets Association). It appeared in 1975 and has been revized several times since then. The latest version forms a part of this appendix. Although it is the code used in many national financial markets there are some central banks which have since developed their own national documents. The current ACI code lists 16 countries which have done this. One of these, London's "Grey Book", is also part of this appendix.

Why did the ACI and the central banks bother to write and promote codes of conduct and why should anyone bother to read them? These questions have been asked and answered very lucidly by the Federal Reserve Bank of New York[1].

"Efficient markets permit buyers and sellers to complete transactions quickly, at low transactions cost, and with minimal effect on market prices. In mature markets, such as foreign exchange or many government securities markets, dealers stand ready to quote two-way prices to wholesale and retail clients while money brokers intermediate between dealers themselves. Over time, conventions develop about, for example, quoting practices and the respective roles of brokers and dealers. Moreover, markets and therefore conventions are constantly evolving, though not necessarily in lock step. New financial products develop because of financial innovation. Advances in trading techniques allow participants to trade in new ways. International banks enter new geographic markets and may not always be aware of local conventions. Moreover, even seemingly innocuous issues create potential uncertainties. The precise roles that market participants play can get blurred at times. For example, a bank may be acting as a principal in one transaction with a customer, but as an agent for the same customer in a different transaction. That bank's fiduciary responsibilities, depending on local laws, may differ dramatically in the two transactions.

The uncertainties noted above, of which many more could be listed, potentially adversely affect the efficiency of the market. A written code of conduct that is thoughtfully written and carefully administered and maintained can be useful in reducing those uncertainties and helping to promote a robust and efficient market. It can contribute to that objective in three very important ways. First, a code may be useful in clarifying roles and responsibilities of dealers, brokers, and customers, and in so doing allow the market to operate faster while reducing potential conflicts because of uncertainties about roles. Second, the code is often part of a broader effort to promote a high level of ethical behaviour, professionalism and honest dealing. Third, a strong code of conduct may be an alternative to government regulation that could be overly burdensome and not conducive to healthy and efficient markets."

[1]Dino Kos, *Codes of Conduct: An Overview*, Federal Reserve Bank of New York, October 1995

The ACI has taken two further steps in its promotion of sound markets and professionalism. First, the ACI's Committee for Professionalism stands ready to "provide impartial and confidential advice to the parties" involved in a dispute. Secondly, more recently, the ACI's educational arm, the ACI Institute, has cooperated with Forex Association Singapore to develop an exam which is available worldwide, an exam which tests candidates' knowledge of the five major codes: London, New York, Tokyo, Singapore and the ACI. The intention is to offer a benchmark in a subject where few exist.

The crucial message being conveyed by the ACI, the central banks and senior market participants is that it is not enough for a market trader simply to make money: the end does not justify the means. There are some reasonable questions which management and central bank supervizors can ask about the means: how much risk was taken to produce a return and how sound was the conduct of the counterparties? This book contains many of the concepts that a thinking banker will need to know when answering these two questions.

The ACI Code of Conduct

Introduction

It was in January 1975 that the ACI published the first Code of Behaviour prepared by the Committee for Professionalism of Forex. Since that time the world's foreign exchange and money markets have grown considerably both in size and complexity, and whilst ethical behaviour itself does not change, this new code of conduct takes into account the many technological changes which have taken place during that time, as well as the introduction of many new financial instruments.

This code **cannot** be a "technical" paper setting out the practicalities of dealing in each and every financial instrument – such information is covered by terms and conditions relating to each instrument which have been published by various authorities.

Nor does this code attempt to deal with legal matters. It is the responsibility of management and staff to ensure that they are aware of legal requirements applicable to transactions they undertake and to operate within them.

Rather, its aim is to set out the manner and the spirit in which business should be conducted in order that the market and its participants may continue to enjoy their current reputation for high standards of professionalism, integrity and ethical conduct. This can only be achieved by the determination of all personnel involved in the market (either directly or indirectly) to act in a manner consistent with these aims. This code is therefore addressed, not only to dealers in both banks and brokers, but to the management of such institutions together with relevant operational support staff. This code should therefore be distributed to all such personnel.

It must be every dealer's ambition to be known, not only for his/her professional expertise, but also for his/her sense of fair play and high standard of ethical behaviour. It is hoped this code of conduct will help in that aim. Inevitably, due to the complexity of the many instruments which comprise today's markets, misunderstandings will occur and disputes will arise. It is essential that the management of the parties involved take prompt action to settle any dispute quickly and fairly. The chairman and members of the Committee for Professionalism are always ready to assist in resolving such disputes by giving impartial confidential advice to the parties concerned, if asked to do so.

The vast majority of disputes referred to the Committee for Professionalism arise from (a) failure of dealers to use **clear, unambiguous terminology** resulting in the parties concerned having different ideas of the amount or the currency dealt in, the value date or period, or even who bought and who sold or (b) failure of back office staff **promptly** and **accurately** to check the counterparty's confirmation.

The Committee for Professionalism **strongly** advises management, dealers and back office staff to pay particular attention, in their own interests to the above matters.

Where there are local restrictions in force or where differences exist between this code of conduct and a code of conduct or similar document issued by the regulatory authority governing the conduct of those transacting business in the financial markets in the centre for which it is responsible, the terms of the local code of conduct shall apply for transactions between institutions in that centre.

The Council of the ACI fully endorses this revised code of conduct and requests all national forex clubs to distribute copies to all relevant banks and brokers in their area for the attention of their **management, dealing and support staff**.

Responsibility for dealing activities

Control of the activities of all personnel engaged in dealing (both dealers and support staff) in both banking and broking firms is the responsibility of the management of such organisations. Management should clearly set out, in writing, the authorisations and responsibilities within which dealing (and support staff) should operate. These might include:

1. General dealing policy including reporting procedures.
2. Persons authorised to deal.
3. Instruments to be dealt in.
4. Limits on open positions, mismatch positions, counterparties, stop-loss limits etc.
5. Confirmation and settlement procedures.
6. Relationships with brokers/banks.
7. Other relevant guidance as considered appropriate.

Dealing at non-current rates

Deals at non-market rates should generally be avoided, as such practices may result in concealment of a profit or loss; in the perpetration of a fraud; **or the giving of an unauthorised extension of credit.** Where, however, the use of non-current market rates may be necessary (as in the swaps market or in certain transactions with corporate clients), they should only be entered into with the prior express permission of senior management, who should ensure that proper controls are in place for the monitoring and reporting of such transactions to avoid the above mentioned problems. **Cash flow implications should be taken into account in the pricing. Spot rates should be fixed immediately within the current spread, to reflect current rates at the time the transaction was done.**

After-hours dealing

Dealing after normal local hours, particularly from premises other than banks' dealing rooms, should only be undertaken with the prior permission of management, who should issue guidelines to their staff on the extent of such dealing (**including names of persons authorised to deal**) and arrangements for the prompt recording and confirmation of such deals.

Position parking

Management should not allow the parking of deals or positions with a counterparty and with the understanding to repatriate these dealing positions at a given moment and at historical rates.

Stop-loss orders

The terms under which such orders are accepted should be explicitly identified and agreed between the parties concerned and be within any management criteria on such orders. Any dealer handling such an order must have adequate lines of communication with the counterparty for use in the event of an extreme price/rate movement or other unusual situation.

Dealing for personal account

Management should consider carefully whether their employees should be allowed to trade for their own account in any of the instruments covered by this Code. Where this is allowed, it is the responsibility of management to ensure that adequate safeguards are established to prevent abuse. These safeguards should reflect the need to prevent insider dealing in any form, and to ensure that no action is taken by employees which might affect the interest of the firm's customers, **or the institution itself.** Whether a dealer is allowed to deal for his own account is first a matter of local regulations and internal matters of the bank. If however dealing for own account is allowed, then, clear written procedures should cover transactions on behalf of their family, other members of the personnel, management included.

Taping

Experience has shown that recourse to tapes proves invaluable to the speedy resolution of differences. The use of recording equipment in the offices of banks and brokers is strongly recommended. All conversations undertaken by dealers and brokers should be recorded together with back office telephone lines used by those responsible for confirming deals or passing payment or other instructions.

When initially installing tape equipment or taking on new clients or counterparties, firms should take steps to inform their counterparties and clients that conversations will be recorded. Tapes should be kept for at least two months. Firms engaged in dealing in longer term interest rate swaps, forward rate agreements or similar instruments where errors may only be found on the date that the first movement of funds is due to take place, may consider it prudent to retain tapes relevant to these transactions for longer periods. Management should ensure that access to tapes, whether in use or in store, is strictly controlled so that they cannot be tampered with.

Entertainment, gifts and gambling

Neither management nor employees should offer inducements to conduct business, or solicit them from the personnel of other institutions. However, it is recognised that gifts and entertainment may be offered in the normal course of business; such gifts or entertainment should not be excessive in value or frequency.

Management should formulate policies in this area which include guidance on the provision and receipt of entertainment and gifts by staff including what may or may not be offered or accepted, together with procedures for dealing with gifts judged to be excessive which cannot be declined without causing offence.

Similar guidelines should be established on gambling with other market participants.

All these activities carry obvious dangers, and where allowed at all, it is strongly recommended that they are tightly controlled. Traders should not be allowed to receive commissions from brokers. Traders must inform Senior Management of any attempt by a brokering firm to break the set rules.

Abused substances (including drugs and alcohol)

Management should take all reasonable steps to educate themselves and their staff about possible signs and effects of the use of drugs and other abused substances.

Any members of staff dependent on such substances are likely to be vulnerable to outside inducement to conduct business not necessarily in the best interests of the firm or the market generally.

Confidentiality

Confidentiality is essential for the preservation of a reputable and efficient market place. Dealers and brokers share equal responsibility for maintaining confidentiality and without explicit permission **from the parties involved,** they should not disclose or discuss any information relating to deals transacted or in the process of being arranged except to or with the counterparties involved.

Care should be taken over the use of open loud-speakers to ensure that no breaches of confidentiality occur.

Individual dealers or brokers should not visit each other's dealing rooms except with the express permission of the management of both parties. Dealers should not deal from within a broker's office nor should brokers arrange deals from outside their own offices. A dealer should not place an order with a broker to find out the name of a counterparty in order to make direct contact to conclude the deal.

Dealing procedures

Both dealers and brokers should state clearly at the outset, prior to a transaction being executed, any qualifying conditions to which it will be subject. These include: where a price is quoted subject to the necessary credit approval; finding a counter-party for matching deals, or the ability to execute an associated transaction. For instance, a dealer may quote a rate which is "firm subject to the execution of a hedging transaction". If a dealer's ability to conclude a transaction is constrained by other factors, for example, opening hours in other centres, this should be made known to brokers and potential counterparties at an early stage and before names are exchanged.

Firmness of quotation

All market participants, whether acting as principal, agent or broker, have a duty to make absolutely clear whether the prices they are quoting are firm or merely indicative. Prices quoted by brokers should be taken to be firm in marketable amounts unless otherwise qualified.

A dealer quoting a firm price (or rate), either through a broker or directly to a potential counterparty, is committed to deal at that price (or rate) in a marketable amount provided the counterparty's name is acceptable.

When dealing in fast moving markets (like spot forex or currency options) a dealer has to assume that a price given to a broker is good only for a short length of time – typically a matter of seconds. However, this practice would offer room for misunder-standings about how quickly a price is deemed to lapse if adopted when dealing in generally less hectic markets, for example forward foreign exchange or deposit markets or when market conditions are relatively quiet. Since dealers have prime responsibility for prices put to a broker, the onus is on dealers in such circumstances to satisfy themselves that their prices have been taken off unless a time limit is placed by the dealer on his interest at the outset (e.g. firm for one minute only). Otherwise, the dealer should feel bound to deal with an acceptable name at the quoted rate in a marketable amount.

For their part, brokers should make every effort to assist dealers by checking with them from time to time whether their interest at a particular price or rate is still current. What constitutes a marketable amount varies from market to market, but will generally be familiar to those operating in that market. A broker, if quoting on the basis of small amounts or particular names, should qualify the quotation accordingly. Where dealers are proposing to deal in unfamiliar markets through a broker, it is recommended that they first ask brokers what amounts are sufficient to validate normal quotations. If their interest is in a smaller amount, this should be specified by the dealer when initially requesting or offering a price to the broker.

In the swap market, considerable use is made of "indicative interest" quotations. When arranging a swap an unconditional firm rate will only be given where a principal deals directly with a client or when such a principal has received the name of a client from a broker. A principal who quotes a rate or spread as "firm subject to credit" is bound to deal at the quoted rate or spread if the name is consistent with a category of counterparty previously identified for this purpose. The only exception is where the particular name cannot be done, for example if the principal has reached its credit limit for that name in which case the principal will correctly reject the transaction. It is not an acceptable practice for a principal to revise a rate which was "firm subject to credit" once the name of the counterparty has been disclosed. Brokers and principals should work together to establish a range of institutions for whom the principal's rate is firm subject to credit.

Concluding a deal

Dealers should regard themselves as bound to a deal once the price and any other key commercial terms have been agreed. However, holding brokers unreasonably to a price is viewed as unprofessional and should be discouraged by management.

Where prices quoted are qualified as being indicative or subject to negotiation of commercial terms, dealers should normally treat themselves as bound to a deal at the point where the terms have been agreed without qualification. Verbal agreements are considered binding, the subsequent confirmation is regarded as evidence of the deal, but should not override terms agreed verbally. The practice of making a transaction "subject to documentation" is not regarded as good practice. In order to minimise the likelihood of disputes arising once documentation is prepared, firms should make every effort to agree all material points quickly during the verbal negotiation of terms and should agree any remaining details as soon as possible thereafter.

Where brokers are involved, it is their responsibility to ensure the principal providing the price or rate is made aware immediately it has been dealt upon. As a general rule, a deal should only be regarded as having been "done" where the broker's contact is positively acknowledged by the dealer A broker should never assume a deal is done without some form of verbal acknowledgement from the dealer. Where a broker puts a specific proposition to a dealer for a price (e.g. specifying an amount and a name for which the quote is required), the dealer can reasonably expect to be told almost immediately by the broker whether the price has been hit or not.

Passing of names by brokers

Brokers should not divulge the names of principals prematurely, and certainly not until satisfied that both sides display a serious intention to transact. Principals and brokers should, at all times, treat the details of transactions as absolutely confidential to the parties involved.

Bank dealers should, wherever possible, give brokers prior indication of counterparties with whom, for whatever reason, they would be unwilling to do business (referring as necessary to particular markets or instruments). At the same time, brokers should take full account of the best interests and any precise instructions of the client. In some instruments, dealers may also wish to give brokers guidance on the extent of their price differentiation across broad categories of counterparties.

In all transactions, brokers should aim to achieve a mutual and immediate exchange of names. However, this will not always be possible. There will be times when one principal's name proves unacceptable to another; and the broker will quite properly decline to divulge by whom it was refused. This may sometimes result in the principal whose name has been rejected, feeling that the broker may in fact have quoted a price or rate which it could not in fact substantiate. In certain centres, in such cases, either the Central Bank or some other neutral body, may be prepared to establish with the reluctant counterparty that it did have business to do at the quoted price and the reasons why the name was turned down, so that the aggrieved party can be assured the original quote was valid without of course, revealing the proposed counterparty's name.

In the deposit markets, it is accepted that principals dealing through a broker have the right to turn down a name wishing to take deposits: this could therefore require pre-disclosure of the name before closing the deal. Once a lender (or buyer) has asked the key question "Who pays?' or "Whose paper is it?" it is considered committed to do business at the price quoted with that name or with an alternative acceptable name if offered immediately. The name of a lender (or buyer in respect of CDs) shall be disclosed only after the borrower's (or issuer's) name has been accepted by the lender (or buyer).

The proposed borrower may decline the lender's name a) when, in the case of "short date" deposits, he (the borrower) is not prepared to repay the deposit prior to advice of receipt of the funds from his correspondent bank or b) when he has no "lending line" for the placer of the funds and does not wish to be embarrassed by being unable to reciprocate.

Additionally, in the case of instruments like CDs, where the seller may not be the same entity as the issuer, the broker shall first disclose the issuer's name to the potential buyer. Once a buyer has asked "Whose paper is it?", the buyer is considered committed to deal at the price quoted. Once the buyer asks "Who sells?", it is considered committed to deal with that particular seller in question (or an alternative acceptable name so long as this name is immediately shown to the buyer by the broker). The name of the buyer shall be disclosed only after the seller's name has been accepted by the buyer. The seller has the right to refuse the particular buyer so long as it is prepared to accept, at that time, sums up to the same amount and at the same price from an alternative acceptable name immediately shown to it by the broker.

Name substitution or switching by brokers

In spot exchange, brokers typically do not reveal the names of counterparties until the amount and exchange rate are agreed upon. It is therefore possible that, after these details are agreed, the name of one counterparty may prove unacceptable to the other due to the unavailability of a credit line. In these circumstances, it is accepted market practice that brokers will attempt to substitute a third name to stand between the two original counterparties to clear the transaction. Because the two offsetting transactions will utilise credit and because they are often executed at an exchange rate that is off-market due to the time it takes to arrange name substitution, such activities should be identified as switching transactions and they should be monitored and controlled. If requested by a broker to clear a transaction through name switching, a dealer must ensure that such activities have the prior approval of senior management, that he or she has the authority to switch names and that any such transactions are executed within policy guidelines. Finally, a dealer must not seek nor accept favours from the broker for switching names.

Payments/settlement instructions

Instructions should be passed as quickly as possible to facilitate prompt settlement. The use of standardised payment instructions between counterparties who trade regularly with each other is recommended as their use can make a significant contribution to reducing both the incidence and size of differences arising from the mistaken settlement of funds.

In some foreign exchange and currency deposit markets, it is not customary for brokers to pass payment instructions where both counterparties are based in the same country as the broker, but the counterparties themselves must exchange instructions without delay.

Whether dealing direct or through a broker, principals should ensure that alterations to original payment instructions, including the paying agent where this has been specifically requested, should be immediately notified to the counterparty, and where a broker has been used and at least one of the principals is in another country, to the broker also. This notification should be supported by written, telex or similar confirmation of the new instructions, receipt of which should be acknowledged by the counterparty concerned. Failure to inform the broker of a change in instructions could clearly place the liability for any ensuing difference with the principal.

Monday morning trading

Trades, whether direct or via a broker, transacted prior to 5.00 am Sydney time, are done so in conditions that are not considered to be normal market-conditions or market hours. Thus the official range in currency markets will be set from 5.00 am Sydney time on Monday morning all year round.

Confirmation procedures

Verbal deal checks

Many dealers now request regular verbal or telex deal checks from brokers (or from other banks with whom they regularly deal by telephone) prior to the exchange and checking of a written or electronically dispatched confirmation. Their use can be an important means of helping to reduce the number and size of differences, particularly when dealing through brokers or for deals involving foreign counterparties. The practice of intra-day deal checks is strongly recommended by the Committee for Professionalism. It is for each firm to agree with their brokers (or counterparties) whether or not it wishes to be provided with this service, and if so, how many such checks a day it requires. If a single check is thought to be sufficient, this should be undertaken towards or at the end of the trading day. As a matter of common sense, the broker (or counterparty) should always obtain acknowledgement from a dealer on completion of the check that all the deals have been agreed or that any identified discrepancies are resolved as a matter of urgency; lack of response should not be construed as acknowledgement.

Confirmation (written or electronic)

Confirmations (whether mailed, telexed or sent by other electronic means) provide an opportunity for dealing errors to be identified and rectified with the minimum of delay and possible cost.

The issue and checking of confirmations is a back office responsibility which should be carried out independently from those who initiate deals. Confirmations must be sent out as quickly as possible (preferably by electronic means) after a deal has been done and should be addressed to the back office or settlement department of the counterparty bank.

The format and content of a confirmation will vary according to the instrument dealt in and reference should be made to any applicable Terms and Conditions published in order to ascertain the correct content and format for any particular instrument. As a minimum, however, all confirmations should include the following information:

(a) Date of transaction
(b) By which means effected (broker, phone, telex, dealing system, etc.)
(c) Name and location of counterparty
(d) Rate, amount and currency
(e) Type and side of deal
(f) Value date, maturity date and all other relevant dates (e.g. exercise date, etc.)
(g) Standard terms/conditions applicable (e.g. FRABBA, BBAIRS, ICOM, etc.)
(h) All other **important,** relevant information

Upon receipt, all confirmations must **immediately** be thoroughly checked and appropriate action taken to rectify any differences. If the counterparty's confirmation is considered incorrect, the counterparty must **immediately** be informed (preferably in writing by electronic means). A new confirmation (or written agreement to a correction) must be requested from and provided by the bank whose original confirmation was incorrect.

Any bank failing to receive a confirmation must query the matter with the back office (or the management) of the counterparty. Where transactions are arranged through a broker, the broker should send a confirmation to each counterparty.

Fraud

Attempts at fraud occur almost daily and many are meticulously planned. Great vigilance is required by all staff, particularly so when calls are received on an ordinary telephone line. It is strongly recommended that the details of all telephone deals which do not include pre-agreed standard settlement instructions, should be confirmed by telex or similar means by the recipient seeking an answer-back to ensure the deal is genuine. Particular care should be taken before paying away funds in favour of a third party.

Money laundering

All banks are reminded of the need to "know their customer" and to take all necessary steps to satisfy themselves that their transactions are not used to facilitate money laundering. As part of the international effort to combat such activities, and in particular drugs related laundering, the Central Bank governors of the Group of Ten countries endorsed, in November 1988, a statement of best practice entitled "The Basle Statement of Principles". The Group of Seven in July 1989 promoted the creation of the Financial Action Task Force (FATF) to reinforce the commitments to combat money laundering. **Firms should adopt appropriate procedures consistent with the G-10 Governor's statement and the FATF recommendations and be well aware of their legal responsibilities in this matter.** Only senior management should decide whether to undertake business with institutions dealing on behalf of clients on a discretionary management basis.

New bank holiday

In the event a country or state declares a new national bank holiday or any other occurrence which would prevent settlement of banking transactions on a specific date in the future, the following procedures should be adopted for adjusting the value date on outstanding foreign exchange transactions maturing on that date:

(a) The new value date will be the first common business day (for both currencies of the contract) following the original value date except where a bank holiday is declared on the last business day of a month, in which case the new value date will be the first common business day (for both currencies) prior to month end (ultimo).
(b) Value dates will not be split.
(c) There will be no adjustment of the exchange rate on outstanding contracts.

Terms and documentation

Documentation should be completed and exchanged as soon as possible after a deal is done, and the use, wherever possible, of standard terms and conditions to facilitate this process is recommended. Standard terms and conditions have been issued by various authorities for many instruments.

When using such agreements, any proposed modifications or choices offered in the agreement must clearly be stated before dealing. When trading any of the products covered by this Code of Conduct, dealers and brokers should make it clear whether or not they propose to use standard terms and where changes are proposed, these should also be made clear. For instruments where standard terms do not exist, particular care and attention should be paid to negotiation of terms and documentation.

In more complex transactions like swaps, dealers should regard themselves as bound to deal at the point where the commercial terms of the transaction are agreed. Making swap transactions "subject to agreement on documentation" is considered bad practice. Every effort should be made to finalise documentation as quickly as possible.

Settlement of differences

If all the procedures outlined above are adhered to, the incidence and size of differences should be reduced: and those mistakes which do occur should be identified and corrected promptly. Nevertheless, mistakes and disputes will arise from time to time, both between two banks when dealing direct with each other or between a bank and a broker. As stated in the introduction, disputes should be routinely referred to senior management for resolution, thereby transforming the dispute from an individual trader to trader or trader to broker issue to an inter-institutional issue.

Where a dispute involves the amount, currency, value date(s), (or any other factor which means that one of the two parties concerned has an "open" or "unmatched" position), it is **strongly recommended** that action should immediately be taken by one of the parties concerned (preferably with the agreement of the other) to "square off" or "neutralise" the position.

Such action shall be seen as an act of prudence to eliminate the risk of further loss resulting from the dispute and shall not be construed as an admission of liability by that party.

On the subject of the settlement of differences by "points" the Committee for Professionalism reiterates its views as follows:

"The Committee for Professionalism recognises that the worldwide foreign exchange markets function smoothly and efficiently with a minimum of official regulation, and is of the opinion that it is in the best interests of all members of our profession to promote and support any market practices, which continue this tradition. The CFP has come to the conclusion that is **not in favour of the settlement of differences by points,** but recognises that in those financial centres where the regulatory authority controls **all** the participants in that market, this practice, properly regulated by the apprehensive authority is acceptable."

The above statement has been specifically endorsed by the Council of ACI.

Commission/brokerage

In countries where brokers charges are freely negotiable, such charges should be agreed only by directors or senior management on each side and recorded in writing. Any deviation from previously agreed brokerage arrangements should be expressly approved by both parties and clearly recorded in writing.

Brokers normally quote dealing prices excluding commission/brokerage charges.

Market terminology

Management should ensure that individual brokers and dealers are aware of their responsibility to act professionally at all times, and as part of this, to use **clear unambiguous terminology.**

The use of clear language is in the interests of all concerned. Management should ensure internal procedures (including retraining if necessary) exist and are monitored to alert individual dealers and brokers who act in different markets (or move from one market to another) to any differences in terminology between markets, and to the possibility that any particular term could be misinterpreted. The use of generally accepted concise terminology is undoubtedly helpful. In those markets where standard terms and conditions have been published individual dealers and brokers should familiarise themselves with the definitions they contain.

The London Code of Conduct

I Introduction

Aims

1 London financial markets have a long-established reputation for their high degree of professionalism and the maintenance of the highest standards of business conduct. All those operating in these markets share a common interest in their health and in maintaining the established exacting standards.

2 The Code is applicable to most wholesale market dealings which are not regulated by the rules of a recognised investment exchange. These typically form part of "treasury"operations and are undertaken in large amounts. A full list of the products covered and the appropriate size criteria are shown in the box overleaf.

3 The Bank of England (the Bank) wishes to sustain the efficient functioning of the London wholesale markets in which these products are traded and to avoid over-burdensome regulation; and believes that this Code is consistent with these objectives.

4 The Code has been developed in close consultation with market practitioners and will continue to be kept under regular review. A fuller description of the Bank's regulatory arrangements covering the wholesale markets, of which this Code is an integral part, is set out in the "Grey Paper" (The regulation of the wholesale markets in sterling, foreign exchange and bullion) available from the Wholesale Markets Supervision Division of the Bank of England.

5 The Code sets out the general standards and controls which the management and individuals at broking firms (including electronic broking firms) and **"core principles"** (banks, building societies plus financial institutions authorised under the Financial Services Act 1986) should adopt when transacting business in the relevant financial products. Furthermore, the Chartered Institute of Public Finance and Accountancy and the Association of Corporate Treasurers commend the Code to their members, which also deal as principal in these markets, as best practice, to which they, too, should adhere.

Distribution

6 It is the responsibility of broking firms/core principals to seek to establish whether their UK based clients/counterparties have a copy of the Code. If they do not, they should send them one or advise them to contact the Bank direct. Where relevant, local authorities plus other institutions and companies in the UK are encouraged to adopt a similar approach.

7 The Bank will seek to make as many as possible **overseas based** firms aware that their wholesale market deals in the London market are undertaken in accordance with the London Code. If broking firms or core principals receive any questions from overseas based firms about their wholesale market deals they should, where appropriate, make them aware of the Code's existence; and that copies can be obtained from the Bank. Non-core principals are encouraged to adopt a similar approach.

Compliance and complaints

8 Compliance with the Code is necessary to ensure that the highest standards of integrity and fair dealing continue to be observed throughout these markets. Breaches by those institutions which they supervise will be viewed most seriously by the Bank and by the Building Societies Commission; any such breaches may be reflected in their assessment of the fitness and propriety of these institutions. In addition, the Securities and Investments Board and the UK Self-Regulating Organisations expect those core principals which they supervise to abide by the Code when dealing in the wholesale markets.

9 If any principal (core or non-core) or broking firm believes that an institution supervised by the Bank has breached either the letter or the spirit of the Code in respect of any wholesale market transaction in which it is involved, it is encouraged – whether or not it is itself supervised by the Bank – to seek to settle this matter amicably with the other party. If this is not possible, the institution which is subject to the complaint should make the complainant aware that it can bring the matter to the attention of the Head of Wholesale Markets Supervision Division of the Bank of England. All such complaints will be investigated by the Bank. As a general rule the Bank will seek evidence from all parties named in the complaint and will wish to discuss this in detail with management of the institution subject to the complaint.

10 Where a breach of the Code by a bank or other firm listed by the Bank under Section 43 of the Financial Services Act (FSA) – a "listed institution" – is established, and depending on how serious it is, the Bank may publicly reprimand individuals and/or the firms involved. It may also restrict a listed institution's activities or, if the breach is sufficiently serious to cast doubt on the competence of the firm or on its integrity, suspend or remove the offending firm from the list. The Bank will seek to promulgate its decisions as widely as it considers appropriate; in so doing the Bank will wish to consider the possible implications of making its findings known to others.

11 Since the compensation fund arrangements established under the FSA do not apply to any exempt business undertaken by listed institutions, if any breaches of the Code are found to have occurred, the offending institution will be expected to consider making appropriate redress to any damaged party or parties, bearing in mind any legal implications of so doing.

Arbitration

12 In order to help resolve differences the Bank is willing, if asked, to arbitrate in disputes between firms it supervises. These arrangements are set out in more detail in paragraph 120.

Products covered by The Bank's wholesale markets arrangements

A: Cash market products
1 Sterling wholesale deposits.
2 Foreign currency wholesale deposits.
3 Gold and silver bullion wholesale deposits.
4 Spot and forward foreign exchange.
5 Spot and forward gold and silver bullion.

B: Instruments which are defined as investments in the Financial Services Act but which are outside the scope of the Investment Services Directive:
6 Over the counter (OTC) options (including warrants) or futures contracts on gold or silver.

C: Instruments which are defined as investments in the Financial Services Act and are within the scope of the Investment Services Directive:

7   Certificates of deposit (CDs), or other debt instruments, issued by institutions authorised under the Banking Act 1987, European authorised institutions, and by UK building societies, with an original maturity of not more than 5 years. (This class of instrument is included in the Financial Services Act under the generic term "debenture".)

8   Bank Bills (or bankers' acceptances)*

9   Other debentures with an original maturity of not more than 1 year (including non-London CDs and commercial paper).

10 Medium-term notes issued under the Banking Act 1987 (Exempt Transactions) (Amendment) Regulations.

11 UK local authority debt (bills, bonds, loan stock or other instruments) with an original maturity of not more than 5 years.

12 Other public sector debt with an original maturity of not more than 1 year (e.g. Treasury bills but **not** gilt-edged securities).

13 Any certificate (or other instrument) representing the securities covered in items 7–12; or rights to and interests in, these instruments.

14 OTC options (including warrants) or futures contracts on any currency (including sterling); interest rate; or items 7–13 above.

15 Interest rate and currency swaps, regardless of their original maturity; forward rate agreements, or any other "contracts for differences" involving arrangements to profit (or avoid loss) by reference to movements in the value of any of the instruments in 7–13 above; or the value of any currency; or in the interest on loans in any currency.

16 Sale and repurchase agreements ("repos"), sale and buybacks and stock borrowing and lending involving debentures, loan stock or other debt instruments, including gilts, of whatever original maturity where repurchase or repayment will take place within twelve months.

Note 1 Instruments subject to the rules of a recognised investment exchange **are not** covered.

Note 2 Instruments denominated in foreign currencies, as well as in sterling **are** covered.

Note 3 Transactions by listed institutions may come within the Bank's supervisory framework even if one of the other parties to the transaction is operating abroad.

Note 4 The regulation of deposit-taking under the Banking Act 1987 is not affected in any way.

Note 5 The Government made clear in January 1988 that ordinary forward foreign exchange (and bullion) transactions fall outside the Financial Services Act; these nevertheless fall within the scope of the Bank's arrangements.

Note 6 Wholesale transactions between core principals in items 1 and 8 are not usually less than £100,000. For items 2 and 4, the usual minimum is £500,000 (or currency equivalent). For bullion (items 3 and 5), the relevant amounts are 2,000 ounces for gold and 50,000 ounces for silver.

Note 7 For items 7, 9–13, and 16, the minimum size of wholesale transactions is £100,000 (or the equivalent in foreign currency). For swaps, options, futures, forward rate agreements (FRAs) and other "contracts for differences" (items 6, 14 and 15) the minimum underlying value is £500,000 (or the equivalent in foreign currency).

* With effect from 1 January 1996, following amendment to the Financial Services Act

II General standards

Core principals and broking firms – and their employees – should at all times abide by the spirit as well as the letter of the Code when undertaking, arranging or advising on transactions in the wholesale markets.

Managers of core principals and broking firms must ensure that the obligations imposed on them and their staff by the general law are observed Management and staff should also be mindful of any relevant rules and codes of practice of other regulatory bodies.

Responsibilities

Of the principal broker

13 All firms (core principals and brokers) should ensure that they and, to the best of their ability, all other parties act in a manner consistent with the Code so as to maintain the highest reputation for the wholesale markets in London.

14 Core principals which conduct non-investment business (see the box on previous page) with private individuals should have internal procedures which set out whether these individuals will be treated as retail customers or as wholesale market participants under the arrangements set out in this Code. The procedures set out in Part IV of this Code may not be relevant, directly, to such business.

15 It is essential that all relevant staff are made familiar with the Code and conduct themselves at all times in a thoroughly professional manner. In particular they must conduct transactions in a way that is consistent with the procedures set out in Part IV of this Code.

16 All firms will be held responsible for the actions of their staff. They must:

– ensure that any individual who commits the firm to a transaction has the necessary authority to do so.

– ensure that employees are adequately trained in the practices of the markets in which they deal/broke; and are aware of their own, and their firm's, responsibilities. Inexperienced dealers should not rely on a broker, for instance, to fill gaps in their training or experience; to do so is clearly **not** the broker's responsibility.

– ensure staff are made aware of and comply with any other relevant guidance that may from time to time be issued by the Bank.

– ensure that employees comply with any other regulatory requirements that may be applicable or relevant to a firm's activities in the wholesale markets.

17 When establishing a relationship with a **new** counterparty or client, firms must take steps to make them aware of the precise nature of firms' liability for business to be conducted, including any limitations on that liability and the capacity in which they act. **In particular, broking firms should explain to a new client the limited role of brokers (see paragraphs 29 and 30 overleaf).**

18 All firms should identify any potential or actual **conflicts of interest** that might arise when undertaking wholesale market transactions and take measures either to eliminate these conflicts or control them such as to ensure the fair treatment of counterparties.

19 All firms should **know their counterparty**. For principals this is essential where the nature of the business undertaken requires the assessment of creditworthiness. Before dealing with another principal for the first time in any product covered by

this Code, core principals should ensure that appropriate steps (see Part III of this Code) are taken.

20 As part of the "know your counterparty" process firms must take all necessary steps to prevent their transactions in the wholesale markets being used to facilitate **money laundering**. To this end firms should be familiar with the Guidance Notes published in 1995.[1] These make clear the very limited responsibilities name passing brokers have in this area; in particular banks (and others that use brokers) should **not** seek to rely on brokers to undertake anything other than identity and location checks on their behalf.

21 As a general rule core principals will assume that their counterparties have the capability to make independent decisions and to act accordingly; it is for each counterparty to decide if it needs to seek independent advice. If a non-core principal wishes to retain a core principal as its financial adviser it is strongly encouraged to do so in writing, setting forth the exact nature and extent of the reliance it will place upon the core principal. All principals should accept responsibility for entering into wholesale market transactions and any subsequent losses they might incur. They should assess for themselves the merits and risks of dealing in these markets. Non-core principals must recognise that it is possible for core principals to take proprietary positions which might be similiar or opposite to their own.

22 It is good practice for **principals**, subject to their own legal advice, to alert counterparties to any legal or tax uncertainties which they know are relevant to a proposed relationship or transaction, in order that the counterparty may seek its own advice if it so wishes.

23 Management of **broking** firms should advise their employees of the need to ensure that their behaviour could not **at any time** be construed as having misled counterparties about the limited role of brokers (see paragraphs 29 and 30 below); failure to be vigilant in this area will adversely affect the reputation of the broking firm itself.

Of the employee

24 When entering into or arranging individual deals, dealers and brokers must ensure that at all times great care is taken not to misrepresent in any way the nature of any transaction. Dealers and brokers must ensure that:

– the identity of the firm for which they are acting and its role is clear to their counterparties/clients to avoid any risk of confusion. This is particularly important, for instance, where an individual dealer acts for more than one company, or in more than one capacity. If so, he must make absolutely clear, at the outset of any deal, on behalf of which company or in which capacity he is acting.

– it is clearly understood in which products they are proposing to deal.

– any claims or acknowledgements about, or relevant to, a particular transaction being considered should, as far as the individual dealer or broker is aware, be fair and not misleading.

– facts believed to be material to completing a specific transaction are disclosed before the deal is done, except where such disclosure would reveal confidential information about the activities of another firm. Unless specifically asked for more information, or clarification, a dealer at a core principal will assume his counterparty has all the necessary information for this decision making process when entering into a wholesale market transaction.

[1] Available from the British Bankers' Association, 10 Lombard Street, London EC3V 9EL.

25 When a deal is being arranged through a broker, the broker should act in a way which does not unfairly favour one client, amongst those involved, over another, irrespective of what brokerage arrangements exist between them and the broking firm.

Clarity of role

Role of principals

26 The role of firms acting as principal is to deal for their own account. **All principals have the responsibility for assessing the creditworthiness of their counterparties or potential counterparties whether dealing direct or through a broking firm. It is for each principal to decide whether or not to seek independent professional advice to assist in this process.**

27 **It is also for the principal to decide what credence, if any, is given to any information or comment provided by a broker to a dealer. Where such information or comment might be interpreted as being relevant to a particular counterparty or potential counterparty, this does not alter the fact that the responsibility for assessing the creditworthiness of a counterparty, whether or not it is supervised, rests with the principal alone.**

28 Some firms may act as agent for connected or other companies as well as, or instead of, dealing for their own account. If so, such agents should:

– always make absolutely clear to all concerned the capacity in which they are acting (e.g. if they also act as principal or broker).
– declare at an early stage of negotiations the party for whom they are acting. It may be considered desirable to set out this relationship formally in writing for future reference.
– ensure that **all** confirmations make clear when a deal is done on an agency basis.
– when acting as agent for an unregulated principal, make clear at an early stage this qualification to potential counterparties; and include this on confirmations.

Role of brokers

29 Typically the role of the specialist wholesale market broking firms in London supervised as such by the Bank is to act as **arrangers** of deals.[1] They:

– bring together counterparties on mutually acceptable terms and pass names to facilitate the conclusion of a transaction.
– receive payment for this service in the form of brokerage (except where a prior explicit agreement between the management of all parties to a deal provides otherwise).
– are **not** permitted, even fleetingly, to act as principal in a deal (even on a "matched principal" basis), or to act in any discretionary fund management capacity.[2]

30 It is accepted that, in providing the service specified in the previous paragraph, individual brokers may be called upon to give advice or express opinions, usually in response to requests from individual dealers. While brokers should be mindful of the need not to reveal confidential information about the market activities of

[1] There are two exceptions to this rule. The first covers the specialist inter-dealer brokers, involved primarily in US Treasury bills, notes and bonds which act as matched principals. The other exception is when name-passing broking firms are investing their own money; in such transactions, brokers must make clear to the relevant counterparties that they are acting as principal.

[2] The relationship between an institution offering a discretionary or advisory management service and its clients in any of the financial products described in the box on pages 284–5 falls outside the scope of this Code and, if it constitutes investment business within the terms of the Financial Services Act 1986, should be conducted in accordance with the requirements of the relevant Self-Regulating Organisation.

individual clients, there is no restriction on brokers passing, or commenting, on general information which is in the public domain. Equally, there is no responsibility upon a broker to volunteer general information of this type. Where information is sought or volunteered individual brokers should exercise particular care. For instance, brokers do not have sufficient information to be qualified to advise principals on the creditworthiness of specific counterparties and to do so is not their role.

III Controls

It is essential that management have in place, and review regularly, appropriate control procedures which their dealing and other relevant staff must follow.

Know your counterparty

It is necessary for a variety of reasons, including firms' own risk control and the need to meet their legal obligations (e.g. on money laundering) for firms to undertake basic "know their counterparty" checks before dealing in any products covered by this Code.

Before agreeing to establish a dealing relationship in any of these wholesale market products, core principals should be mindful of any reputational risks which might arise as a result, and whether these risks might be greater when undertaking such transactions with non-core principals. In the absence of firm evidence to the contrary, non-core principals should be regarded as end-users (i.e. "customers") of the wholesale markets.

31 In order to minimise the risks which they face it is desirable for core principals to have in place a clearly articulated approval process for their dealers and salespersons to follow before dealing for the first time in any wholesale market product with counterparties. This process, which should be appropriately monitored by management, should apply both when granting an initial dealing line for a product, and subsequently if changing or extending it to other wholesale products. Such a process might include the following considerations, which will need to be tailored to the type of transaction being considered:

With all counterparties
–   What information is available to the core principal on the legal capacity of the counterparty to undertake such transactions? Is this information sufficient to make an informed decision on the legal risks it might face if it undertakes such business with the counterparty?

With customers
–   Who initiated the request for the product relationship? Might this decision have been influenced by any product **advice** given by the core principal?
–   If advice is given was this subject to a written agreement between the parties; if not, should it be? Are both parties clear what reliance the customer is placing upon that advice?
–   What, if any, are the legal responsibilities the core principal might owe to the customer to whom advice is given in subsequently undertaking transactions in that product? For instance, management might ask itself if it is being asked to advise on the customer's whole portfolio – which might put it in a different legal position than if it were advising on only part of the portfolio.
–   Are there potential conflicts between the firm's interests and those of the potential customer? If there are how should they be managed; and does the customer need to be alerted?

– Have appropriate legal agreements between the core principal and the customer been enacted? Do they make clear the respective responsibilities of both companies for any losses? Do they make clear which party is responsible for decisions to close-out trades undertaken?

32 **Procedures should be in place to ensure that the information available to banks and other core principals,** upon which they will base their judgement on whether or not to open/extend a dealing relationship with a particular customer, **is carefully assessed on a broad product by product basis.**

33 Once a customer dealing relationship has been established in one, or more, wholesale market product(s) it is **strongly recommended that management at both parties periodically review it,** against the above criteria. It is also in their own interest for core principals to review periodically the totality of their business relationship with each customer against the same criteria.

Additional arrangements for small investors
The Bank believes that it is in the interest of banks and other listed institutions for management to consider most carefully whether to grant or extend dealing facilities in OTC wholesale market products to "small investors" (i.e. individuals or small business investors as defined under SFA rules).

34 The expectation at the time the FSA was introduced was that individuals (or other small investors) would not normally be dealing in the wholesale OTC markets, which are primarily for core principals and other professionals such as large corporates, that regularly use the markets and which should have professionally trained staff able to undertake such transactions on their behalf.

35 It is more likely, therefore, that small investors will ask for **advice** on the particular product being considered (for instance in terms of its risk profile, how this might differ from exchange traded instruments with which they might be more familiar, or how to value its worth over time, etc). It is the Bank's view (shared by the SIB) that where this is so they should **not** automatically be granted a new or extended dealing line for this product. If the product being considered is a derivative and/or leveraged, the Bank believes that it is in the interest of banks and other listed institutions to have in place a written agreement, which makes clear which products are concerned and the extent to which any reliance can be placed by the small investor on the advice given.

36 Where an FSA exempt product is involved (items 6–16 in the box on pages 284–5) small investors should also be advised that by seeking to conduct such business with a s 43 listed institution they would not have the protection of the FSA. The provisions set out in paragraph 21 above would apply.

37 The Bank believes it prudent for core principal to maintain, as accurately as they can, records of conversations – both internal or with the investor– material to their relationship. Where these are in written form, records must be kept in line with statutory requirements. Where tapes are the only record of specific transactions, management should consider very carefully whether some or all of these should be retained for a similar length of time to written records.

Dealing mandates

38 There has been growing interest in the use of dealing mandates as a means of clarifying the extent of a relationship between core principals and their customers, and their respective responsibilities. That in turn could help reduce the scope for

errors. In the Bank's view it is appropriate for core principals to consider the merits of establishing dealing mandates to govern their relationship with non-core principals, but it is unlikely that mandates would be necessary between core principals. When deciding whether to initiate a mandate it is important that proper consideration is given by both parties to the manner in which the mandate is to be structured and subsequently administered.

39 It is good practice for both parties to agree what the mandate should and should not cover. To aid this process associations like the ACT and BBA may be able to guide their members on common practice. Where a mandate has been initiated, both parties should review it periodically; as a general rule, the onus is on the counterparty to notify the core principal promptly of any change necessary to an existing mandate.

40 While they can have a useful role in improving internal controls dealing mandates should **not** be used as a vehicle to pass all responsibility to another counterparty. They should not, therefore, weaken the standard set out in paragraph 16 – that all firms will be held responsible for the actions of their staff. Firms must, in particular, ensure that any individual who commits the firm to a transaction has the necessary authority to do so, and is aware of the terms of any mandate that has been agreed.

Confidentiality

41 Confidentiality is essential for the preservation of a reputable and efficient market place. Principals and brokers share equal responsibility for maintaining confidentiality. Principals or brokers should not, without explicit permission, disclose or discuss, or apply pressure on others to disclose or discuss, any information relating to specific deals which have been transacted, or are in the process of being arranged, except to or with the parties directly involved (and, if necessary, their advisers) or where this is required by law or to comply with the requirements of a supervisory body.

42 Where confidential or market sensitive information is routinely shared by a London based firm with other branches/subsidiaries within its group it is for management to review periodically if this is appropriate. Where it is, the Bank believes that London management should be responsible and accountable for how such information is subsequently controlled – in particular they should make clear that such information should **at all times** continue to be treated as being subject to the confidentiality provisions of the Code. It is a responsibility of management to ensure that all relevant personnel are aware of, and observe, this fundamental principle.

43 Care should be taken over the use of open loudspeakers in both brokers' offices and principals' dealing rooms to ensure that they do not lead to breaches of confidentiality.

44 Situations arise where sales/marketing staff from core principals visit the offices of their customers; during such visits the customer may wish to arrange a transaction via the sales/marketing representative. Subject to proper controls this is perfectly acceptable. However, individual dealers or brokers should **not** visit each other's dealing rooms except with the express permission of the management of both parties. In particular a principal's dealer should **not** deal from within the offices of a broker or another principal. Brokers should never conduct business from outside their own offices. The only exception to these general rules might be when it is necessary for two unconnected institutions to share the same facilities

as part of their agreed contingency arrangements. In such circumstances management should ensure appropriate arrangements are in place to protect counterparty confidentiality.

45   A principal should not place an order with a broker with the intention of ascertaining the name of a counterparty in order to make direct contact to conclude the deal; neither should direct contact be made to increase the amount of a completed trade arranged through a broker.

Location of back office functions

46   There is a growing trend towards locating front and back office functions in physically separate locations; indeed a number of the branches of international banks in London have relocated and consolidated their back office functions in their home country. Others have back offices outside London. The Bank's view is that there should be no objection to banks consolidating back offices in a single location, even if that were overseas – provided that there are individuals in London with whom any deal or settlement queries can be resolved quickly.

47   At the same time the banking supervisors have reviewed whether it is still necessary in all cases, on control grounds, to maintain a physical segregation of back and front office staff within banks. They have concluded that whilst in most cases physical segregation is preferable, a lack of such segregation may be acceptable provided that it can be demonstrated that appropriate management controls are in place. For instance lack of segregation may be acceptable where computer logical access controls are in place. **Even so, it is essential that a strict segregation of duties between staff in the front and back office is maintained**, and especially that confirmations are sent direct to back office staff (see also paragraph 98 below).

Taping

48   Experience has shown that recourse to tapes proves invaluable to the speedy resolution of differences and disputes. The use of recording equipment in the offices of voice brokers and principals has become common; other means for monitoring "conversations"are embodied within electronic broking systems now used in the markets. **The Bank strongly recommends taping by principals and brokers of all conversations by dealers and brokers** together with back office telephone lines used by those responsible for confirming deals or passing payment and other instructions. The Bank expects firms which it supervises to use tapes. Any which do not tape all their front plus relevant back office conversations should review this management policy periodically and be prepared to persuade the Bank that there are particular reasons for them to continue with such an approach. This review should be repeated annually. Failure to tape will normally count against a firm if it seeks to use the arbitration process described in paragraph 120 to settle a difference, or is the subject of a complaint.

49   When initially installing tape equipment, or taking on new clients or counterparties, firms should take the necessary steps to inform them that conversations will be recorded. **Tapes should be kept for at least two months, and preferably longer.** Experience suggests that, with the growing involvement of the private banking divisions within core principals in selling wholesale products to small investors, taping of all conversations by salesmen/account officers in these areas is in the interests of core principals. The longer tapes are retained the greater the chances are that any subsequent disputes over transactions or where advice has been given, can be resolved satisfactorily. **Tapes which cover any transaction about which**

there is a dispute should be retained until the problem has been resolved. Management should ensure that access to taping equipment and tapes, whether in use or in store, is strictly controlled so that they cannot be tampered with.

Deals at non-current rates

There is now widespread recognition that, as a general rule, deals at non-market rates should not be undertaken.

50 Banks and other listed firms are strongly discouraged from undertaking deals involving rolling-over an existing contract at the original rate. These should only be undertaken, if at all, on rare occasions and then after most careful consideration by both parties and approval, on a deal by deal basis, by their senior management. Senior management must ensure that proper procedures are in place to identify and bring to their attention all such deals **when they are proposed** so that they can be made fully aware of the details before reaching a decision on whether a particular trade should go ahead on this basis. Before reaching such a decision, senior management should seek written confirmation from the counterparty, also at senior management level, of the reasons for the transaction. This is essential not only because of the potential credit risk implications of rolling-over deals at original rates but also because failure to use current rates could result in the principal unknowingly participating in the concealment of a profit or loss, or in perpetration of a fraud. In order to provide a clear audit trail, there should be an immediate exchange of letters between the senior managements of both parties to any such deals to demonstrate that the above procedures have been followed.

51 However, if management accept that the application of non-market rates can be necessary to create deal structures which satisfy the legitimate requirements of counterparties, they should ensure proper controls are in place to prevent such arrangements from concealing fraud, creating unacceptable conflicts of interest, or involving other illegal activity. It is particularly important to ensure that there is no ambiguity in such transactions over the amounts which each counterparty is to pay and receive. It should, for instance, be possible to demonstrate from the documentation available to both parties that the combination of cashflows, coupons, and foreign exchange rates etc., used in such transactions produces a result that is consistent with the current market price for a straightforward transaction of similar maturity. **It is therefore essential that appropriate documentation is in place before any such deals are undertaken and that this is reviewed, by senior management, regularly so that they can satisfy themselves whether it remains appropriate to undertake further transactions on this basis.**

52 A specific area where there is sometimes pressure to conduct deals at non-current rates is in the foreign exchange market. In particular pressure can be placed on dealers undertaking a foreign exchange swap to avoid the immediate fixing of the spot price underlying the trade. **This practice is judged by practitioners in the London market to be unethical and is not appropriate practice for UK based institutions. Spot rates should be determined immediately after completion of the foreign exchange swap transaction.**

Dealing with unidentified principals

53 There has been a growing trend towards discretionary management companies dealing in wholesale market products on behalf of their clients. For its own commercial reasons a fund manager may not wish to divulge the name of its client(s)

when concluding such deals. Since this practice raises important considerations, particularly in terms of banks' ability to assess their credit risk to particular counterparties and to meet supervisory requirements on large exposures, the Bank is in discussions with the relevant market associations about it; and may in due course seek views from other supervisors in Basle on this practice. In the interim, before any institution transacts business on this basis its senior management should decide, as a matter of policy, whether they judge it appropriate to do so. In doing so, they should consider all the risks involved. They should fully document the decision which they reach.

After-hours dealing

54 Extended trading after normal local hours has become accepted in some markets, most notably foreign exchange. Dealing after hours into other centres forms an integral part of the operations of many firms both in London and elsewhere. Such dealing can involve additional hazards – whether undertaken direct or via a broker. For example, when dealing continues during the evening from premises other than the principals' dealing rooms, one of the principals involved might subsequently forget, or deny, having done a deal. Management should therefore issue clear guidelines to their staff, both on the kinds of deal which may be undertaken in those circumstances and on the permitted limits of any such dealing. All deals should be confirmed promptly – preferably by telex or similar electronic message direct to the counterparty's offices – and carefully controlled when arranged off-premises. Management should consider installing answerphone facilities in the dealing area which dealers should use to record full details of all off-premises trades. These should be processed promptly on the next working day.

Stop-loss orders

55 Principals may receive requests from branches, customers and correspondents to execute transactions – for instance to buy or sell a currency – if prices or rates should reach a specified level. These orders, which include stop-loss and limit orders from counterparties desiring around-the-clock protection for their own positions, may be intended for execution during the day, overnight, or until executed or cancelled. Management should ensure that the terms of such orders are explicitly identified and agreed, and that there is a clear understanding with the counterparty about the obligation it has assumed in accepting such orders. Moreover, management needs to establish clear policies and procedures for its traders who accept and execute stop-loss and limit orders. Management should also ensure that any dealer handling such an instruction has adequate lines of communication with the counterparty so that the dealer can reach authorised personnel in case of an unusual situation or extreme price/rate movement.

Conflicts of interest
Dealing for personal account

56 Management should consider carefully whether their employees should be allowed to deal at all for own account in any of the products covered by this Code. Where allowed by management, it is their responsibility to ensure that adequate safeguards are established to prevent abuse. These safeguards should reflect the need to maintain confidentiality with respect to non-public price-sensitive information and to ensure that no action is taken by employees which might adversely affect the interests of the firm's clients or counterparties.

Deals using a connected broker

57 Brokers have a legal obligation to disclose the nature and extent of any material conflict between their own interests and their responsibilities to clients. To safeguard the independence of brokers they should give all their clients formal written notification of any principal(s) where a material connection exists (unless a client explicitly waives its rights to this information in writing); and notify any subsequent changes to this list of principals as they occur. For the purposes of this Code, a material connection would include situations where the relationship between the parties could have a bearing on the transaction or its terms, as a result for example of common management responsibilities or material shareholding links, whether direct or indirect. The Bank regards a shareholding of 10% or more in a broker as material; but, depending on the circumstances, a smaller holding may also represent a material connection.

58 Any deals arranged by a broker involving a connected principal must be at arm's length (i.e. at mutually agreed rates which are the same as those prevailing for transactions between unconnected counterparties).

Marketing and incentives

59 When listed institutions are operating within the boundaries of the Section 43 arrangements, they will not be subject to advertising or cold-calling rules since these would be inappropriate in such professional markets. Nevertheless listed institutions should take care to ensure that any advertisements for their services within the exempt area are directed so far as possible towards professionals.

60 In recent years a number of foreign exchange electronic broking services have begun operating in London. Understandably such firms have considered a range of marketing arrangements, in the form of incentives, to generate liquidity in their systems. After consultation through the Joint Standing Committee it was concluded that the principle that brokers should not make payments to banks for using their services should be strictly maintained. As with conventional voice brokers, the provision of discount arrangements is a legitimate marketing technique, even if these involve cross-product subsidisation between different parts of the same group.

Entertainment, gifts and gambling

61 Management or employees must neither offer inducements to conduct business, nor solicit them from the personnel of other institutions. However it is recognised that entertainment and gifts are offered in the normal course of business and do not necessarily constitute inducements. Nevertheless this is an area where the Bank receives a surprisingly high number of complaints about the potentially excessive nature of entertainment being offered. In response the Bank consulted practitioners during 1994 on how best to help facilitate a consistent approach across the London market. This reconfirmed that management should have a clearly articulated policy towards the giving/receipt of entertainment (and gifts), and ensure it is properly observed. It should include procedures for dealing with gifts judged to be excessive but which cannot be declined without causing offence. The policy should be reviewed periodically. In developing and implementing its policy, management should have regard to the potential adverse impact on the reputation of the firm, and the London market generally, of any adverse comment/publicity generated by any entertainment (or gifts) given or received.

62 The following general pointers have been identified which management ought to consider including as part of their policy:

- Firms should have in place arrangements to monitor the type, frequency and cost of entertainment and gifts. Periodic control reports should be made available to management.
- Authorisation and control procedures should be clear and unambiguous in order to ensure proper accountability.
- Policies should contain specific reference to the appropriate treatment for gifts (given and received). This policy should specifically preclude the giving (or receiving) of cash or cash convertible gifts.
- In determining whether the offer of a particular gift or form of entertainment might be construed as excessive, management should bear in mind whether it could be regarded as an improper inducement, either by the employer of the recipient or the supervisory authorities. Any grey areas should be cleared **in advance** with management at the recipient firm(s).
- Firms should not normally offer entertainment if a representative of the host company will not be present at the event.

63 These procedures should be drawn up bearing in mind that the activities of dealers of some of the principals active in the markets may be governed by statute. For instance, offering hospitality or gifts to officers and members of local authorities and other public bodies is subject to the provisions of legislation that carries sanctions under criminal law. One of the most onerous requirements of this legislation is that any offer or receipt of hospitality is, prima facie, deemed to be a criminal offence, unless the contrary is proved.

64 Similar guidelines should also be established on gambling with other market participants. **All these activities carry obvious dangers and, where allowed at all, it is strongly recommended that they are tightly restricted.**

Abused substances (including drugs and alcohol)

65 Management should take all reasonable steps to educate themselves and their staff about possible signs and effects of the use of drugs and other abused substances. The judgement of any member of staff using such substances is likely to be impaired; dependence upon drugs etc. makes them more likely to be vulnerable to outside inducement to conduct business not necessarily in the best interests of the firm or the market generally and could seriously diminish their ability to function satisfactorily.

IV Dealing principles and procedures: a statement of best practice

Scope

Deals in the London wholesale markets (defined by the products covered in the box on pages 284–5) should be conducted on the basis of this Code of Conduct.

66 Whilst this Code is designed for the London markets, its provisions may extend beyond UK shores, for example where a listed UK broker arranges a deal involving an overseas counterparty. Where deals involving overseas counterparties are to be made on a different basis in any respect, for example because of distinct local rules or requirements, this should be clearly identified at the outset to avoid any possible confusion.

Overseas market conventions

The trading of currency assets in London should follow recognised trading conventions that have been established internationally or in specific overseas markets, provided they do not conflict with the principles of this Code.

67 Where foreign currency-denominated short-term securities issued overseas are traded in London, there may be important differences in dealing practice compared with the trading of London instruments, partly reflecting the way the instruments are traded in their domestic markets. The London Code is intended to be complementary to any generally accepted local standards and practices for such instruments traded in London. The Bank would expect firms trading these instruments in London to abide by any such local conventions.

Procedures

Preliminary negotiation of terms

Firms should clearly state at the outset, prior to a transaction being executed, any qualifing conditions to which it will be subject.

68 Typical examples of qualifications include where a price is quoted subject to the necessary credit approval; finding a counterparty for matching deals; or the ability to execute an associated transaction. For instance principals may quote a rate which is "firm subject to the execution of a hedge transaction". For good order's sake it is important that firms complete deals as quickly as possible; the onus is on both sides to keep each other informed of progress or possible delays. If a principal's ability to conclude a transaction is constrained by other factors, for example opening hours in other centres, this should be made known to brokers and potential counterparties at an early stage and before names are exchanged.

69 In the Euronote and commercial paper markets, principals should notify investors, at the time of sale, of their willingness or otherwise to repurchase paper. Investors should also be notified, before the sale, of any significant variation from the standard terms or conditions of an issue.

Undertaking derivative transactions with end-users (i.e. "customers" of the market)

It is important, before derivative transactions are undertaken with a customer, that dealers are satisfied that appropriate "know your counterparty" procedures (see section III above) have been implemented for the product under consideration.

70 When a core principal is dealing with any customer of the market in leveraged or derivative products it is good practice for its dealers to assist their opposite number by using clear concise terminology. It is however the responsibility of each party involved to seek clarification, before concluding a deal, on any points about which they are not clear. Each party should also consider whether it would be helpful for the core principal to send by electronic means (telex or fax) a pre-deal message setting out the terms upon which the deal will be priced and agreed by both parties. While this may not be judged appropriate for some customers (e.g. an experienced large corporate), **it is likely to be helpful to send pre-deal messages to small investors (as defined earlier)**. Such a message may also be particularly useful, for instance, where the product involved is relatively new to the customer; or where the individual dealer acting on behalf of the customer is not the regular contact point for undertaking such trades with that customer. The sending or receipt of such a message is not a substitute for the confirmation procedures described below.

71 The existence, or not, of such a message should not however be taken as undermining in any way the principle that each party must accept responsibility for entering into such trades and any losses that they might incur as a result of doing so. There are, of course, circumstances in which this principle might be brought into question; for instance if the dealer at the core principal had deliberately misled the customer by knowingly providing false and/or inaccurate information at the time the deal was being negotiated. It is therefore very important that great care is taken not to mislead or misinform.

72 To help minimise the scope for error and misunderstanding the Bank strongly recommends that management require their dealers to use standard pre-deal check lists of the key terms that they need to agree when entering into leveraged and/or derivative transactions.

Firmness of quotation

All firms, whether acting as principal, agent or broker, have a duty to make absolutely clear whether the prices they are quoting are firm or merely indicative. Prices quoted by brokers should be taken to be firm in marketable amounts unless otherwise qualified.

73 A principal quoting a firm price (or rate) either through a broker or directly to a potential counterparty is committed to deal at that price (or rate) in a marketable amount provided the counterparty name is acceptable. In order to minimise the scope for confusion where there is no clear market convention, dealers quoting a firm price (rate) should indicate the length of time for which their quote is firm.

74 It is generally accepted that when dealing in fast moving markets (like spot forex or currency options) a principal has to assume that a price given to a broker is good only for a short length of time – typically a matter of seconds. However, this practice would be open to misunderstandings about how quickly a price is deemed to lapse if it were adopted when dealing in generally less hectic markets, for example the forward foreign exchange or deposit markets, or when market conditions are relatively quiet. Since dealers have prime responsibility for prices put to a broker, the onus in such circumstances is on dealers to satisfy themselves that their prices have been taken off, unless a time limit is placed by the principal on its interest at the outset (e.g. "firm for one minute only"). Otherwise, the principal should feel bound to deal with an acceptable name at the quoted rate in a marketable amount.

75 For their part brokers should make every effort to assist dealers by checking from time to time with them whether their interest at particular prices (rates) is still current. They should also do so when a specific name and amount have been quoted.

76 What constitutes a marketable amount varies from market to market but will generally be familiar to practitioners. A broker, if quoting on the basis of small amounts or particular names, should qualify the quotation accordingly. Where principals are proposing to deal in unfamiliar markets through a broker, it is recommended that they first ask brokers what amounts are sufficient to validate normal market quotations. If their interest is in a smaller amount, this should be specified by the principal when initially requesting a price from or offering a price to the broker.

77 In the swap market, considerable use is made of "indicative interest" quotations. When arranging a swap an unconditional firm rate will only be given where a principal deals directly with a client, or when such a principal has received the name of a client from a broker. A principal who quotes a rate or spread as "firm

subject to credit" is bound to deal at the quoted rate or spread if the name is consistent with a category of counterparty previously identified for this purpose (see also paragraph 82 below). The only exception is where the particular name cannot be accepted, for example if the principal has reached its credit limit for that name, in which case the principal will correctly reject the transaction. It is not an acceptable practice for a principal to revise a rate which was "firm subject to credit"once the name of the counterparty has been disclosed. Brokers and principals should work together to establish a range of institutions for whom the principal's rate is firm subject to credit.

Concluding a deal
Principals should regard themselves as bound to a deal once the price and any other key commercial terms have been agreed Oral agreements are considered binding. However, holding brokers unreasonably to a price is viewed as unprofessional and should be discouraged by management.

78 Where quoted prices are qualified as being indicative or subject to negotiation of commercial terms, principals should normally treat themselves as bound to a deal at the point where the terms have been agreed without qualification. Oral agreements are considered binding; the subsequent confirmation is evidence of the deal but should not override terms agreed orally. The practice of making a transaction subject to documentation is **not** good practice (see also paragraphs 107–109). In order to minimise the likelihood of disputes arising once documentation is prepared, firms should make every effort to agree all material points quickly during the oral negotiation of terms, and should include these on the confirmation. Any remaining details should be agreed as soon as possible thereafter.

79 Where brokers are involved, it is their responsibility to ensure that the principal providing the price (rate) is made aware immediately it has been dealt upon. As a general rule a deal should only be regarded as having been "done" where the broker's contact is positively acknowledged by the dealer. A broker should never assume that a deal is done without some form of oral acknowledgement from the dealer. Where a broker puts a specific proposition to a dealer for a price (i.e. specifying an amount and a name for which a quote is required, the dealer can reasonably expect to be told almost immediately by the broker whether the price has been hit or not.

Passing of names by brokers
Brokers should not divulge the names of principals prematurely, and certainly not until satisfied that both sides display a serious intention to transact. Principals and brokers should at all times treat the details of transactions as absolutely confidential to the parties involved (see paragraph 41 above).

80 To save time and minimise frustration, principals should wherever practicable give brokers prior indication of counterparties with whom, for whatever reason, they would be unwilling to do business (referring as necessary to particular markets or instruments). At the same time brokers should take full account of the best interests and any precise instructions of the client.

81 To save subsequent awkwardness, principals (including agents) have a particular obligation to give guidance to brokers on any particular features (maturities etc.) or types of counterparty (such as non-financial institutions) which might cause difficulties. In some instruments, principals may also wish to give brokers guidance on the

extent of their price differentiation across broad categories of counterparties. Where a broker is acting for an unlisted (or unsupervised) name he should disclose this fact as soon as possible; the degree of disclosure required in such a case will usually be greater. For instance, credit considerations may require that such names be disclosed to a listed principal first (as in the swap market), in order that the listed principal may quote a rate at which it is committed to deal. Equally, disclosure of difficult names may be necessary since this may influence the documentation.

82 In all their wholesale market business, brokers should aim to achieve a mutual and immediate exchange of names. However this will not always be possible. There will be times when one principal's name proves unacceptable to another and the broker will quite properly decline to divulge by whom it was refused. This may sometimes result in the principal whose name has been rejected feeling that the broker may in fact have quoted a price (rate) which it could not in fact substantiate. In such cases, the Bank will be prepared to establish with the reluctant principal that it did have business to do at the quoted price and the reasons why the name was turned down, so that the aggrieved party can be assured the original quote was valid without, of course, revealing the reluctant party's name.

83 In the sterling and currency deposit markets, it is accepted that principals dealing through a broker have the right to turn down a name wishing to take deposits; this could therefore require predisclosure of the name before closing the deal. Once a lender has asked the key question "who pays", it is considered committed to do business at the price quoted with that name, or an alternative acceptable name if offered immediately. The name of a lender shall be disclosed only after the borrower's name has been accepted by the lender. Conversely, where a borrower is taking secured money there may be occasions when it will wish to decline to take funds, through a broker, when the lender's name is passed.

84 In the case of instruments like CDs, where the seller may not be the same entity as the issuer, the broker shall first disclose the issuer's name to the potential buyer. Once a buyer has asked "whose paper is it", the buyer is considered committed to deal at the price quoted. Once the buyer asks "who sells" it is considered committed to deal with the particular seller in question (or an alternative acceptable name, so long as this name is immediately shown to the buyer by the broker). The name of the buyer shall be disclosed only after the seller's name has been accepted by the buyer. The seller has the right to refuse the particular buyer, so long as it is prepared at that time to sell the same amount at the same price to an alternative acceptable name immediately shown to it by the broker.

85 In the CD markets a price quoted is generally accepted as good for any name "on the run".

Use of intermediaries
Brokers must not interpose an intermediary in any deal which could take place without its introduction.

86 An intermediary should only be introduced by a broker where it is strictly necessary for the completion of a deal, most obviously where a name switch is required because one counterparty is full of another's name but is prepared to deal with a third party. Any fees involved in transactions involving intermediaries must be explicitly identified by the broker and shown on the relevant confirmation(s).

87 Where a broker needs to switch a name this should be undertaken as promptly as possible, bearing in mind that this may take longer at certain times of the day; or

if the name is a particularly difficult one; or if the deal is larger than normal. In no circumstances should a deal be left overnight without acceptable names having been passed.

Confirmation procedures
Prompt passing, recording and careful checking of confirmations is vital to minimise the possibility of errors and misunderstanding whether dealing direct or through brokers. Details should be passed as soon as practicable afterdeals have been done and checked upon receipt. The passing of details in batches is not recommended. For markets where standard terms are applicable e.g. under standard documentation, it is recommended that confirmations conform to the formats specified for the market or instrument concerned.

(a) Oral deal checks
An increasing number of practitioners find it helpful to undertake oral deal checks at least once a day, especially when using a broker.

88 Particularly when dealing in faster moving markets like foreign exchange, but also when dealing in other instruments which have very short settlement periods, many principals now request regular oral deal checks – whether dealing through brokers or direct – prior to the exchange and checking of a written or electronically dispatched confirmation. Their use can be an important means of helping to reduce the number and size of differences particularly when dealing through brokers or for deals involving non-London counterparties. It is for each firm to agree with its broker(s) whether or not it wishes to be provided with this service; and, if so, how many such checks a day it requires. When arbitrating in disputes, the Bank will take into account the extent to which principals have sought to safeguard their interests by undertaking oral checks.

89 If a single check is thought to be sufficient, the Bank sees merit in this being undertaken towards the end of the trading day as a useful complement, particularly where late deals are concerned, to the process of sending out and checking confirmations.

90 As a matter of common sense, the broker should always obtain acknowledgement from a dealer on completion of the check that all the deals have been agreed or, if not, that any identified discrepancies are resolved as a matter of urgency. Lack of response should not be construed as acknowledgement.

(b) Written/electronic confirmations
In all markets, the confirmation provides a necessary final safeguard against dealing errors. Confirmations should be dispatched and checked carefully and promptly, even when oral deal checks have been undertaken. The issue and checking of confirmations is a back office responsibility which should be carried out independently from those who initiate deals.

91 A confirmation of each deal must be sent out without delay. This is particularly essential if dealing for same day settlement. As a general rule the Bank believes all participants in the wholesale markets should have, or be aiming to have, in place the capability to dispatch confirmations so that they are received and can be checked within a few hours of when the deal was struck. Where the products involved are more complex, and so require more details to be included on the confirmation, this may not be possible; nevertheless it is in the interest of all concerned that such deals are confined as quickly as is practicable. The Bank recommends that principals should enquire about any confirmations which have not been received with in the expected timescale.

92 It is not uncommon in the derivatives markets, and perfectly acceptable if the two principals involved agree, for only **one** party (rather than both) to the deal to send out a confirmation. But where this is so, it is imperative not only that the recipient checks it promptly, but that it also in good time responds to the issuer of the confirmation agreeing/querying the terms. For good order's sake it would also be imperative that the issuer of the confirmation has in place procedures for chasing a response if one is not forthcoming within a few hours of the confirmation being sent.

93 All confirmations should include the trade date, the name of the other counterparty and all other details of the deal, including where appropriate the commission charged by the broker. Some principals include their own terms and conditions of trading on their written confirmations. To avoid misunderstandings, any subsequent changes should be brought specifically to the attention of their counterparties.

94 In many markets, it is accepted practice for principals to confirm directly all the details of transactions arranged through a broker; the broker should nevertheless also send a confirmation to each counterparty.

95 All principals are reminded that the prompt sending and checking of confirmations is also regarded as best practice in deals not arranged through a broker, including those with corporates and other customers.

96 Wherever practicable the Bank wishes to discourage the practice in some markets of sending two confirmations (e.g. an initial one by telex, fax or other acceptable electronic means) followed by a written confirmation, which if posted could easily not arrive until after the settlement date and could cause confusion and uncertainty. For this reason, the Bank believes that wherever practicable a single confirmation should be sent promptly by each party, if possible by one of the generally accepted electronic means now available (notably the ACS system, SWIFT, fax or telex). Where this is not practicable, for instance in more complex derivative transactions, firms should indicate (e.g. on the preliminary confirmation) that a more detailed written version is to follow. The Bank does not believe that it is good practice to rely solely on an oral check.

97 It is vital that principals check confirmations carefully and immediately upon receipt so that discrepancies can be quickly revealed and corrected. Firms that check within a few hours of receipt would be complying with best practice.

98 As a general rule, confirmations should not be issued by or sent to and checked by dealers. This is a back office function. Where dealers do get involved in these procedures they should be closely controlled. The most common instance where it may sometimes be thought helpful to mark a copy of the confirmation for the attention of the person who has arranged the deal, in addition to the back office, is in markets requiring detailed negotiation of terms (notably those involving contracts for differences). Certain automated dealing systems produce confirmations automatically; provided these are received in the back office no additional confirmation need be sent.

99 Particular attention needs to be paid by all parties when confirming deals in which at least one of the counterparties is based outside London, and to any consequential differences in confirmation procedure.

Payment / settlement instructions
Instructions should be passed as quickly as possible to facilitate prompt settlement. The Bank strongly recommends the use of standard settlement instructions; their use

can make a significant contribution to reducing both the incidence and size of differences arising from the mistaken settlement of funds.

100 The use of standard settlement instructions (SSIs) continues to increase in London. International acceptance of the benefits of many SSIs is an important next step. In order to facilitate still greater usage of SSIs the BBA now maintains a directory of London based institutions that use them. The Bank wishes to encourage firms that it supervises, that do not already do so, to draw up plans to move towards using SSIs as soon as possible. A major advantage of using SSIs is that they remove the need to confirm payment details by phone.

101 The guidelines set out in Schedule 2, which have been drawn up in consultation with practitioners, set out a framework which it is hoped principals will aim to adopt when using SSIs for wholesale market transactions. The guidance notes emphasise that SSIs should only be established via confirmed letter or authenticated SWIFT message, and **not** by SWIFT broadcast. While many firms comply with this guidance, difficulties have been encountered where some insist on using SWIFT broadcasts. Having raised the matter with SWIFT it is clear that broadcast messages remain unsuitable for the purpose of changing SSIs and are non-binding on recipients. SWIFT is currently looking at developing a new message for this purpose. In the interim, however, the majority view is that banks which receive notice from a counterparty of the amendment of an SSI by a SWIFT broadcast should be free to act upon such notice if they so wish. They should seek authentication of the message by way of sending confirmation of the arrangement, making clear when and for what deals the new instructions will be implemented. Until that process is complete the original instructions will be deemed still to be operative.

102 It has been the practice in the domestic sterling market that brokers pass payment instructions. In view of the increasing use of SSIs, the domestic sterling market should be moving away from requiring this service from brokers. Brokers should therefore only be expected to pass payment instructions in very unusual circumstances or in certain deposit markets where the counterparty is a non-core principal (such as a local authority).

103 Similarly brokers do not pass payment instructions in the foreign exchange and currency deposits market where the counterparties are both in the UK. It is for banks to agree with brokers the basis on which they will be able to pass such instruction for deals using a non-UK counterparty; all such instructions should be passed with minimum delay. It is intended that, with the hoped for increasing use of SSIs internationally, brokers will cease providing payment instructions involving overseas counterparties in due course.

104 Where SSIs are not being used, principals should ensure that any alterations to original payment instructions, including the paying agent where this has been specifically requested, should be immediately notified direct to the counterparty. This notification should be supported by written, telex, or similar confirmation of the new instructions.

105 While it is important that payment instructions are passed quickly, it is equally important that principals have in place appropriate procedures for controlling the timing of their instructions to correspondent banks to release funds when settling wholesale market transactions. A recent survey by G-10 central banks suggested that there is a wide gap between the best and worst controls practised in the markets; failure to maintain effective controls over payment flows

can significantly increase the risks that institutions face when dealing in the OTC wholesale markets.

Fraud

106 There is a need for great vigilance by all staff against attempted fraud. This is particularly so where calls are received on an ordinary telephone line (usually in principal to principal transactions). As a precautionary measure, it is strongly recommended that the details of all telephone deals which do not include pre-agreed standard settlement instructions should be confirmed by telex or similar means without delay by the recipient, seeking an answer-back to ensure the deal is genuine.

Terms and documentation

It is now common for wholesale market deals to be subject to some form of legal documentation binding the two parties to certain standard conditions and undertakings. The Bank endorses the use, wherever possible, of such documentation (which typically will take the form either of signed Master Agreements exchanged between the two parties or can take the form of standard terms). Core principals should have procedures in place to enable documentation to be completed and exchanged as soon as possible.

107 It is in the interest of all principals to make every effort to progress the finalisation of documentation as quickly as possible. In some markets, such as repo, or in other circumstances such as those described in paragraphs 31 and 51, documentation should be in place before any deals are undertaken. More generally, however, the Bank believes the aim should be for documentation to be in place within three months of the first deal being struck. Failure to agree documentation within this timescale should cause management to review the additional risks that this might imply for any future deals with the counterparty concerned. Factors which may influence managements' views include whether they can take comfort on their legal position from the mutual confirmation of terms with a particular counterparty; or where the delay is in putting in place multiple master agreements for products that are, in the interim, subject to previously agreed documentation.

108 Some documentation in common usage provides for various options and/or modifications to be agreed by mutual consent. These must be clearly stated before dealing. Firms should make clear at an early stage, when trading any of the above mentioned products, if they are not intending to use standard terms documentation. Where changes are proposed these should also be made clear. For other wholesale instruments, where standard terms do not yet exist (e.g. barrier options), particular care and attention should be paid to the negotiation of terms and documentation.

109 Some outstanding transactions might still be subject to old documentation (e.g. the 1987 ISDA) that results in one-way payment provisions. The use of such provisions is **not** recommended. Banking supervisors worldwide have indicated that such transactions will not be eligible for netting for capital adequacy purposes and the Bank supports moves to amend such clauses where they are still in existence. Non-core principals are encouraged to cooperate with core principals in this objective.

Stock lending and repos

Where sale and repurchase (or stock borrowing and lending) transactions are entered into, proper documentation and prior agreement of key terms and conditions are essential.

110 The Bank expects core principals to abide by the relevant codes drawn up by market practitioners. When undertaking stock lending transactions the Stock Borrowing and Lending Committee Code of Guidance should apply. With the advent of a gilt repo market the Gilt Repo Code of Best Practice should be adhered to.

111 The Gilt Repo Code will apply not only to gilt repo, but also to other transactions involving gilts which have similar effect and intent, including secured lending (of money and gilts) under the gilt-edged stock lending agreement; lending of gilts against collateral; and buy/sellbacks (whether or not under a Master Agreement). The Bank also believes that the general standards set down in the Gilt Repo Code will be relevant when undertaking other, non-gilt, repo activity covered by the London Code.

Assignments or transfers
Assignments should not generally be undertaken without the consent of the parties concerned.

112 Assignments have become increasingly common in the derivatives market. Principals who enter into any wholesale market transaction with the intention of shortly afterwards assigning or transferring the deal to a third party should make clear their intention to do so when initially negotiating the deal. It is recommended that the confirmation sent by the principal should specify any intent to assign and give details of the procedure that will be used. The subsequent documentation should also make provision for assignment.

113 When a principal is intending to execute such a transfer it must obtain the consent of the transferee before releasing its name. If the principal proposes to use a broker to arrange the transfer, consent from the transferee for this to happen must also be obtained. The transferee has an obligation to give the principal intending to transfer sufficient information to enable the transaction to be conducted in accordance with the principles of best practice set out elsewhere in the Code. Where the transaction is conducted through a broker, this information should likewise be made available to him. In particular the information from the transferee should include details of the type of credit the transferee is prepared to accept, and whether he is seeking any sort of reimbursement for the administrative costs that might be incurred. Principals and brokers arranging a transfer or assignment should also agree the basis or pricing the transfer at an early stage of the negotiations. When arranging assignments, it is important for participants to observe the general principle set out elsewhere in the Code that there should be mutual disclosure of names. Finally it should be noted that proper, clear documentation is as important for transfers as for the origination of deals.

Settlement of differences
If all the procedures outlined above are adhered to, the incidence and size of differences should be reduced; and those mistakes which do occur should be identified and corrected promptly. Failure to observe these principles could leave those responsible bearing the cost, without limit on size or duration, of any differences which arise. Except in the foreign exchange market, all differences must be settled in cash.

114 In all the wholesale markets (including foreign exchange) if a broker misses a price he is required by the Bank to offer to close the deal at the next best price if held to the deal. The broker must then settle the difference arising by cheque (or, if both sides agree, points if it is a foreign exchange transaction); **principals**

should always be prepared to accept this cash settlement since to do otherwise would put the broker in breach of the Code. It is unprofessional for a dealer to refuse to accept a difference cheque and insist the deal is honoured; individual brokers facing this situation should advise their senior management who, if necessary, should raise the matter with management of the client. The Bank is keen to be advised of any persistent offenders.

115 Where brokers are used to arrange derivative products like barrier options, they should not be held liable for disputes between principals that arise where there is a disagreement over whether a certain spot level has or has not been reached in sufficient quantity to trigger the option. Nor should brokers be cited as independent referees in such transactions unless they have explicitly agreed to do so before the deal is struck.

116 As noted above, the prompt despatch and checking of confirmations is of paramount importance. Non-standard settlement instructions should be particularly carefully checked, and any discrepancies identified promptly upon receipt, and notified direct to the counterparty, or to the broker (in circumstances described earlier).

117 Where difference payments arise because of errors in the payment of funds, principals are reminded that it is the view of the Bank and the Joint Standing Committees that they should not benefit from undue enrichment by retaining the funds. Technological developments have resulted in faster and more efficient mechanisms for the delivery and checking of confirmations. This means that when brokers pass payment instructions that cannot be cross-checked against direct confirmation details, their liability in the event of an error should be limited to 24 hours from when the deal was struck. This limit on the broker's liability is not intended to absolve brokers of responsibility for their own errors; rather it recognises that once payments do go astray the broker is limited in what action it can directly take to rectify the situation.

118 In the foreign exchange and currency deposit markets arrangements have been drawn up to facilitate the payment of differences via the Secretary of the Foreign Exchange Joint Standing Committee.[1] In the foreign exchange market only, and only with the explicit consent of principals, brokers may make use of "points" to settle differences. Even then their use will only be permitted if arrangements for management control, recording and reporting of points consistent with the requirements laid down by the Bank (see Annex 1) have been established.

119 Listed broking firms must agree their own procedures with the Wholesale Markets Supervision Division of the Bank before using "points". The informal use of "points" between individual dealers and brokers is not acceptable. Using "points" in lieu of cash to settle differences is not permitted in any market other than foreign exchange. As a matter of prudent housekeeping, all differences should normally be settled within 30 days from the date the original deal was undertaken.

Arbitration procedure

120 The Bank is prepared to arbitrate in disputes between firms it supervises about the application of the Code, or current market practice, to specific transactions in wholesale market products. As a condition for doing so the Bank will expect

---

[1] All requests for settlement via these arrangements should be marked for the attention of The Secretary, Foreign Exchange Joint Standing Committee, Bank of England Dealing Room (HO-G), Bank of England, Threadneedle Street, London EC2R 8AH. They should be accompanied by a written report of the circumstances resulting in the difference.

the parties to have exhausted their own efforts to resolve the matter directly. All parties must then first agree to the Bank taking such a role and to accept its decision in full and final settlement of the dispute. In doing so, the Bank may draw on the advice and expense of members of the Joint Standing Committees or other market practitioners as it feels appropriate. Requests for arbitration should be addressed to the Bank's Wholesale Markets Supervision Division. The Bank will not normally arbitrate in any dispute which is subject to, or is likely to be subject to, legal proceedings. Paragraphs 48 and 49 of the Code, on taping, and paragraphs 88-90, on oral deal checks, are especially relevant to firms considering recourse to these arrangements.

Commission/brokerage
Brokers' charges are freely negotiable. Principals should pay brokerage bills promptly.

121 Where the services of a broker are used it is traditional practice for an appropriate brokerage package to be agreed by the directors or senior management on each side. Any variation on a particular transaction from those previously agreed brokerage arrangements should be expressly approved by both parties and clearly recorded on the subsequent documentation; this should be the exception rather than the rule. Under no circumstances should a broker pay cash to a principal as an incentive to use its service (see also early section on Marketing).

122 Although brokers normally quote dealing prices excluding commission/brokerage charges, it is perfectly acceptable, and not uncommon, in some derivative markets for the parties to agree that the broker quotes rates gross of commission and separately identifies the brokerage charge. Equally there may be circumstances when the broker (or principal) and client may agree on an acceptable net rate; if so it is important that the broker (or principal) subsequently informs the client how that rate is divided between payments to counterparties and upfront commission. In such cases it is essential that all parties are quite clear that this division will be determined no later than the time at which the deal is struck; and that a record is kept.

123 The Bank is aware that some principals fail to pay due brokerage bills promptly. **This is not good practice** and can significantly disadvantage brokers since overdue payments are treated by the Bank, for regulatory purposes, as a deduction from their capital base.

Market conventions
Management should ensure that individual brokers and dealers are aware of their responsibility to act professionally at all times and, as part of this, to use clear, unambiguous terminology. This is even more important when dealing with non-core principals, whose staff may be less experienced in dealing in these markets.

124 The use of clear language is in the interests of all concerned. Management should establish internal procedures (including retraining if necessary) to alert individual dealers and brokers who act in different markets (or move from one market to another) both to any differences in terminology between markets and to the possibility that any particular term could be misinterpreted. The use of generally accepted concise terminology is undoubtedly helpful. In those markets where standard terms and conditions have been published individual dealers and brokers should familiarise themselves with the definitions they contain.

125 Standard conventions for calculating the interest and proceeds on certain sterling and currency instruments, together with market conventions regarding brokerage, are set out in Schedule 1.

Market disruption/bank holidays

126 There have been instances of general disruption to the wholesale markets which have, in turn, resulted in interruptions to the sterling settlement systems and consequent delays in sterling payments. It has been agreed by the Joint Standing Committees that in such unexpected circumstances the Bank should determine and publish the interest rate(s) which parties to deals affected by such interruptions should use to calculate the appropriate interest adjustment (unless all the parties to the deal agree instead on some other arrangement – such as to continue to apply the existing rate of interest on the original transaction or as provided for in the relevant documentation). The Bank shall have absolute discretion in its determination of any interest rate(s), and shall not be required to explain its method of determining the same and shall not be liable to any person in respect of such determination.

127 Occasionally unforeseen events mean that market participants will have entered into contracts for a particular maturity date only to find, subsequently, that that day is declared a public holiday. It is normal market practice in London to extend contracts maturing on a non-business day to the next working day. But to minimise possible disputes market participants may need to agree settlement arrangements for such deals with their counterparties in advance.

Schedule 1: Market conventions

1 Calculation of interest and brokerage in the sterling deposit market

Interest
On CDs and deposits or loans this is calculated on a daily basis on a 365-day year.

Interest on a deposit or loan is paid at maturity, or annually and at maturity, unless special arrangements are made at the time the deal is concluded.

On secured loans the discount houses and Stock Exchange money brokers do not pay interest at intervals of less than 28 days. The current general practice is to calculate at the close of business on the penultimate working day interest outstanding on secured loans to the last working day of each calendar month and to pay the interest thereon on the last working day of the month.

Brokerage
All brokerage is calculated on a daily basis on a 365-day year and brokerage statements are submitted monthly.

2 Calculation of interest in a leap year
The calculation of interest in a leap year depends upon whether interest falls to be calculated on a daily or an annual basis. The position may differ as between temporary and longer-term loans.

Temporary loans
Because temporary loans may be repaid in less than one year (but may, of course, be continued for more than a year) interest on temporary money is almost invariably calculated on a daily basis. Thus any period which includes 29 February automatically

incorporates that day in the calculation; in calculating the appropriate amount of interest, the number of days in the period since the last payment of interest is expressed as a fraction of a normal 365-day year, not the 366 days of a leap year, which ensures that full value is given for the "extra" day.

Examples:

Assume last previous interest payment 1 February (up to and including 31 January) and date of repayment I April (in a leap year). Duration of loan for final interest calculation = 29 days (February) + 31 days (March) = 60 days.

Calculation of interest would be

$$P \times \frac{r}{100} \times \frac{60}{365} =$$

Assume no intermediate interest payments. Loan placed 1 March and called for repayment 1 March the following year (leap year). Total period up to and including 29 February = 366 days. Calculation of interest would be

$$P \times \frac{r}{100} \times \frac{366}{365} =$$

This is in line with banking practice regarding interest on deposits which is calculated on a "daily" basis and no conflict therefore arises.

Longer-term loans

The following procedure for the calculation of interest on loans which cannot be repaid in less than one year (except under a TSB or building society stress clause) was agreed between the BBA and the Chartered Institute of Public Finance and Accountancy on 12 December 1978.

(a) Fixed interest

The total amount of interest to be paid on a longer-term loan at fixed interest should be calculated on the basis of the number of complete calendar years running from the first day of the loan, with each day of any remaining period bearing interest as for 1/365 of a year.

Normal practice for the calculation of interest in leap years is to disregard 29 February if it falls within one of the complete calendar years. Only when it falls within the remaining period is it counted as an additional day with the divisor remaining at 365.

Example: $3\frac{1}{2}$ year loan, maturing on 30 June of a leap year.

First 3 years' interest: $P \times \dfrac{r}{100} \times 3 =$

Final 6 months' interest: $P \times \dfrac{r}{100} \times \dfrac{182}{365} =$

Certain banks, however, require additional payment of interest for 29 February in all cases, and it was therefore agreed that:

– both the original offer or bid, and the agents confirmation, must state specifically if such payment is to be made; and
– the documentation must incorporate the appropriate phraseology.

Interest on longer term loans should be paid half-yearly, on the half-yearly anniversary of the loan or on other prescribed dates and at maturity. **To calculate half yearly interest payments** the accepted market formula is:

$$P \times \frac{r}{100} \times \frac{d}{365} =$$

Where d = actual number of days

Although, with the agreement or both parties, the following is sometimes used:

$$P \times \frac{r}{100} \times \frac{1}{2} =$$

(b) Floating rate
Interest on variable rate loans, or roll-overs, which are taken for a fixed number of years with the rate of interest adjusted on specific dates, should be calculated in the same manner as for temporary loans.

3 Brokerage and other market conventions in the foreign exchange and currency deposit markets

Brokerage

(a) General (foreign exchange and currency deposits)
Brokerage arrangements are freely negotiable.

These arrangements should be agreed by directors and senior management in advance of any particular transaction.

(b) Currency deposits
Calculation of brokerage on all currency deposits should be worked out on a 360-day year.

Brokers' confirmations and statements relating to currency deposits should express brokerage in the currency of the deal.

In a simultaneous forward-forward deposit (for example one month against six months), the brokerage to be charged shall be on the actual intervening period (in the above example, five months).

Other market conventions

(a) Currency deposits

Length of the year
For the purpose of calculating interest, one year is in general deemed to comprise 360 days; but practice is not uniform in all currencies or centres.

Spreads and quotations
Quotations will normally be made in fractions, except in short-dated foreign exchange dealings, where decimals are normally used.

Call and notice money
For US dollars (and sterling), notice in respect of call money must be given before noon in London. For other currencies, it should be given before such time as may be necessary to conform with local clearing practice in the country of the currency dealt in.

4 Calculations in the foreign currency asset markets

Euro-commercial paper (and other such instruments)

The net proceeds of short-term interest-bearing and discount Euro-commercial paper, on which interest is determined on a 360-day basis, are calculated in the same manner as those for short-term, interest-bearing and discount CDs.

Formula for non-interest bearing Euronotes quoted on a "discount to yield" basis:

$$\frac{N}{1 + \dfrac{(Y}{(100} \times \dfrac{M)}{360)}} = \text{Purchase consideration}$$

where

N = Nominal amount or face value
Y = Yield
M = Number of days to maturity

Example:

A Euronote with a face value of US$5 million and with 90 days to run is sold to yield 7.23% per annum.

$$\frac{5,000,000}{1 + \dfrac{(7.23 \times 90)}{(36,000)}} = \$4,911,229.53$$

US Treasury bills (and other US discount securities such as bankers' acceptances and commercial paper)

The quoted trading rates for such assets are discount rates. The price of the asset is calculated on the basis of a 360-day year.

The market price (Pm) on a redemption value of $100 can be calculated as follows:

$$Pm = 100 - \frac{(M \times D)}{(360)}$$

where
M = days to maturity or days held
D = discount basis (per cent).

Schedule 2: Guidelines for exchanging standard settlement instructions (SSIs)

These guidelines have been drawn up by the Bank of England in consultation with practitioners. While the parties to SSIs are free to agree changes to the detail on a bilateral basis, it is hoped that this framework will be useful and as such followed as closely as possible.

When **establishing** SSIs with a counterparty for the first time these should be appropriately authorised internally before being issued. It is desirable that SSIs be established by post (and issued in duplicate, typically under two authorised signatories). However authenticated SWIFT message can also be used if necessary.

Cancellation or amendment of a standard instruction should ideally be undertaken by authenticated SWIFT; tested telex is also an acceptable means when cancelling or making amendments. SWIFT broadcast is **not** an acceptable means for establishing, cancelling or amending SSIs.

A mutually agreed **period of notice** for changing SSIs should be given; typically this will be between 10 working days and one month. Some parties may also wish to provide for changes to be made at shorter notice in certain circumstances.

Recipients have a responsibility to acknowledge acceptance (or otherwise) of the proposed/amended SSI within the timescale agreed (see above). Failure to do so could result in a liability to compensate for any losses which result. In the case of written notification this should be undertaken by the recipient signing and returning the duplicate letter.

Recipients should also confirm the precise date on which SSIs will be activated (via SWIFT or tested telex).

Instructions should be issued for each currency and wholesale market product. Each party will typically nominate only one correspondent per currency for foreign exchange deals and one per currency for other wholesale market deals. The same correspondent may be used for foreign exchange and other wholesale market deals.

As a general rule, all outstanding deals, including maturing forwards, should be settled in accordance with the SSI in force at their value date (unless otherwise and explicitly agreed by the parties at the time at which any change to an existing SSI is agreed).

The SSI agreement for each business category should contain the following:

- the nature of the deals covered (for example whether they include same day settlement or only spot/forward forex deals).
- confirmation that a single SSI will apply for all such deals with the counterparty.
- the effective date.
- confirmation that it will remain in force "until advised".
- recognition that no additional telephone confirmation of settlement details will be required.
- recognition that any deviation from the SSI will be subject to an agreed period of notice.

When operating SSIs on this basis, the general obligations on both parties are to ensure that:

- they apply the SSI which is current on the settlement date for relevant transactions.
- confirmations are issued in accordance with the London Code of Conduct; the aim should be to send them out on the day a deal is struck.

confirmations are checked promptly upon receipt in accordance with the London Code. Any discrepancies should be advised by no later than 3.00 pm on the business day following trade date, if not sooner.

Annex 1: Operating a dual broking system in the London foreign exchange market

Notice issued by the Bank of England, 24 October 1989[1]

1 The Bank's enquiries of foreign exchange market participants in March 1989 established that opinion was divided on use of the "points" system in London.[2]

---

[1] The bank introduced a complementary Notice (February 1994) to all banks and brokers setting out the detailed requirements for brokers operating a "points" broking system in London; copies are available from the Wholesale Markets Supervision Division at the Bank of England. Note: this Notice may be amended from time to time

[2] Examples of typical situations generating "negative" and "positive" points are set out in the Appendix

The Bank has considered with the FECDBA and the Joint Standing Committee the kind of steps necessary to allow those institutions wishing to retain the use of points to do so, whilst ensuring that points are not used in deals with banks which reject this system. It has been agreed that the following general arrangements will be established.

2　Management in all banks (and other active market participants) will be expected to have internal rules for their dealers to minimise the scope for differences and to discourage dealers from acting unprofessionally, for example by "stuffing" brokers.

Participating banks

3　Each broking firm will approach all their clients (based in the UK or overseas) at the appropriate management level to establish whether, in order to be provided as far as possible by the broker with the current firm price service, they are prepared to sign a client letter accepting the broker's involvement in points arrangements. Those banks which do agree client letters are referred to here as "participating banks".

4　Banks which explicitly accept the use of points in this way will be assumed to have given their informed consent to the practice. The arrangements described here are deemed satisfactory in the foreign exchange market because it is a professional market in which best execution is not normally expected. Obviously in abnormal circumstances, where a broker agrees to provide best execution to a client or the client is not a market professional or the broker performs an advisory or discretionary function[1] to a client, there must be full disclosure to the client of the broker's interest and explicit informed prior consent.

5　Signing such a client letter will **not** of itself commit any bank to **lending** points to brokers or to the use of positive points in lieu of cash payment for any differences. Any such decision should be taken quite separately by management and would require appropriate record keeping and reporting arrangements to be established.

Non-participating banks

6　For "non-participating banks" which decline to provide a client letter, a broking firm will need to consider on a case-by-case basis whether it is prepared to continue to provide a broking service, and if so on what terms. Where a service continues to be provided, the broking firm will be required to take the following steps to ensure that these banks are not unwittingly involved in deals where there is an undisclosed benefit to the broker:

(i)　The broker will advise the management of the non-participating banks that it may no longer provide as firm a price service; banks will be expected to take steps to inform their dealers that the broker cannot be held to a price. Any attempts to "stuff" a broker should in the first instance be brought to the attention of management in the broking firm; they in turn should raise it at the appropriate level with the bank(s) concerned. Any bank dealers attempting to pressurise a broker should be subject to internal disciplinary procedures. Furthermore, if necessary, brokers will have recourse to the Bank of England to complain.

(ii)　Each broking firm will establish to the Bank of England's satisfaction appropriate arrangements to enable it to distinguish non-participating from participating banks. The precise means by which this distinction is achieved are likely to vary between broking firms depending, inter alia, on the number of non-participating

---

[1] See paragraphs 29 and 30 of the July 1995 Code regarding the role of brokers.

clients each broker has; the manner in which they receive a service (whether over an open voice box system or over an ordinary telephone line); and the number and volume of deals involved.

(iii) Any differences payable by the broker resulting from mistakes will normally be settled by cheque; where London banks are concerned, it is recommended that cheques be paid through the established FECDBA mechanism.[1] As a matter of equity, banks should also accept that any differences resulting from mistakes on the part of their dealers should be payable to the broker through the same procedures.

(iv) An up-to-date list of names distinguishing participating from non-participating banks will be maintained by the broker, with copies provided to all appropriate members of staff. The Bank of England will also be provided with a copy of the current list.

(v) Any "cross-overs" involving a non-participating bank will, subject to acceptability of names, be completed either at a mutually acceptable middle rate or by the introduction of an intermediary bank; if an intermediary is introduced, none of the benefit to it from such a deal will accrue to the broker.

(vi) In the event of a "name switch" becoming necessary involving one or more non-participating banks, the broker will reserve the right to adjust the brokerage charges to compensate. Any such adjustment should be arranged between management in both the broking firm and the bank(s) concerned.

7 Management in broking firms active in forex have indicated to the Bank that this framework forms an acceptable basis for accommodating banks' differing requirements for broking services. Its operation will be kept under close review by the Bank and by the Joint Standing Committee, and the first six months of operation will be regarded as experimental.

8 The Bank will require brokers to maintain records of deals involving points, including any such deals arranged involving correspondent brokers. These must ensure that accurate and verifiable points' tallies are kept on a deal by deal basis, and must be backed by rigorous management systems and controls. These requirements have been discussed with the broking firms concerned and are set out in a separate paper which has been provided to all listed brokers for implementation to the Bank's satisfaction.

9 The Bank accepts that on rare occasions individuals will inevitably make mistakes, when (positive) points may wrongly be taken by a broker from a deal involving a non-participating bank. Systems will therefore need to be in place in each broking firm to identify any such errors promptly and to ensure that full rectification takes place immediately so that no positive points accrue to the benefit of the broker. Any such adjustment will leave the original deal undisturbed. The Bank will monitor closely the frequency of any such errors in each firm; if they reveal an inability to distinguish participating from non-participating banks, the Bank may require a broking firm to give up the use of points altogether.

Arrangements for monitoring participating banks

10 In parallel to these arrangements for brokers, the Banking Supervision Division of the Bank will wish to be notified by those UK authorised banks which decide that they may be prepared to accept positive points to settle differences arising with broking firms. They will wish to discuss with these banks from time to time how

---

[1] See paragraph 118 of the July 1995 Code for details of the arrangements which superseded the FECDBA mechanism.

these arrangements will work, including importantly the record keeping arrangements in place to enable individual transactions involving points (both negative and positive) to be identified.

Appendix: Examples of situations giving rise to points in foreign exchange dealing

"Negative Points"

1 Suppose a broker quotes sterling at $1.8030/1.8035. Bank A hits the $1.8030 bid for 5 mn. However, before the broker could let Bank A know, this price had been withdrawn by the market maker who had originally indicated to the broker a willingness to deal at the rate. The market for sterling has moved to $1.8025/1.8030.

2 When told that the bid price of $1.8030 was no longer available, the trader at Bank A insists on selling 5 mn at the original price.

3 Suppose the broker accepts responsibility for not withdrawing the price quickly enough, or values highly his relationship with Bank A, and therefore agrees to be held to the price. He searches the market and finds Bank B (a participating bank) who is willing to help the broker by agreeing to buy from Bank A at $1.8030 (and hopefully sell to the current bidder in the market at $1.8025); the broker is committed to make good the $2,500 loss which results from Bank B doing the two trades. This dealer has lent the broker 25 "points" (i.e. 5 "points" per 1 mn in a 5 mn deal).

"Positive Points"

4 The $2,500 (25 "points") obligation of the broker in the above example to Bank B could obviously be settled in cash if Bank B so wished. Or Bank B may be prepared to see it reduced by the broker's ability to put to Bank B other transactions that produce a profit to Bank B's dealing position of at least $2,500. This might be achieved in various ways, one of which is as follows.

5 Suppose at some later time the market for sterling stands at $1.8070/75. This might reflect prices put into the broker as follows: Bank A bidding at 1.8070; Bank C is offering at 1.8075. Suppose two unrelated Banks, X and Y, simultaneously have a respective need to sell/buy 5 mn. Bank X hits the 1.8070 bid; Bank Y the 1.8075 offer. The broker now has these latter two banks committed to deal in opposite directions at overlapping rates (in this example equal to the market spread). The broker may, at its discretion, offer both these deals to Bank B.

6 The consequences of this would be:

(i) Bank X has sold sterling at the (market) rate desired;
(ii) Bank Y has bought sterling at the (market) rate desired;
(iii) by being given both deals Bank B earns a profit of $2,500 equal to the spread; it may, or may not, decide to reward the broker for this "service" in the form of offsetting these "positive points" against the 25 negative points the broker owes.

Annex 2: London instruments

The London Code of Conduct defines best market practice for secondary transactions. The act of issuing debentures (including CDs, commercial paper and medium-term notes) is not an investment activity under the Financial Services Act

1986, but such primary issues are expected to comply with the Bank's market guidelines. The Bank believes that as great a degree of homogeneity as possible at the primary issuing stage in the short-term paper markets assists good order in those markets. It reduces the scope for investor confusion about the nature of the instrument being traded and thereby facilitates market trading.

Such homogeneity is achieved in the CD market by the Bank's guidelines on Certificates of Deposit in London, together with a booklet issued by the British Bankers' Association setting out in detail the requirements covering the issuance of CDs. These identify the standard terms and conditions under which London CDs are issued. A similar degree of homogeneity is also achieved in the sterling Commercial Paper and Medium-Term Note markets through both the Bank's Market Notice incorporating guidelines on this subject and the underlying statutory instrument which provides exemptions from the deposit-taking prohibition in the Banking Act and therefore permits regular issuance by non-deposit-taking entities.

Copies of the Bank's current notices on CDs, and Commercial Paper and Medium-Term Notes, may be obtained from the Bank's Gilt-Edged and Money Markets Division (telephone 0171-601 3100); any questions on either of these subjects may also be directed to the Bank on the same number.

The Bank is willing to co-operate with market participants in any of the other wholesale markets where similar standards and homogeneity would be desirable.

GLOSSARY

Abandon Where an option holder chooses not to exercise his option.

American style An option that may be exercised into its underlying instrument on any business day until expiry (see also *European style*).

Arbitrage The purchase or sale of an instrument and the simultaneous taking of an equal and opposite position in a related market, when the pricing is out of line.

Arbitrageur A trader who takes advantage of profitable opportunities arising out of pricing anomalies.

At market An order to buy/sell at the current trading level, generally used in the exchange traded market.

At the money option (ATM) An option with an exercise price at the current market level of the underlying. For example, this could be ATMF – at the money forward.

Average rate option An option where the settlement is based on the difference between the exercise price and the average price of the underlying over a predetermined period. Also known as **Asian** options.

Basis point One hundredth of one percent (0.01%).

Bear market A falling market.

Best The broker can buy or sell at the "best" price available at his or her discretion.

Bid The wish to buy.

Black and Scholes The original, commercially available option pricing model used by many market practitioners, written by Black and Scholes in 1972.

Broken date A value date that is not a regular forward date.

Broker An individual or a firm that acts as an intermediary, putting together willing sellers and willing buyers for a fee (brokerage).

Bull market A rising market.

Call option An option that gives the holder (buyer) the right but not the obligation to buy the underlying instrument at a pre-agreed rate (exercise price) on or before a specific future date.

Cash settlement Where a product is settled at expiry, based on the differential between the fixed/guaranteed price and the current price underlying instrument.

Compound option An option on an option. The holder (buyer) has an option to purchase another option on a pre-set date at a pre-agreed premium.

Covered writing Where an option is sold against an existing position.

Cross rate The exchange rate for one non–US dollar currency against another non–US dollar currency, e.g. DEM/JPY.

Day trade A position opened and closed within the same trading day.

Default Failure to perform on a foreign exchange transaction or failure to pay an interest obligation on a debt.

Delta The sensitivity of an option premium to changes in the price of the underlying currency, also known as the "hedge ratio."

Discount The margin by which the forward exchange rate (dollarwise) is less expensive than the near date.

End/end Swap transaction for settlement on the last business day of a month against the last business day of a future month.

European style An option which may be exercised only on the expiry date (see also *American style*).

Exchange traded A transaction where a specific instrument is bought or sold on a regulated exchange, e.g. LIFFE, MATIF, IPE, NYMEX, SIMEX.

Exercise The conversion of the option into the "underlying;" to make use of the right to enter into a specific obligation.

Exercise price/strike price The price at which the option holder has the right to buy/sell the underlying instrument.

Exotic options New generation of option derivatives, including look-backs, barriers, baskets, ladders, etc.

Expiry The date after which an option can no longer be exercised.

Expiration date The last date on which an option can be exercised.

Expiration time The latest time on the expiration date when the seller will accept a notice of exercise (usually 3 pm London time/10 am New York time).

Extrinsic value The amount by which the premium on an option exceeds the intrinsic value, also known as time value.

Fair value For options, this is the premium calculated by an option pricing model such as that written by Black and Scholes. For futures, it is the level where the contract should trade, taking into account cost of carry.

Forward foreign exchange All foreign exchange transactions over two business days from transaction date for periods of one month onward fixed at time of dealing. See also *Short dates*.

Hedge A transaction that reduces or mitigates risk.

Historical volatility An indication of past volatility in the marketplace.

Holder The buyer of the option.

Implied volatility The volatility implied by the market price of the option.

Indication only Quotations which are not firm.

In the money option (ITM) An option with an exercise price more advantageous than the current market level of the underlying.

Intrinsic value One of the components of an option premium. The amount by which an option is in the money.

LIBOR The London Inter-Bank Offered Rate. The interbank rate used where one bank offers money to another. It is also the benchmark used to price many capital market and derivative transactions.

LIBID The London Inter-Bank Bid Rate. The rate at which one bank will bid for money from another.

LIFFE London International Financial Futures Exchange.

Limit order An order given at a certain price.

Liquid market An active marketplace where selling and buying occur with minimal price concessions.

Liquidation The closing of an existing position.

Long More purchases than sales.

Mark-to-market A process where both OTC and exchange-traded contracts are revalued on a daily basis.

Mine The dealer takes the offer which has been quoted by the counterparty. It must be qualified by the amount.

Mio One million.

Naked option An option position taken without having the underlying commodity.

Notice of exercise Notification by telex, fax, or phone which must be given irrevocably by the buyer to the seller of the option prior or at the time of expiry.

Offer The wish to sell.

Open position Difference between total spot and forward purchases and sales in a currency on which an exchange risk is run.

Option An agreement between two parties that gives the holder (buyer) the right but not the obligation to buy or sell a specific instrument at a specified price on or before a specific future date. On exercise the seller (writer) of the option must deliver, or take delivery of, the underlying instrument at the specified price.

Orders Firm order given by a dealer to a counterparty to execute a transaction under certain specified conditions, e.g. limit order, stop-loss order, etc.

OTC or over the counter A bilateral transaction between a client and a bank, negotiated privately between the parties.

Out of the money option (OTM) An option with an exercise price more disadvantageous than the current market level of the underlying. An out of the money option has time value but no intrinsic value.

Outright The purchase or sale of a currency for delivery on any date other than spot (not being a swap transaction).

Overnight–today/tomorrow Swap transaction for settlement on a transaction date to or against the next business day after transaction date.

Par Where the price is the same on both sides of the swap.

Point/pip The last decimal place of the quotation.

Premium options The cost of the option contract. It is made up of two components: intrinsic value and time value.

Premium currency The margin by which the currency (dollarwise) is more expensive than the near date.

Price quotation: Either in the form of a premium, e.g. a percentage of the principal amount, or in the form of a volatility quotation, which can be input into the pricing model.

Price transparency Where a transaction is executed on the floor of an exchange, and every participant has equal access to the trade.

Put option An option that gives the holder (buyer) the right but not the obligation to sell the underlying instrument at a pre-agreed strike rate (exercise rate) on or before a specific future date.

Short More sales than purchases.

Short dates Foreign exchange deals for a broken number of days up to the one month date.

Sold short Someone who has sold a commodity without previously owning it.

Spot foreign exchange A transaction to exchange one currency for another at a rate agreed today (the spot rate), for settlement in two business days from transaction date.

Spot/next Swap transaction for settlement on the second business day against the third business day after transaction date.

Spread The difference between buying and selling rates.

Square Purchases and sales of currency are equal.

Stop-loss order Becomes an order at best after a certain rate has been reached or passed or dealt depending upon the specified conditions previously agreed between the parties.

Straddle A combination of a Put and a Call option with the same strike and same expiry date. Long the straddle – both options are purchased simultaneously. Short the straddle – both options are sold simultaneously.

Strangle A combination of a Put and a Call option with equally out of the money strikes and the same expiry date. Long the strangle – both options are purchased simultaneously. Short the strangle – both options are sold simultaneously.

Strike price/exercise price The price at which the option holder has the right to buy or sell the underlying instrument.

Swap The simultaneous purchase and sale of identical amounts of a currency for different value dates. Not to be confused with derivatives swap transactions.

Swaption An option into a predetermined swap transaction – can be payers or receivers, American or European.

Technical analysis A graphical analysis of historical price trends, used to predict likely future trends in the market. Also known as "charts."

Theoretical value The fair value of a futures or option contract (see *Fair value*).

Time value The amount (if any) by which the premium of an option exceeds the intrinsic value. Also known as intrinsic value.

Tom/next Swap transaction for settlement on the next business day against the second business day after transaction date.

Traded option An option contract bought or sold on a regulated exchange.

Underlying The asset, future, interest rate, FX rate, or index upon which a derivative transaction is based.

Value today Same day value.

Value tomorrow Value the next working day or business day.

Volatility One of the major components of the option pricing model, based on the degree of "scatter" of the underlying price when compared to the "mean average exchange rate." Statistically speaking, the standard deviation in the logarithm of the underlying price expressed as an annual rate.

Warrant An option which can be listed on an exchange, generally longer than one year. Many capital market issues have warrants embedded in them.

Writer The seller of an option.

Yard One thousand million (billion).

Your risk Quoted rates are subject to change at the risk of the receiver.

Yours Opposite to mine. The dealer gives at the bid which has been quoted by the counterparty. It must be qualified by the amount.

INDEX

For further information about derivatives markets contact:

Francesca Taylor at TAYLOR ASSOCIATES, a specialist financial training company, designing training and development programmes for clients with needs associated with derivatives, capital markets, FX and money markets, and treasury techniques. Both banks and corporations benefit from the dedicated training programmes. All the trainers are ex-market practitioners.

Client-awareness courses are also available from Taylor Associates in understanding and recognising money laundering problems and the abuse of derivatives, accounting, credit evaluation and general finance.

Courses include:

Foundation course in derivatives
Options, Swaps and Futures. The course explains in clear language, the products, applications and risks of using derivatives, the differences between OTC and exchange rate products, and the various underlying asset groups.

Workshops in:
Using Interest Rate Derivatives
Using Currency Derivatives
Using Equity Derivatives
Using Energy Derivatives
Money Laundering

Corporate Sales Training
Giving the corporate sales team the skills to understand the client's annual report and accounts, identify marketing and selling opportunities, as well as listening and observation skills, both on the telephone and face to face. Importance is placed on getting the client to agree to the deal without any undesirable pressure and ultimately closing the deal.

Post to: Taylor Associates, 31 Abbotstone Road, London, SW15 1QR, UK
Telephone/Fax : 0181 780 9518
E-Mail : francesca@taylorassociates.co.uk
Web site: http://www.taylorassociates.co.uk